CW00435171

Studies in Public Choice

Volume 31

Series editor

Randall G. Holcombe, Tallahassee, USA

Founding Editor

Gordon Tullock, Fairfax, VA, USA

For further volumes:
http://www.springer.com/series/6550

Bernard Grofman · Alexander H. Trechsel
Mark Franklin
Editors

The Internet and Democracy in Global Perspective

Voters, Candidates, Parties, and Social Movements

 Springer

Editors
Bernard Grofman
School of Social Sciences
Center for the Study of Democracy
  University of California
Irvine, CA
USA

Mark Franklin
Department of Political Science
MIT
Cambridge, MA
USA

Alexander H. Trechsel
Department of Political and Social Sciences
European University Institute (Fiesole)
Florence
Italy

ISSN 0924-4700
ISBN 978-3-319-04351-7   ISBN 978-3-319-04352-4   (eBook)
DOI 10.1007/978-3-319-04352-4
Springer Cham Heidelberg New York Dordrecht London

Library of Congress Control Number: 2014933542

Printed on acid-free paper

Springer is part of Springer Science+Business Media (www.springer.com)

Preface and Acknowledgments

This book originated as a cooperative project between the European Union Democracy Observatory (EUDO) at the European University Institute's (EUI) Robert Schuman Center for Advanced Studies (RSCAS) and the Center for the Study of Democracy (CSD), School of Social Sciences, University of California, and Irvine (UCI). This collaboration led to two conferences, one in Fiesole at the EUI, June 3–4 2010, and one in Laguna Beach, California, hosted by CSD in May 14–15, 2011. Most of the papers in the volume were drawn from one or the other of these two conferences. The idea for the joint project came in a conversation between Mark Franklin, then at the EUI, and Bernard Grofman, and it quickly led to Alexander Trechsel's involvement in the project. Alexander Trechsel was the Director of EUDO and Bernard Grofman Director of CSD at the time the conferences were held. The "Internet and Democracy" seemed like an ideal project for international institutional cooperation because of its timeliness, and because of the centrality of its topic to both EUDO and CSD. Additional funding for the Laguna Beach conference came from the Jack W. Peltason (Bren Foundation) Endowed Chair held by Bernard Grofman. We are grateful for logistic support at UCI from CSD's Administrator, Shani Brasier; at the EUI we are grateful to the financial support offered by EUDO and the academic and administrative help offered by Valentina Bettin, Andrea Calderaro, Amy Chamberlain, and Ingo Linsenmann.

We owe very special thanks to Rachel Gibson, a leading scholar of political communication, for writing a comprehensive Preface to the volume that places its papers in the context of recent scholarship on the Internet. Her preface plays the role that the more customary form of editors' introduction plays in most edited volumes, since we regard her as far more knowledgeable about the literature on the Internet and politics than any of the three co-editors. In this editors' introduction, we will simply note the central features of this book and the vision that inspired it.

Looking at the many excellent papers that were given at the two conferences the editors sought to put together a small set of first-rate papers that reflected two kinds of diversity: diversity in the nature of the actors using computer-mediated communications to get their message across and/or to identify and coordinate those with shared ideas (e.g., candidates, parties, activist groups and social movements, and public interest groups seeking to disseminate reliable information about election choices), and diversity across sites. We are especially pleased that we have research dealing not only just on the USA, the UK, and across Europe, but also on Canada and Brazil, as well as on Iran, Tunisia, and Egypt, and that we have studies that look at both local and national elections.

Because we did not have any paper at the conferences that dealt with voting in actual elections using the Internet, and we believe this to be a mode of voting that will grow dramatically in future importance, we were pleased to add to the volume the chapter by Nicole Goodman "Internet Voting in a Local Election in Canada" on Canada's pioneering use of Internet voting for local elections, and to make that paper our opening chapter. Her paper shows the promise of this method. The chapter by Garzia, Trechsel, Vassil, and Dinas "Indirect Campaigning: Past, Present and Future of Voting Advice Applications" is a review of another important innovation in the use of the Internet, Voting Advice Applications (VAAs), which is at the moment far more visible in its implementation in Europe than in the USA. The idea of a VAA is simple: ask candidates or parties to answer questions about where they stand on key issues (or, as is done most commonly, have experts code their positions) and store these responses online in a publicly accessible way. Then allow voters to input their own answers to this same set of questions, and provide an algorithm that tells the voters which candidates or parties are closest, in sum, to their own positions. Providing information about the breadth of their use and reviewing the present research literature on the political consequences of access to VAAs, Garzia et al. demonstrate that they appear to have increased turnout, and voter knowledge and sense of political involvement, though they sound a note of caution in terms of waiting for validation of results from more controlled experiments. But they also note that voter responses to VAAs provide an incredible new data source for those studying voter's cognitive processes, since the sample sizes are often much much larger than for traditional surveys.

The next four chapters take us away from Internet uses that are motivated primarily by a concern for improving citizen information and participation, to ones with a goal of persuasion in favor of and/or mobilization on behalf of a candidate, party or cause. While these chapters are primarily descriptive, which is appropriate given how fast changing campaign technologies have been and how little we know about the spread of these technologies, the authors also try to come to grips with assessing the impact of these new technologies, albeit in a very preliminary fashion.

"Indirect Campaigning: Past, Present, and Future of Voting Advice Applications" and "Digital Media and the 2010 National Elections in Brazil" deal with candidates and parties. In the Gilmore and Howard chapter, looking at national legislative elections and other elections in Brazil, they find, for higher levels of office, what to our eye, are remarkably high levels of use of media such as Facebook and Twitter, with the creation of candidate website now being essentially universal. But they also point out that the use of these technologies are, by and large, not that sophisticated, especially in being able to take advantage of feedback or tailoring messages to narrowly targeted audiences. Moreover, for the lower chamber of the legislature, where they had a representative sample of 20 %

of the viable candidates "only 40 % of candidates nationwide for the lower house had any form of online campaign presence. Candidate websites, by and large, had simple structures and tended to have only a few pages of information on the candidate." For candidates from minor parties, they do find some evidence of a link between success and Internet use, especially the use of Twitter, because Brazil is a society where "mobile phone use is as extensive," but recognize that assessing causality is difficult. The next chapter, by Jensen and Anstead, on campaigning for parliament in the UK, contrasts the use of "new media" at the national level, as used in communications from party leaders, and that at the constituency level, where individual candidates send messages and create sites for supporters and those in search of more information. In particular, they contrast top–down communication strategies with ones that are more interactive. Their key finding is that, "while a predominantly command and control structure of the campaign operates at the national level, communications at the local level are more horizontal and personal in nature."

"Campaigns and Social Media Communications: A Look at Digital Campaigning in the 2010 U.K. General Election" and "Virtual Power Plays: Social Movements, Internet Communication Technology, and Political Parties" deal with the use of the Internet by social movements, from groups seeking to take over an existing major political party or shift its political direction to ones that are seeking regime change. The Rohlinger, Bunnage, and Klein chapter deals with social movements such as the Tea Party Movement and MoveOn that reflect very different political attitudes. As the authors note, social movements have been neglected in the literature on elections in part because of an historic division of labor between sociologists, who study movements, and political scientists who study elections, yet social movements can be vital participants in the political process such that it is hard to understand election outcomes and the nature of campaigning without examining closely their role. This is especially true in very recent elections in the USA when we look at organizations like the Tea Party Movement or MoveOn, but alanalyzesso for the 2013 national Italian elections, where the "Movimento 5 Stelle" of Beppe Grillo, by heavily relying on an Internet platform for its campaign, gained a quarter of all votes. The study by Rohlinger, Bunnage and Klein is characteristic of much new social research in combining multiple methodologies, e.g., large n (e.g., of Internet communication patterns), elite interviewing, and participant observation. They show how "savvy organizations can use ICT in ways that can ultimately help activists transform a party." They also show that, despite important similarities in their use of information communication technologies, the two organizations have very different styles of use, with the latter more top-down and the former more participatory and bottom up. Thus, the contrast they make between variation in ICT use in the two different political organizations parallels in an intriguing way the contrast drawn in ICT use between national and localized campaigns by Jensen and Anstead. The last chapter, by Ritter and Trechsel, like the previous chapter by Rohlinger, Bunnage and Klein, is remarkably timely. It deals with a debate within academia triggered by press and activist bloggers claims of the critical importance of the Internet as a coordinating device in the events leading to Arab Spring, especially the regime change in Tunisia and Egypt. Ritter and Trechsel note that "even among those sociologists and political scientists who have focused on agency in revolutions, few contributions have been devoted to the role of information and communication technology (ICT) in the process of regime change, nonviolent or otherwise." They claim that this neglect is "mainly due to two interrelated facts: first, the study of revolutions ... tilted heavily toward structural analyses that leave little room for the role of the actual revolutionaries, and even less for their communication tactics. Second, and perhaps more important ..., nonviolent revolutions remain severely understudied." These authors argue that "successful use of ICTs [such as the Internet and cell phone tweets] seems to be correlated with nonviolent revolutions in particular, not their violent counterparts." They posit two interrelated factors: domestic mobilization and the potential for global awareness. But they also call attention to historical parallels such as the use of the telegraph in the Iranian "Tobacco Revolution" of 1891 and the remarkable distribution of over 1,00,000 cassette tapes recording messages by the Ayatollah Khomeini in the prelude to the 1970s Iranian Revolution. Such historical examples suggest we should not overstate the importance of "contemporary" communication technology. Ritter and Trechsel provide a carefully nuanced bottom line: While they argue that, "in both Tunisia and Egypt, ICTs played an important role in the very early stages of the revolutions," they also assert that, while "bloggers continued to report on the progression of the protests and announced meeting points and times for planned demonstrations, ... mobilization in the latter part of the revolution would likely have occurred even without the participation of online activists."

While no set of six papers could possibly do justice to the rapidly growing literatures in multiple disciplines on the communication uses of the Internet and other contemporary information technologies in politics, and the prospects of ICTs advancing the cause of democracy, we believe that the six papers in this volume, along with Rachel Gibson's survey of the literature, will provide the reader with an excellent introduction to the topic. We are happy to offer this collection as what we believe will be a very useful contribution to one of the most exciting areas of current research in the social sciences.

Contents

Introduction   1
Rachel Gibson

Internet Voting in a Local Election in Canada   7
Nicole J. Goodman

Indirect Campaigning: Past, Present and Future of Voting
Advice Applications.   25
Diego Garzia, Alexander H. Trechsel, Kristjan Vassil and Elias Dinas

Digital Media and the 2010 National Elections in Brazil   43
Jason Gilmore and Philip N. Howard

Campaigns and Social Media Communications:
A Look at Digital Campaigning in the 2010 U.K. General Election . . .   57
Michael J. Jensen and Nick Anstead

Virtual Power Plays: Social Movements, Internet Communication
Technology, and Political Parties   83
Deana A. Rohlinger, Leslie A. Bunnage and Jesse Klein

Revolutionary Cells: On the Role of Texts, Tweets,
and Status Updates in Unarmed Revolutions   111
Daniel P. Ritter and Alexander H. Trechsel

References   129

Index   143

Introduction

Rachel Gibson

Abstract This volume provides an important update to our current understanding of politics and the Internet in a variety of new contexts, both geographically and institutionally. The subject of e-democracy has morphed over the years from the speculative and optimistic accounts of Rheingold (1993) and Negroponte (1996) who foresaw a future of heightened direct citizen involvement in political decision making and an increasingly "withered" state apparatus, to more prosaic investigations of party and governmental website content and micro-level analyses of voters' online activities. These latter studies painted a more muted and "normalized" picture of adaptation. Rather than leveling the communications and participation playing field, most studies concluded that existing patterns of bias and power distribution were being repeated online.

Introduction

This volume provides an important update to our current understanding of politics and the Internet in a variety of new contexts, both geographically and institutionally. The subject of e-democracy has morphed over the years from the speculative and optimistic accounts of Rheingold (1993) and Negroponte (1996) who foresaw a future of heightened direct citizen involvement in political decision making and an increasingly "withered" state apparatus, to more prosaic investigations of party and governmental website content and micro-level analyses of voters' online activities. These latter studies painted a more muted and "normalized" picture of adaptation. Rather than leveling the communications and participation playing field, most studies concluded that existing patterns of bias

R. Gibson (✉)
University of Manchester, Manchester, UK
e-mail: Rachel.Gibson@manchester.ac.uk

B. Grofman et al. (eds.), *The Internet and Democracy in Global Perspective*,
Studies in Public Choice 31, DOI: 10.1007/978-3-319-04352-4_1,
© Springer International Publishing Switzerland 2014

1

and power distribution were being repeated online. The larger parties were operating better sites and attracting more links (Gibson et al. 2003a; Gibson et al. 2003b; Margolis and Resnick 2000) and at the individual level any mobilizing effects of Internet use were seen as limited and linked to prior levels of engagement (Bimber 1999; Norris 2001). Indeed 10 years into the Web revolution, a meta-analysis of studies searching for individual-level effects concluded that the best that could be said was that "...there is little evidence to support the argument that Internet use is contributing to civic decline." And that while the effect of Internet use on engagement is positive, "the average positive effect is small in size" (Boulianne 2009, p. 203).

One area where the Internet did appear to be directly linked with a promise of genuine change was in the arena of protest and e-activism. Accounts emerged of how the new technologies were being used to coordinate anti-government, populist movements such as the Zapatistas in Mexico, the infamous anti-capitalist "Battle in Seattle," the global anti-war movements/protests during the Iraq war, and the anti-government protests in the 2004 Spanish elections (Bonchek 1995; Capling and Nossal 2001; Rheingold 2002; Bennett 2003; della Porta and Mosca 2005; della Porta et al. 2006; Earl 2006; Pickerill 2003; Gillan and Pickerill 2008; Meikle 2002). From a theoretical perspective, the Internet was seen as particularly suited to mobilizing collective action given its capacity for reducing organizational and coordination costs (Pickerill 2003; Bimber et al. 2005). More recently the protests in Tunisia, Egypt, and the so-called Arab Spring have given rise to greater optimism for the role of technology in fomenting democratic transitions and citizen engagement (Khamis 2011; Khondker 2011; Norris 2012).

Across all of these accounts, whether they focus on the systemic, institutional, or individual level, one central question that has recurred and structured the debate is whether the Internet is essentially a leveling communication tool that elevates the profile of the smaller and more marginalized players in the political system? Or whether it is a medium that simply reinforces existing power and participatory biases?

This is certainly a central concern that the studies assembled here attempt to address from various starting points within and outside the electoral arena. More specifically, the work presented here contributes to this debate and widens it in a number of important ways. Nicole Goodman's chapter turns to re-examine that old "chestnut" of digital politics—Internet voting—and revisits the core debates in a new context—Canada. Using a very rich over time dataset from one municipality she reveals the growing importance of the technology in Canadian elections, and a picture of both normalization and equalization or mobilization. Her research shows that despite the fact that the most common users of Internet voting are drawn from the ranks of the already mobilized, in that they are older and of higher socio-economic status, its roll-out has actually prompted some of the less engaged or nonvoting members of public to cast a ballot. Whether this leads them onto further action remains to be seen.

Remaining in the electoral arena but taking us several steps prior to the act of voting are the chapters of Garzia et al. and also Jensen and Anstead. Together these chapters move us nicely through the funnel of e-campaign causality. The latter outlines the rising tide of social media stimuli that parties and candidates now need to produce in order to appeal to voters. In an acknowledgment of the methodological challenges raised by the volume of data that these new digital tools generate, the authors provide a series of case studies of local-level adoption of Twitter and Facebook within UK constituencies during the 2010 election. In particular they ask how use of these new media by candidates opened up the traditional top-down command and control structure of party campaign communications and released a more horizontal and personal mode of adoption at the local level. Through social media, they argue, campaigns can create tools and "spaces" where supporters can help them in a self-directed manner, so the individual defines the parameters of their own engagement. Thus, while there is still an emphasis on national message management by national officials, a primary contribution of these media is to empower the grassroots and provide a platform through which campaigns can integrate their voices and ideas into its messaging and organization.

Having gained some insight into direct uses of the internet and particularly social media technologies by candidates in elections, Garzia et al. switch the readers' attention to a crop of new digital tools that allow for a more indirect online communication with voters—Voter Advice Applications or VAAs. VAAs function as quasi-official policy dissemination channels for parties according to the authors. More generally they form an important part of the new "postmodern" campaign environment in which nonparty actors assume an authoritative role in communicating election information to voters. A key contribution of these sites to the campaign landscape is their capacity for lowering voters' information costs. By condensing and filtering party messages into their bare essentials the sites serve as increasingly important "one stop shops" that citizens can consult to ensure that they are voting "correctly," or in accordance with their true issue preferences. Surveying the literature on VAAs to date the chapter makes the fascinating point that despite their overt focus on facilitating voter choice, their real impact may ultimately lie in their effect on political parties that are now scrambling to take positions on issues they previously ignored from the electorate, and even changing their policy stance in response to voters expressed preferences.

The chapter of Gilmore and Howard keeps us within the electoral arena but moves us away from the more established democracies of Europe to a developing nation—Brazil. Despite the relatively unmapped terrain covered by the authors, the chapter returns us to questions of normalization and equalization by investigating whether digital media offers any competitive advantage to underdogs—namely minor party candidates and challengers against their major party and incumbent rivals who command higher profile and more resources? The answer is a relatively unqualified affirmative with digital media seen as forming a valuable new tool for the lesser known candidates to counteract the traditional dominance of the powerful and resource rich incumbent coalition candidates. Following the logic of Jensen and Anstead the tools provide an inexpensive, if not free, option that can help them reach establish new constituencies. In addition, while not conclusively proving any causal effect they do note that those incumbents who lost office are less likely to have invested in internet campaigning than their successful colleagues. Furthermore, for challenger candidates using digital media was particularly important. Winning challenger candidates, especially at the level of lower house for deputies were found to have aggressive digital media campaigns.

The chapter of Deana Rohlinger and her colleagues extends the lens of the previous chapters from the formal political arena and contrasts the adaptation of political parties to the arrival of Internet with that of social movements In a bold and compelling argument they claim that not only are new ICTs particularly well suited to advancing the agenda of less formal political actors, but that the way they do so is by opening up a new and more direct channel of influence on political parties'. Using a rich assembly of qualitative data drawn from two key recently formed U.S. social movements—MoveOn.org and the Tea Party Movement—the authors show how these groups' skillful use of the Internet has allowed them to challenge and encroach on the Democrat and Republic parties' support base and agenda much more effectively in the post-digital era. This happens in a two-fold manner. First, they have greater access to funds, political advertising, and organizational support base to support their own efforts. In addition, they have an enhanced ability to mobilize behind the more unconventional candidates that can spring up in the American primary system and challenge the preferred party choice.

In the chapter "Revolutionary Cells: On the Role of Texts, Tweets, and Status Updates in Nonviolent Revolutions", our attention is shifted entirely out of the conventional arena by Ritter and Trechsel in their analysis of the role of online communication in fomenting nonviolent revolutions. Their question is a simple one, but one of great importance to the study of Internet and democracy. Specifically, they ask whether there is a causal link between new ICTs and revolutionary success? In an innovative analysis they compare use of old information and communication technologies of telephone and cassette recordings to oust the Shah of Iran in the 1970s with two more recent examples from the Middle East–North African region that relied on the digital media—Tunisia and Egypt. While the tools used in both uprisings were highly effective in achieving their ends the difference for the authors lies in the much wider global reach afforded to the Arab Spring revolutionaries. The rapid internationalization of the dissent through the medium of Twitter and Facebook generated a widespread movement of solidarity that was hard for established democratic governments to ignore. The subsequent calls for meaningful change and peaceful transition from influential figures such as the U.S. President helped stemmed the tide of violent domestic suppression that might otherwise have taken place, and set up what the authors see as a digital "feedback loop" that accelerated the revolution.

References

Bennett WL (2003) Communicating Global Activism: Strengths and Vulnerabilities of Networked Politics. Inf Commun Soc 6(2):143–168

Bimber B (1999) The Internet and citizen communication with government: does the medium matter? Polit Commun 16(4):409–428

Bimber B, Flanigan AJ, Stohl C (2005) Reconceptualizing collective action in the contemporary media environment. Commun Theor 15(4):365–388

Boulianne S (2009) Does internet use affect engagement? A meta-analysis of research. Polit Commun 26(2):193–211

Bonchek M (1995) Grassroots in cyberspace: using computer networks to facilitate political participation. Paper presented at the annual meeting of the Midwest Political Science Association, Chicago IL. <http://www.scribd.com/doc/82147418/Grass-Roots-in-Cyberspace-Bonchek-1995> Accessed 20 Jan 2013

Capling A, Nossal KR (2001) Death of distance or tyranny of distance? The internet, deterritorialization, and the anti-globalization movement in Australia. Pac Rev 14(3):443–465

della Porta D, Mosca L (2005) Global-net for global movements? A network of networks for a movement of movements. J Public Policy 25(1):165–190

della Porta D, Andretta M, Mosca L, Reiter H (2006) Globalization from below: transnational activists and protest networks. University of Minnesota Press, Minneapolis

Earl J (2006) Pursuing social change online: the use of four protest tactics on the internet. Soc Sci Comput Rev 20:1–16

Gibson RK, Margolis M, Resnick D, Ward SJ (2003a) Election campaigning on the WWW in the US and UK: a comparative analysis. Party Polit 9(1):47–76

Gibson R, Nixon P, Ward S (2003b) Net gain? Political parties and the internet. Routledge, New York

Gillan K, Pickerill J (2008) Transnational anti-war activism: solidarity, diversity and the internet in Australia, Britain and the United States after 9/11. Aust J Polit Sci 43(1):59–78

Khamis S (2011) The transformative egyptian media landscape: changes, challenges and comparative perspectives. Int J Commun 5:1159–1177

Khondker HH (2011) Role of the new media in the Arab spring. Globalization 8(5):675–679

Margolis M, Resnick D (2000) Politics as usual? The cyberspace revolution. Sage, London

Meikle G (2002) Future active: media activism and the internet. Routledge, New York and London

Negroponte N (1996) Being digital. Hodder & Stoughton, London

Norris P (2001) Digital divide: civic engagement, information poverty, and the internet. Cambridge University Press, Cambridge

Norris P (2012) The impact of social media on the Arab uprisings: the facebook, twitter, and youtube revolutions. Paper presented at the joint sessions of the ECPR, Antwerp, Belgium, 10–15 Apr

Pickerill J (2003) Cyberprotest: environmental activism on-line. Manchester University Press, Manchester

Rheingold H (2002) Smart mob: the next social revolution. Basic Books, Cambridge

Rheingold H (1993) The virtual community: homesteading on the electronic frontier. Addison Wesley, Reading, http://www.rheingold.com/vc/book/intro.html

Internet Voting in a Local Election in Canada

Nicole J. Goodman

Abstract In the past decade, Internet voting has been used in hundreds of binding elections at multiple levels of government throughout the world. Though many European jurisdictions have established well-developed online voting models, Canada is quickly emerging as an important research case. To date, there have been more instances of remote Internet voting in local Canadian elections than any other country. There have been more than two million remote Internet voting opportunities in over 90 local Canadian elections. This chapter analyzes the effects of online ballots by examining the City of Markham, Ontario as a case study. Using survey data from the 2003, 2006, and 2010 Markham municipal elections, a 2010 survey of candidates and other municipal data were applicable, the chapter considers which electors are using Internet voting, its potential to positively impact voting turnout, whether it is encouraging the participation of reported nonvoters, and assesses the implications for candidates and campaigns.

Introduction

For the past two decades, the deployment of Internet voting programmes has been growing worldwide. This growth has intensified in recent years because of rising Internet penetration, public use of the World Wide Web, and increasing government willingness to make use of the Internet in public service delivery. While some projects and trials have failed, others have been effectively implemented and developed, observing positive outcomes and receiving favorable feedback from stakeholders. To date, Canada, Estonia, and Switzerland represent some of the most advanced and refined Internet voting models, each at different levels of government.

N. J. Goodman (✉)
McMaster University, Hamilton, ON, Canada
e-mail: ngoodma@mcmaster.ca; Nicole.goodman@utoronto.ca

B. Grofman et al. (eds.), *The Internet and Democracy in Global Perspective*,
Studies in Public Choice 31, DOI: 10.1007/978-3-319-04352-4_2,
© Springer International Publishing Switzerland 2014

Canada, in particular, has quickly emerged as a local leader in Internet voting having offered more instances of online ballots in binding municipal elections than any country or jurisdiction throughout the world. Notably in Ontario, the October 2010 local elections offered about 800,000 potential voters the option of casting a ballot online in 44 municipalities and townships across the province. Of these communities, the City of Markham is the largest and, having offered online ballots in three consecutive election cycles, it is also one of the most established. This article provides a brief overview of the growing phenomena of remote Internet voting in Canada with a special emphasis on the City of Markham. Relying on attitudinal data collected in the Markham elections of 2003, 2006, and 2010 and research collected by Elections Canada and Intelivote Systems Inc., this article considers who is making use of online voting, the impact of Internet ballots on turnout, and finally, implications for candidates and election campaigns. Findings suggest that frequent voters are most likely to be receptive to online ballots and supports evidence from previous research that middle-aged electors are most inclined to make use of Internet voting (Alvarez et al. 2009; Internet Voting Workshop 2010). Finally, there is evidence that remote Internet voting has the potential to engage some electors with noncommittal voting records, particularly young people.

Remote Internet Voting

There are multiple types and forms of voting that use the Internet or an electronic machine to submit ballots. Alvarez and Hall (2004) identify four ways in which Internet voting can take place, including machines in polls (both in an electors' assigned poll or those that may be used in any polling place even if unassigned to the potential voter), kiosks, and voting from remote locations. Electronic machines have also been used to cast ballots, but these do not use Internet technology. Of these different online voting methods, this article focuses on instances of remote Internet voting[1] because this approach offers electors the greatest potential accessibility and convenience and therefore has the most potential to positively impact electoral participation. Polling place Internet voting, for example, may actually increase the opportunity cost of voting for some electors because it requires that they travel to the polls and involves learning a new voting method. Kiosks and other Internet machines are also less accessible than voting from home or work, even if made available in public places. Furthermore, most people associate the term *Internet voting* with voting online from remote locations such as home or work and do not often think of kiosks or machines in polling places (Mercurio 2004). Finally, the accessibility remote Internet voting offers most

---

[1] For purposes of stylistic relief 'remote Internet voting' is used synonymously throughout this article with 'Internet voting', 'online voting', 'Internet ballots', and 'online ballots'.

closely resembles other services provided online that are actively used by citizens, including banking, shopping, and government services (e.g., renewing passports) (Goodman et al. 2010).

Methodology

The primary data for this chapter come from a series of attitudinal surveys carried out by Delvinia, a Toronto-based company that partnered with the City of Markham in three local elections since 2003 to orchestrate marketing and voter outreach initiatives. This includes three exit poll surveys of online voters from 2003, 2006, and 2010 as well as a 2010 survey of candidates.[2] Data from Elections Canada and a special national survey conducted through Delvinia's AskingCanadians Panel provide broader insight into the effects of the Internet voting in Canada. Information was also gathered from key officials within certain municipalities to ensure accuracy and completeness. Finally, data from other municipalities that offered remote Internet voting in the 2010 Ontario municipal elections was made available by Intelivote, a Nova Scotia-based company, which conducted the alternative voting portion of the election (Internet and telephone) for 34 of the 44 cities and towns that chose to offer electronic voting methods in that election.

The Growth of Internet Voting in Canada

The first occurrence of Internet voting in Canada was a national New Democratic Party (NDP) leadership vote in 2003. Shortly after a group of 12 Ontario cities and townships offered online ballots in their 2003 elections.[3] This marked the first instance where Internet voting was made available in a binding government election in Canada. Since then the use of Internet voting in local Canadian elections has expanded significantly. About 60 municipalities in two provinces (Ontario and Nova Scotia) have successfully deployed Internet voting programs in their communities and have plans to continue its use. In the 2010 Ontario municipal elections, for example, 44 cities and townships made remote Internet voting available to about 800,000 potential voters (or one-tenth of the provincial electorate) totaling a growth rate of about 73 % over three consecutive election cycles. Taken together, there have been over 2 million Internet voting opportunities in over 90 municipal elections. These figures represent more instances of online

---

[2] For additional information about specific samples or methods used in conducting the surveys please see the Appendix.

[3] These include Champlain, Clarence-Rockland, East Hawkesbury, Hawkesbury, Markham, North Dundas, North Glengarry North Stormont, South Dundas, South Glengarry, South Stormont, and the Nation (Goodman 2010).

voting in binding elections than any other country or jurisdiction, making Canada a world leader in Internet voting at the municipal level.

Recent news suggests expansion locally and at other levels of government. A majority of the eligible electors in municipalities in the province of Nova Scotia were offered the option to vote remotely by Internet and telephone in their October 2012 elections. Of those participating in the elections that offered e-voting,[4] over 63 % of voters cast their ballots electronically (Smith 2012). Large municipalities in other provinces have also expressed an interest in offering Internet voting. The largest city in British Columbia, Vancouver, for example, approved the use of Internet ballots in the advance polls of its 2011 election, but the proposal was blocked by jurisdictional issues between levels of government prior to implementation (Pearce 2011).[5]

Though no tests or trials are confirmed at the provincial level, some provinces have been actively researching the benefits and drawbacks of online ballots. In Ontario specifically, the passage of the *Election Statute Law Amendment Act* (Bill 231) in May 2010 provides the province with the authority to test an electronic voting method pending approval from the Ontario Legislative Assembly and the province's Chief Electoral Officer (CEO). It also gives the provincial elections agency, Elections Ontario, the directive to report back to government on the feasibility of "network voting"[6] in Ontario by 2013 (Pollock 2011). The passage of this legislation provides the basis for a supportive legal framework and contributes toward creating a culture of support for Internet voting as an alternative voting method.

At the federal level, Canada's national election agency, Elections Canada, committed to trialing Internet voting as part of its Strategic Plan 2008–2013. This decision reflects amendments made in 2001 to the Canada *Elections Act*,[7] which allow the CEO to test an electronic voting system in a by-election or general election (Kohoko 2011). The trial requires the parliamentary approval prior to implementation, which Elections Canada plans to seek sometime after the 2015 election. In the meantime, the agency will continue researching and monitoring Internet voting in other jurisdictions.

---

[4] E-voting here refers to casting a ballot remotely by Internet or telephone. Both Internet voting and telephone voting were offered as alternative voting methods by 14 Nova Scotia municipalities in their October 2012 local elections.

[5] Though passed by city council, Vancouver was required to pass a by-law and have its online voting plan approved by the province given that it was incorporated before the British Columbia and is therefore governed under the *Vancouver Charter* and not the provincial municipal elections legislation (Kohoko 2011). With an electorate of 410,000 Vancouver would have been the largest Canadian municipality to offer online ballots in a binding election to date (Pearce 2011).

[6] The term 'network voting' will allow Elections Ontario to conduct a trial including any one of the following voting methods—telephone, fax, Internet, and possibly SMS (text message) or a multi-platform trial including a combination of electronic methods. Decisions regarding whether a trial will take place, and if so its scope, are to be determined in the coming weeks (Pollock 2011).

[7] These changes were made in 2000.

Aside from developments in government elections, the use of Internet voting remains strong in other types of elections as well. Many unions are increasingly opting for online ballots in their elections and there is significant uptake among political parties. Online ballots were used by the federal New Democratic and Liberal parties to elect their leaders in March 2012 and April 2013, respectively. Provincial leadership contests have also gravitated toward online voting in recent years. Some notable party elections using Internet ballots include: the Saskatchewan NDP, the Ontario NDP, the British Columbia NDP, and Liberal Party,[8] the Alberta Party and Alberta Liberal Party, as well as the New Brunswick Liberal Party (Smith 2012).

The expansion of Internet voting in Canada is well suited given the robust levels of public support for the alternative voting method. Data from a 2011 national survey indicates that about 85 % of Canadians support the introduction of Internet voting as a complementary method of voting in elections. A similar majority also reports being likely to make use of online ballots if introduced, at all levels of government (Delvinia 2011). Data from voters who cast ballots over the Internet in the Ontario municipality of Markham (Delvinia 2003, 2007, 2011) also suggests increasing support for Internet voting at other levels of government. Notably, 99 % of those surveyed reported being likely to vote online in a provincial or federal election if it were an option.

Taken together, growth in the number of Canadian municipalities that offer online ballots in binding local elections, strong public support for the policy change, and increasing interest on the part of governments and election agencies suggest Canada is a hot spot for Internet voting development. The frequency of elections with an Internet voting option and prospects for expansion make Canada an important research case, particularly for other jurisdictions considering the introduction of online voting. By critically examining the City of Markham as a case study, and bringing in other examples and cases where relevant, this article sheds the light on the impact of Internet voting on an election and the effects of online ballots for voters and candidates.

Markham

Markham is the largest Ontario municipality to offer Internet voting and the only major district to do so in three consecutive binding elections. Online ballots were made available to Markham electors in advance polls for 5 days in 2003, 6 days in 2006, and 7 days in 2010. The Markham model operates on a two-step process, which requires electors to register to vote online before they are able to cast a ballot.

---

[8] The Liberal winner was also declared the new provincial premier.

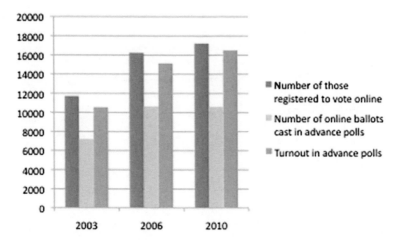

Fig. 1 Online registrants, ballots cast, and advance turnout in Markham elections. Data provided by the City of Markham (Turpin 2011a)

All eligible electors are sent a voter notification card by mail and receive a second card by registered mail upon completing the online registration process. This involves using a unique PIN (a randomly generated numeric credential), creating a seven-digit personal pass code (that must also be numeric), and entering their birth date.[9] The second mail out contains another unique PIN to be used along with the personal passcode electors create during the registration process in order to vote (Turpin 2011b).

Voter satisfaction with Markham's Internet voting system has been consistently high (about 99 %) in all three elections. In 2010, for example, those that reported being "very satisfied" increased 10 % from previous years.[10] In addition to strong levels of satisfaction, with each election the number of Internet voting registrants in Markham has grown and a majority of advance poll voters have chosen to cast their ballots online (see Fig. 1) (Turpin 2011a). Although the number of online ballots cast decreased very slightly (by less than 100 votes) in 2010, overall advance turnout noted a small increase.[11] On the whole Markham electors have responded favorably to Internet voting by making use of the alternative voting method and offering positive reviews of the system.

---

[9] This process differs slightly from the one used in 2003 and 2006, whereby electors were required to create a unique security question and did not have to submit their birth date. This was a new security measure for 2010 (Turpin 2011b).

[10] This increase in reported satisfaction may have something to do with the changes Markham made to the voting process (Delvinia 2011).

[11] Reasons for the decrease could be many, notably a different online voting marketing approach.

Who is Making Use of Internet Voting?

Many speculate that the incorporation of technology into the political process will encourage the participation of young people (Norris 2001; Milner 2010). However, data analyzing the use of Internet ballots by age group shows that it is not the youngest cohort that votes online most frequently, but rather more established electors. Analysis of Estonian e-voting by age in the 2007 federal election shows that those aged 25–49 were most likely to cast a ballot online (Alvarez et al. 2009). Data collected by Elections Canada confirm this finding in all Estonian elections with an online ballot component except the 2009 European Parliamentary elections, where those aged 50–59 were just as likely to vote online as those aged 30–49. In addition, data from a referendum in Geneva in 2004 find that voters aged 30–39 were the most popular users of online voting. Finally, a 2004 election in the Netherlands revealed that those aged 40+, and particularly voters aged 60–69 made the most use of online ballots (Elections Canada 2011). While these results are mixed, they suggest that the youngest cohort (aged 18–24) is not as likely to actively use Internet voting as older generations of electors. This lower rate of use, however, may have more to do with the fact that young people are less likely to participate electorally than with the appeal of online ballots (Pammett and LeDuc 2003).

Canadian data reveals a pattern somewhat similar to that found in European elections, although overall use of Internet voting in Canada is most prevalent among middle-aged electors (Goodman 2010). Results from Markham show that those aged 35–64 are the strongest Internet voting users in all election years and suggest that online ballots are growing in popularity among older voters while use is waning among younger voters (see Fig. 2). Since 2003, there has been a notable spike in use of Internet voting among those aged 55 and older. Similar findings of use by age group have also been observed in Nova Scotia municipalities (Goodman 2010). Though data from additional election years is needed prior to drawing any broad conclusions, these findings may reflect the simple aging of committed Internet voters. They could also be an indication of greater Internet penetration and use among older generations.

Comparing Markham to other Ontario municipalities and townships (for which data on Internet voting use is available in 2010) reveals a noticeable difference in use by age between younger and middle-aged voters (see Fig. 3).[12] Those aged 50 and older are considerably or at least moderately more likely to make use of online ballots in all 34 communities. This offers further support that middle-aged and older electors appear most likely to use online voting and is interesting for a number of reasons. First, it goes against popular perception that younger electors should be the target group of Internet voting initiatives. Though this difference in use could perhaps be explained in part by patterns of voting behavior, notably the fact that older electors are known to vote at higher rates than younger citizens, it still depicts

---

[12] The data was grouped into these age categories because that is how it was made available.

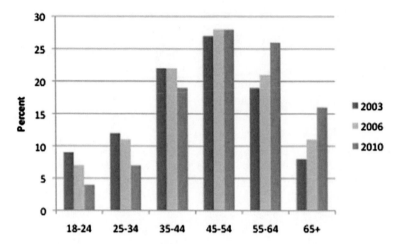

Fig. 2 Age of Internet voters in Markham. Data drawn from the 2003, 2006, and 2010 Markham online voting studies conducted by Delvinia, and the City of Markham, and 2010 age data from Intelivote Systems Inc

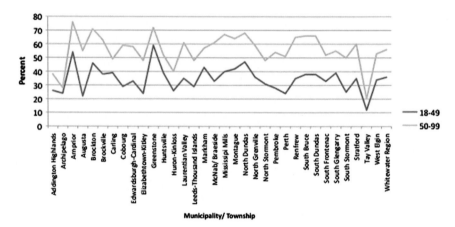

Fig. 3 Age of Internet voters in 33 Ontario municipalities. Data taken from Intelivote Systems Inc

a trend in use among those 50 and older. It may be that the extension of online voting is more about making the electoral process convenient for middle-aged and older electors and less about serving as a tool of engagement for the younger generation. This is also interesting given the fact that older electors in Markham report being less familiar with computers and using the Internet less than their younger counterparts (Delvinia 2011). It may be that a high level of use and familiarity with the Internet are not such powerful preconditions to using online voting.

Finally, it is curious that Internet voters in Ontario municipalities seem to be slightly older than online voters in Europe.[13] This may have something to do with the higher rate of Internet penetration in Canada (see Goodman 2010).

Turnout and Use of Internet Ballots

Proponents of Internet voting are quick to cite increases in turnout as a primary benefit of online ballots. Critics, however, are more hesitant and suggest that increases are not guaranteed and may be marginal at best. Existing literature has found it difficult to establish a causal link between the extension of Internet voting and turnout as more data is needed to clarify whether there is indeed a relationship. Currently, most of this research examines Estonian elections. Trechsel et al.s' (2010) analysis of turnout and Internet ballots in Estonia's 2009 local elections, for example, shows that turnout may have been 2.6 % lower had online ballots not been an option. By contrast, Bochsler's (2010) examination of Estonia's 2007 national parliamentary elections concludes that the increase in turnout from 2003 to 2007 can be explained by other factors and that Internet ballots seem to be used by those people who would have otherwise voted in polling stations. Additional data and turnout simulation is required to obtain a clearer picture. The case of Markham produces mixed results finding some support for Bochsler's conclusions, but also suggesting potential to increase turnout, albeit not every time.

Although turnout has not increased substantially in every Markham election where Internet voting was made available, advance polls noted a 300 % increase from 2000 to 2003 and a further 43 % rise in 2006 (Goodman 2010). As noted earlier, there was a less than 1 % decrease of advance online ballots in 2010, but overall turnout was down slightly as well (from 38 to 36 %), probably due to an uncompetitive race where the incumbent was perceived to be the clear victor early on (Froman 2010). Despite the lack of gains in 2010, the number of online registrants increased 6 % and, on the whole, advance turnout in Markham has been transformed as a consequence of Internet voting. For example, before 2003 a typical advance turnout was a couple thousand votes, but since the introduction of Internet ballots it averages about 10,000. Though the impact on overall turnout is marginal, Markham electors are making use of Internet ballots and turning out to the advance polls in much higher numbers.[14]

Looking to other Canadian municipalities the effect of Internet voting on turnout is mixed, although voters are clearly making use of online ballots more so, in fact, than telephone or paper options. Comparing turnout rates from 21 municipalities that offered Internet voting for the first time in 2010–2006

---

[13] An exact breakdown of online participation by the same age categories would confirm this.

[14] If online voting were made available throughout the entire voting period including election day, its impact on overall turnout would be more easily evaluated.

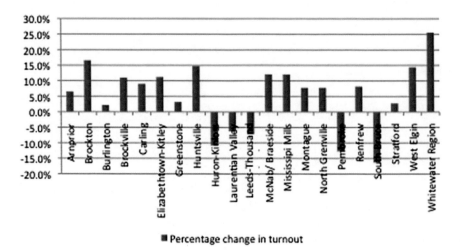

Percentage change in turnout

Fig. 4 Percentage change in turnout from 2006 to 2010 in Ontario municipalities. Data taken from Intelivote Systems Inc. and Hewitt (2011)

participation levels reveals a turnout increase in 16 and a decrease in 5 (see Fig. 4). Though there are many other contextual factors that affect turnout, and so which could be responsible for fluctuations in electoral participation, the decreases suggest that Internet voting is not a panacea for all the causes of declining turnout, while the increases imply that for some the added accessibility and convenience offered by Internet voting encourages turnout.

Examining the methods of voting used in municipalities that offered alternative voting options such as remote Internet and telephone voting reveals that remote Internet voting is the most popular method of casting a ballot in a majority of municipalities and townships across Ontario (see Fig. 5).[15] The data in Fig. 5 shows that in 2010 a minority of voters opted for traditional paper ballots, while Internet ballots were consistently popular in all communities. Though this does not shed light on turnout per se, it does illustrate that voters are making use of the service and in many municipalities and townships the accessibility of online voting has been cited as accounting for modest increases in overall turnout (Delvinia 2011; Goodman et al. 2010). In the City of Burlington, for example, where Internet voting was only offered in advance polls, advance turnout increased by more than 40 %. The impact on overall turnout was only about 2 %, but the extension of Internet voting had an important effect on the advance portion of the election (Hewitt 2011).

---

[15] Please note that this is not a comprehensive list of all municipalities and townships that offered remote Internet voting in the 2010 Ontario local elections. The data shown was collected by Intelivote Systems Inc., the remote Internet and telephone service provider for a number of municipalities, and supplied by Dean Smith, CEO/President.

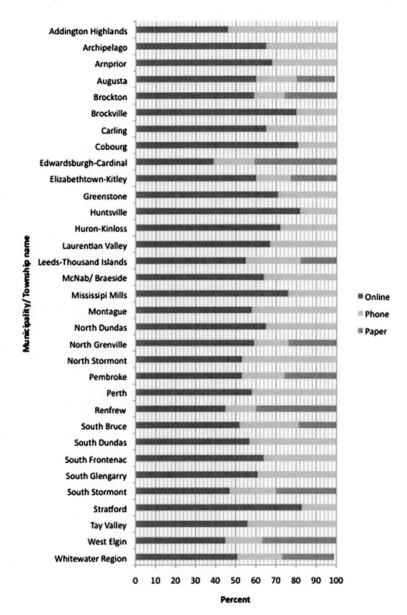

Fig. 5 Methods of voting in 33 Ontario municipalities and townships, 2010. Data taken from Intelivote Systems Inc

Turnout, Nonvoters, and the Ability of Internet Voting to Engage the Young

Another approach to gauging whether the extension of remote Internet voting has a positive effect on electoral participation is to assess its impact on respondents who report having noncommittal voting records.[16] If the option of online voting can successfully promote participation among those who had not participated previously or had taken part sporadically it could have a positive affect on turnout. In Markham, 9 % of Internet voters in 2010 reported having not voted in 2006. Similarly, 21 % of 2006 voters claimed they had not voted in 2003, and 25 % of 2003 online voters said they did not vote in the 2000 municipal election (Delvinia 2003, 2007, 2011). These figures suggest that the extension of remote Internet voting may have the potential to encourage the electoral involvement of nonvoters or those who participate in elections less frequently. The fact that the number of previous nonvoters decreased 12 % between 2006 and 2010 could be attributed to the fact that less young people (who vote at lower rates than older electors and are more likely to report noncommittal voting records) made use of Internet voting in the 2010 election. Similar findings about reported nonvoters making use of Internet voting has been detected in Estonia (Alvarez et al. 2009; Goodman et al. 2010).

To get a better sense of the relationship between reported voting record and whether online voters would have cast a ballot had Internet voting not been an option, the question "If you didn't have the option to vote by Internet, would you still have voted?" is correlated with an additive scale constructed from responses to "Considering elections at all levels of government, since you became eligible to vote would you say you have participated in...federal elections, provincial elections, and municipal elections?" Based on their responses online voters were divided into three categories: frequent voters (those who report voting "in all elections" were given a value of 1.00), occasional voters (those who report voting 'in some elections' or 'from time to time' were given a value of 2.00), and nonvoters (voters who said they 'never' vote were given a value of 3.00).[17] Responses were then added together producing a nine-point scale. Using Kendall's tau-b to assess whether there is a relationship between the two variables reveals a strong positive correlation between the two (tau-b = 0.359; sig. = 0.000), meaning that people who are more likely to be voters or who have committed past voting records are more likely to be receptive to Internet voting. This result is consistent with Bochsler's (2010) finding in Estonian elections that Internet voters primarily include those already keen to take part electorally, but does it mean online voting has little to no capacity to persuade less committed or nonvoters to participate?

---

[16] This includes nonvoters and those who say that they vote 'occasionally'.

[17] See Trechsel (2007) or Breuer and Trechsel (2006).

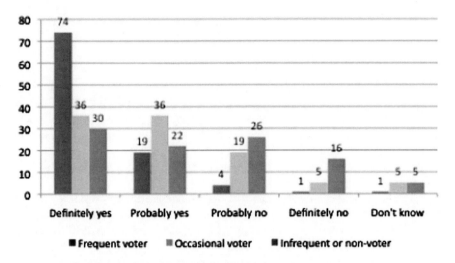

Fig. 6 Likelihood of voting if Internet ballots not been available, by voting record. Data drawn from the 2010 Markham online voting study conducted by Delvinia

To gain more insight as to whether Internet ballots can motivate less committed electors to vote, the scale was reduced to three categories.[18] Examining responses by percentage to the question, 'If you didn't have the option to vote by Internet, would you still have voted?' (see Fig. 6) shows that infrequent or nonvoters were most likely to say that they would not have cast a ballot if Internet voting were not available (Delvinia 2011). Occasional voters were slightly more certain about their likelihood of voting, but about 26 % said they 'probably' would not have or 'definitely' would not have participated (Delvinia 2011). These figures show that the certainty of voting without the option of online ballots decreases as the voting record becomes less committed. This could be because occasional and infrequent/ nonvoters are always less sure about whether they will cast a ballot in an election, however it might also be an indication that Internet voting can encourage some nonvoters and (fewer) occasional voters to participate during election time.

Noting that the youngest online voters are least likely to participate and hence most likely to belong to the occasional and infrequent/nonvoting categories it is useful to assess responses to this question by age group. Grouping responses into "yes" and "no" categories by age reveals that the youngest online voters (aged 18–24) are twice as likely as any other group to say they "probably" would not have or "definitely" would not have voted had Internet ballots not been an alternative voting method. Not surprisingly, the likelihood of voters saying they

---

[18] Values in the scale ranged from 3.00 to 9.00. Since 1.00 had been used to represent the response "vote in all elections' a score of 3.00 represented a frequent voter. 2.00 represented voting 'in some elections' or 'from time to time" so values of 4.00, 5.00, and 6.00 were grouped together to symbolize the occasional voter. Finally, 'never' voting received a score of 3.00 so values of 7.00, 8.00, and 9.00 were clustered together to signify an infrequent or nonvoter.

would not have voted without the online option decreases with age. Although data indicates that young people use online voting less, it may be that Internet ballots have potential to encourage some young noncommittal voters to participate electorally. More research is needed to determine if this is the case.

Overall, however, data indicates that those who report voting "frequently" are most likely to be receptive to casting a ballot online. This group appears to be older, committed voters. Despite these findings, the fact that many young reported nonvoters say that they voted because of Internet ballots merits further investigation. While the trend could certainly be that frequent older voters are the highest users and most drawn to the method of online voting, it might also appeal to some noncommitted voters, particularly young ones.

Analysis of a special national survey of Canadian electors produces similar findings regarding the potential of Internet voting to encourage the participation of young people. Taking all electors into account, 53 % of respondents indicated agreement with the statement "If Internet voting were available I would be more likely to vote in elections." Evaluating agreement with this statement by age shows that young people especially say they would be more likely to cast a ballot if they could do so online, offering nearly double the support of other cohorts.[19] While young people may merely be "saying" they will be more likely to participate, with no intended follow-through, consistent response patterns in these two surveys suggests there may be something to the fact that the youngest segment of the electorate expresses overwhelmingly (especially comparative to other age groups) that Internet ballots would promote their electoral participation. Again, the fact that their rate of use is lower than other age groups may be linked to their weak inclination to participate and does not mean that online voting is not a motivating factor in promoting the electoral involvement of young people (Pammett and LeDuc 2003).

Impact on Candidates and the Campaign

Aside from its impact on electors and turnout in advance polls, the introduction of Internet voting in Markham has also affected candidates and the nature of the campaign. 38 of a potential 44 candidates completed a voluntary survey following the election to shed light on the incorporation of Internet voting in the electoral process.[20] 78 % of candidates surveyed said they believed the presence of Internet voting in the advance polls affected the campaign. Explaining this impact their comments centered on three main aspects: turnout, accessibility and convenience, and shortening of the campaign. A majority of candidates expressed noting an

---

[19] This data comes from a different survey, which includes an oversample of youth aged 18–26 from across Canada collected by Delvinia.

[20] This survey was carried out by and is the property of Delvinia.

increase in participation while canvassing, which they attributed to Internet voting. Some observed that online ballots were particularly useful in promoting the youth vote, especially for those young people away at school. Many other comments mentioned the accessibility and convenience of online ballots and how being able to vote when 'busy' or 'away' provided an opportunity of involvement for electors who might otherwise have abstained. Finally, some made comments about how online voting shortened the campaign given the large number of voters that chose to vote by Internet in the advance polls. Candidates observed that some campaign information went out too late, since when canvassing they encountered many constituents who had already voted.

Candidates were specifically asked to recount how many people they encountered while campaigning that reported already having voted and how many of these voters indicated they had cast online ballots. About 80 % of candidates said they did connect with online voters while canvassing or carrying out other campaign-related activities. Notably, over 40 % reported having encountered 10 or more online voters during the campaign period. The fact that advance poll voting in Markham is up substantially from pre-Internet voting levels and that candidates came in contact with so many electors who had already cast online ballots suggests that Internet voting has an impact on the campaign, particularly with respect to informing, canvassing, and mobilizing voters. It is interesting that more candidates did not comment on campaign changes, but instead focused on the issue of turnout and the positive effect they observed.

While Internet voting may not have a large effect on turnout, or even a marginal effect in all elections, it is telling that so many candidates emphasized that Internet voting had an observable impact on participation, notably because they rationalize it makes the voting process more accessible for certain groups of electors (e.g., those away, students at college or university, and those too busy with work or family obligations to vote at a traditional poll). Evidence from the capital city of Nova Scotia, Halifax, suggests that Internet voting also shortened its election campaign, with many municipal candidates reporting the need to get information out to electors much sooner (Goodman 2010). Additional research is needed to more fully explore the impact of Internet voting on the campaign and candidate functions during the campaign, particularly with respect to advance polls. If the changes to advance turnout in Markham and the feedback from this survey are any indication, Internet voting has potential to positively impact participation and create a shorter, more top-heavy campaign, whereby the first few weeks could become more important than the last, depending on the number of Internet voters.

Conclusion

Overall, looking at the case of Markham and some other Ontario municipalities where relevant, several observations are apparent. First, middle-aged and older electors who have committed voting records are the most likely to make use of

Internet voting. Similarly, Internet voting is most likely to attract committed voters. These findings, however, should not be taken as evidence that Internet voting has no positive effect on turnout. Though frequent voters may be most receptive to Internet voting, findings suggest that online ballots encourage some infrequent/nonvoters to participate, notably young people. More evidence is needed, but turnout statistics suggest that in many cases the *initial* extension of online ballots can have a positive impact on electoral participation, even if reported committed voters cast a large portion of those ballots.

Third, there is evidence to suggest that the youngest infrequent/nonvoters can be drawn into the electoral process through the extension of online ballots. Despite the fact that this group votes at the lowest rates and is least likely to make use of Internet voting generally, the largest portion of those that are attracted to participate electorally through Internet voting come from the 18 to 24 age group. Though voting by Internet is by no means a systemic fix for apathy or other social and political causes of nonvoting, and the numbers are small, there does seem to be some potential for engagement among less committed voters, particularly young people. Given that the habit of voting now seems to be developing later in life, if at all, the promise of engaging some young people in the electoral process earlier is hopeful, especially if it could establish voting as a custom for future elections.

Finally, candidate commentary suggests that when Internet voting is offered in advance polls the campaign is shortened and therefore, the need to get information out becomes more important at the outset of the campaign. In situations where Internet ballots are offered in advance polls this could mean that the first few weeks of a campaign turn out to be the most important, whereas the last few weeks become significantly less so. Furthermore, a majority of candidates stressed that the option of online ballots seemed to encourage participation. Although it is anecdotal, this offers support that Internet ballots can positively impact voting turnout.

On the whole, the findings of this article are mostly favorable for the use of Internet voting as an alternative voting method in elections, but more research is needed to refine conclusions and solidify results. Analysis highlights popular usage patterns, especially among older voters who report being less Internet savvy. It also presents evidence that online voting has potential to encourage some nonvoters to take part, notably the youngest nonvoters. Furthermore, findings suggest that although online ballots are not a broad-based solution for turnout decline, electoral participation can experience modest increases when they are made available. These increases are likely the result of the enhanced accessibility and convenience offered by remote electronic voting methods. While condensing the campaign may or may not be taken as a positive influence, there are many other electronic mediums that have penetrated electoral politics and are currently transforming the ways in which traditional campaigns are run (e.g., Twitter, Facebook, and YouTube). The advent of Internet voting is consistent with the breakthrough of other technologies and Web applications in politics and as such may be a welcome addition to the electoral arena for many electors. There is much to be learnt about the extension of Internet voting, but some initial results suggest it is a useful complementary voting method to offer in elections.

Acknowledgements I would like to thank Jon Pammett and Bernard Grofman for their valuable comments. The research and data for this chapter was in large part provided by Delvinia, a Toronto-based digital strategy and customer experience design firm that has been played an important role in helping Markham develop its Internet voting approach and outreach strategy. I sincerely thank Adam Froman, CEO, for the use of the data his company collected over the past three election cycles in Markham. For more information about Delvinia's research and data collection regarding Internet voting please contact Susan O'Neill, Public Relations Manager, via email at soneill@delvinia.com. I would also like to thank Elections Canada for kindly sharing their research and Dean Smith, President of Intelivote Systems Inc. for offering some municipal data his company has collected in past elections.

References

Alvarez RM, Hall TE (2004) Point, click and vote: the future of internet voting. Brookings Institution Press, Washington

Alvarez RM, Hall TE, Trechsel AH (2009) Internet voting in comparative perspective: the case of Estonia. PS: Polit Sci Polit 42:497–505

Bochsler D (2010) Can internet voting increase political participation? Remote electronic voting and turnout in the Estonian 2007 parliamentary elections. In: Prepared for presentation at the conference 'Internet and Voting', Fiesole, June 3–4

Breuer F, Trechsel AH (2006) Report for the council of Europe, E-voting in the 2005 local elections in Estonia. European University Institute, Florence

Delvinia (2003) Internet Voting and Canadian Democracy in Practice: The Delvinia Report on Internet Voting in the 2003 City of Markham Municipal Election

Delvinia (2007) Understanding the Digital Voter Experience: The Delvinia Report on Internet Voting in the 2006 City of Markham Municipal Election

Delvinia (2011) eDemocracy and citizen engagement: The Delvinia Report on Internet Voting in City of Markham.

Elections Canada (2011) Canada Municipal Jurisdiction Graphs

Froman A (2010) CEO, Delvinia. Personal interview, 21 Oct 2010

Goodman N (2010) Internet voting in Canadian municipalities: what can we learn? CEU Polit Sci J 5(4):492–520

Goodman N, Pammett JH, DeBardeleben J (2010) A comparative assessment of electronic voting, report prepared for elections Canada

Hewitt L (2011) Clerks Technology Analyst, City of Burlington. Personal Communication, 6 May 2011

Kohoko D (2011) Manager, Alternative Voting Methods, Elections Canada. Personal communication, 14 April 2011

Mercurio B (2004) Democracy in decline: can internet voting save the electoral process? John Marshall J Comput Inf Law 12(2):101–143

Milner H (2010) The internet generation: engaged citizens or political dropouts. Tufts University Press, Medford

Norris P (2001) Digital divide: civic engagement, information poverty, and the internet. Cambridge University Press, Cambridge

Pammett JH, LeDuc L (2003) Explaining the turnout decline in Canadian federal elections: a new survey of non-voters. Ottawa, Elections Canada. http://www.elections.ca

Pearce B (2011) Deputy Chief Election Officer, City of Vancouver. Personal Interview, 5 May 2011

Pollock S (2011) Program Manager, Event Readiness, Elections Ontario. Personal Interview, 10 May 2011

Smith D (2012) President, Intelivote. Personal Communication, 30 Nov 2012

Trechsel AH (2007) E-voting and electoral participation. In: de Vreese C (ed) Dynamics of referendum campaigns—an international perspective. Palgrave, London, pp 159–182

Trechsel A, Robert S, Kristjan V (2010) Internet voting in Estonia: a comparative analysis of four elections since 2005, report prepared for the directorate general of democracy and political affairs and the directorate of democratic institutions, Council of Europe

Turpin C (2011a) Legislative Coordinator, City of Markham. Personal Communication, 12 April 2011

Turpin C (2011b) Legislative Coordinator, City of Markham. Personal Interview, 25 April 2011

Indirect Campaigning: Past, Present and Future of Voting Advice Applications

Diego Garzia, Alexander H. Trechsel, Kristjan Vassil and Elias Dinas

Abstract Voting Advice Applications (VAAs) have become an integral part of many electoral campaigns in modern democracies. VAAs allow users to compare, on the Internet, their political preferences with the positions of parties and candidates prior to an election. In recent elections in Switzerland, the Netherlands, and Germany, more than a quarter of the respective electorates used such an online-tool. This contribution explains the logic behind VAAs, retraces their historical development and diffusion, discusses the most recent findings on the impact such tools can have on political behavior of citizens, as well as on political parties themselves, and finally offers a look into the future of online voting advice applications.

Introduction: The Logic of Voting Advice Applications

Voting Advice Applications (hereafter: VAAs) have nowadays turned into a widespread feature of electoral campaigns in Europe and beyond (Walgrave et al. 2008, 2009; Cedroni and Garzia 2010; Trechsel and Mair 2011; Vassil 2011). According to Walgrave et al. (2008) in 2007 there was at least one such application running in 15 European countries out of the 22 they surveyed. Five years later, a reassessment of the spread of VAAs mapped the presence of (at least) one such tool in all but two countries of the EU27 (Garzia et al. 2012). Over the last few years, VAAs have also been developed for elections in North America (Dufresne et al. 2012) as well as in emerging democracies such as Tunisia, Morocco and Egypt (Wall et al. 2012).

D. Garzia · A. H. Trechsel (✉) · K. Vassil · E. Dinas
European University Institute, Florence, Italy
e-mail: Alexander.Trechsel@EUI.eu

B. Grofman et al. (eds.), *The Internet and Democracy in Global Perspective*,
Studies in Public Choice 31, DOI: 10.1007/978-3-319-04352-4_3,
© Springer International Publishing Switzerland 2014

In some countries—including the Netherlands, Germany, Switzerland, Finland, and Belgium—the incorporation of VAAs into the electoral process is almost self-evident. In the run-up to the 2012 parliamentary election in the Netherlands, 4.9 million users resorted to the Dutch VAA *StemWijzer*. If these 4.9 million users corresponded to individual Dutch voters, this figure would mean that over 40 % of all voters casting a vote in the 2012 general elections (9.4 million) would have been exposed to this VAA. Similarly impressive figures come from Switzerland, where almost one million voting advices were provided by the national VAA *smartvote* during the federal election of 2007 (Ladner et al. 2010) and over one million in 2011 (Pianzola et al. 2012). In absolute numbers, the German *Wahl-O-Mat* launched before the national elections in 2009 has been used by the largest number of users ever: 6.7 million (Marschall et al. 2010). VAAs have not only been deployed at the national level. For the 2009 EP election, a pan-European VAA was conceptualised and put in place by the European University Institute led *EU Profiler* consortium.[1] In only 6 weeks of online presence, prior to the elections of June 7 2009 the *EU Profiler* was able to attract more than 2.5 million unique visitors (Breuer 2010; Trechsel and Mair 2011).

Although different in some respects (for a review, see Garzia et al. 2012), VAAs share a common underlying principle: they help users casting a vote by comparing their policy preferences on major issues with the programmatic stances of political parties on the same issues. The nuclear component of every VAA that enables this comparison is a political issue statement, e.g. "Social programs should be maintained even at the cost of higher taxes" (Cf. Fig. 1a). Each user can express her agreement or disagreement with each particular statement. The number of issue statements used varies from one VAA to another, but it usually ranges between 10 and 70. The resulting issue preferences of the user are then matched with the positions of the parties. The party positions are usually extracted by the developers of the VAA, sometimes even in association with the political parties running in the campaign. In some cases, such as in the Swiss or Luxemburgish VAAs, the positions of individual candidates are also offered on the respective platforms. After comparing the user's profile with that of each party (or candidate), the application produces a "voting advice", usually in the form of a rank-ordered list, at the top of which stands the party closest to the user's policy preferences (Cf. Fig. 1b). Various forms of graphical representations of the overlap between users and parties exist, such as compasses or spider-grams. However, most VAAs include at least the rank-ordered list, sometimes called "match list".

As they have emerged in numerous countries—and given their increasing popularity among voters—VAAs have started to constitute a relevant object of

---

[1] The *EU Profiler* consortium consists of the European University Institute (EUI) in Florence, the Amsterdam-based company *Kieskompas* and the NCCR Democracy (University of Zurich/ Zentrum für Demokratie Aarau)/*Politools* network. The project has been led by the Robert Schuman Centre for Advanced Studies (RSCAS), part of the European University Institute (EUI) and developed under the auspices of the EUI-based European Union Democracy Observatory (EUDO).

Fig. 1 Example of a VAA statement (*left*); the 'voting advice' provided in the results screen (*right*) *Source* http://www.euprofiler.eu

social science research. The academic literature on campaign innovations locates the spread of VAAs within a broader trend in the post-modern campaigning environment, i.e. the growing presence of non-party actors who "communicate" in electoral campaigns without running themselves for office (Farrell and Schmitt-Beck 2008). Whereas the vote advice from the VAA can be thought of as a form of political communication, it must be also noted that these advices differ considerably from most of the messages that are received via electoral campaigning. Unlike most of the campaign messages, VAA advices are in fact not persuasive in nature (Stiff and Mongeau 2003), since it is up to the voter to initiate the process of acquiring the information (i.e. the voting advice) out of her own self-interest. Moreover, VAAs offer an explicit ranking of viable options with an implication that this ranking is tailored according to one's preferences. The ability of VAAs to reduce the costs of information before an election is one of the keys to understand their growing success among voters (Alvarez et al. 2012).

With a growing part of the electorate resorting to these tools during election times, academic interest has progressively arisen with respect to the effect of these tools on voters as well as on parties and candidates. The aim of the present chapter is to map the existing VAA studies and to outline an agenda for these increasingly prominent tools and their role within contemporary democracies. The Section "History and Diffusion of VAAs: From *StemWijzer* to *EU Profiler*" describes the history and the diffusion of VAAs over the last two decades—from the paper-and-pencil *StemWijzer* in the Netherlands to the pan-European, continent-wide *EU Profiler*. It then presents the key literature regarding the effects of VAAs on the main actors of election campaigns (i.e. parties and candidates) as well as voters. Next, it highlights the potential contribution of VAA-generated data to the study of party politics and representation in contemporary European democracies. The Section "Introduction: The Logic of Voting Advice Applications" is devoted to a reflection on the future of VAAs in the light of their growing relevance in the pre-electoral sphere.

History and Diffusion of VAAs: From *StemWijzer* to *EU Profiler*

What can be considered the "ancestor" of all VAAs—the *StemWijzer*—was developed in 1989 by the Dutch *Stichting Burgerschapskunde* (SBK: Citizenship Foundation) in collaboration with the *Documentatiecentrum Nederlanse Politieke Partijen* (DNPP: Documentation Centre of Dutch Political Parties) and the faculty of Political Management of the University of Twente. The *StemWijzer* package consisted in a booklet containing 60 statements taken from political party programs and a diskette, and was primarily aimed for junior high-school education. The booklet was fairly popular, especially in the educational sector. However, not more than 50 floppy-disc copies were sold. Eventually, the creators of *StemWijzer* started considering the possibility to exploit the full potential of emerging ICTs. An internet-based *StemWijzer* was released a few years later, on the occasion of the 1998 Dutch parliamentary elections. Despite the rather wide outreach of the project and publicity invested into the *StemWijzer,* its use among Dutch voters remained rather limited. In that year, only 6,500 voters used the internet-based version of the VAA. The intention of its creators to persist in their effort—supported by the parallel spread of internet access among the population at large— proved to be a winning choice after all. During the two consecutive elections in 2002 and 2003, strongly tainted by the extraordinary rise and subsequent murder of Pim Fortuyn, *StemWijzer* grew into the most used political application on the internet by Dutch voters. From 50 sold booklets in 1989, via the 6,500 online users in 1998, the number of users now reached the figure of two million, only to reach about five million during the following elections (de Graaf and Jochum 2010). Based on these figures, the most recent versions of *StemWijzer* were used by the equivalent of roughly one out of two Dutch voters.

With the beginning of the new millenium, the highly successful experience of *StemWijzer* made its incursion into several other countries. This is he case of Germany, where *Wahl-O-Mat* was fielded for the first time in 2002 and attracted more than 20 million users ever since (Marschall et al. 2010). Further versions of the Dutch pioneering VAA also appeared in Bulgaria (*Glasovoditel*) and Switzerland (*Politarena*). The Swiss application was "challenged" already in 2003 by *smartvote,* a VAA developed by Politools. The first version of *smartvote* provided over 255,000 voting advices as compared to the 135,000 issued by *Politarena*. In only four years, the use of *smartvote* had increased almost fourfold, with roughly one million voting advices issued in 2007 (Ladner et al. 2010). Besides Switzerland and Germany, Belgium (Flanders) has also been inspired by the Dutch example. In 2004, the Flemish public broadcaster VRT launched *Doe de Stem Test!*—a VAA for the regional elections of that year. Due to its intrinsic connection with the homonym TV-show, the Flemish VAA was able to issue over 840,000 voting advices during that campaign (Walgrave et al. 2008). A similar media-driven development can be observed in the case of Finland. There, the Finnish public broadcasting company developed the first VAA already in 1996. Following this example, Helsingin Sanomat (the largest daily newspaper in the country) built its own application for the 1999 European Parliamentary elections. In 2001, as many as eleven different VAAs were available to Finnish voters. This figure rises up to over twenty during the 2007 election campaign, with the most popular among these applications attracting over one million users (Ruusuvirta and Outi 2010).

Most recently, VAAs continued to mushroom across Europe and beyond. Focusing only on VAA versions that have been developed for national level elections, over 40 online tools of this kind have been implemented in Europe (Garzia et al. 2012). In some nations, more than one VAA has been launched, in particular among the early-movers, leading to sometimes fierce competition between several VAA providers. The Dutch *Kieskompas* is a telling example in this respect. Developed as an open attempt to overcome the shortcomings inherent to the *StemWijzer* methodology, it evolved into one of the most established VAA applications in the Netherlands. Furthermore, its producers have implemented similar VAAs in various political settings across Europe (i.e. Portugal, Sweden) and beyond (i.e. Israel, Turkey, Marocco, Tunisia) (Wall et al. 2012).

An empirically based explanation for the huge territorial spread of VAAs builds on the "snow-balling" model. The early success of VAAs in certain countries, and most notably in the Netherlands and Germany, was in fact among the main driving forces behind the creation of the Network of European Citizenship Education (NECE)—a group encompassing agencies and NGOs in the field of citizenship education from 25 European countries, and serving as a forum for the dissemination of national VAA projects (Garzia et al. 2012). In 2009, the so far most ambitious and largest VAA in terms of territorial spread and number of parties was offered to citizens across 30 countries during the European Parliamentary elections. Led by the European University Institute in Florence (Italy) and relying on the support of over 130 collaborators organised in country teams, the *EU Profiler* also served as a channel of dissemination of the VAA idea to other European countries. With the coding of more than 270 political parties across the European Union on 30 political issues, the *EU Profiler* project stands indeed as the largest-scale transnational VAA endeavor to date. The making of *EU Profiler* brought about a number of technical and methodological innovations in the field. Suffice it to say that, for the first time, the location of party positions across *all* member states of the European Union was determined interactively with the parties themselves (Trechsel and Mair 2011—cf. "5. Impact on the Discipline: Party Politics and Democratic Representation"). With more than 2.5 million users visiting the website in order to compare their views with those of the parties and over 900,000 voting advices issued in only 6 weeks (Breuer 2010) the *EU Profiler* project has set a new standard for the development of transnational VAAs.

Impact on Electoral Competition: Parties and Party Systems

Related to the impressive spread of VAAs throughout political systems is their growing impact on political parties, exemplified by the large-scale interaction of these partisan actors with the makers of *EU Profiler* (Cf. "5. Impact on the Discipline: Party Politics and Democratic Representation"). There are good reasons to assume that VAAs exert influence on the parties. In fact, parties and their positions on the statements are at the core of these tools. Furthermore, parties themselves are involved in the process of production of the statements in certain VAAs, e.g. the German *Wahl-O-Mat* (Marschall et al. 2010). The same goes for candidate-level VAAs such as the Swiss *smartvote* (Ladner et al. 2010).

Especially for VAAs that ask party representatives to authorize their party position on statements, their sheer existence may have a number of potential effects. First, the development of a VAA may lead parties to adopt positions on issues they previously ignored or tried to avoid (de Graaf and Jochum 2010) and it may help them to "reshape" their positions in light of the questions asked by VAA producers. The progressive diffusion of VAAs among the respective electorates has also led parties to pay increasing attention to this new format of political communication. Real world evidence shows that parties have become rather sensitive to the potential effects of these tools on users/voters. This can go as far as in the case of some parties that consciously synchronise the drafting of their party manifesto with the questionnaires developed by VAA producers. Especially larger parties in heavy-VAA-user countries have built an entire "team" to interface with the growing demands coming from VAA-makers. In some instances (e.g. The Netherlands, Belgium) parties have even recruited personnel for their campaign team in order to make sure that responses to the statements are answered "knowledgeably and professionally" (Krouwel et al. 2012).

At times, voters' reaction to VAAs can even instigate changes in parties' own political positions. In the Belgian campaign of 2003, for instance, the public broadcasting corporation's VAA revealed that

> a massive majority of users were in favour of restricting the rules on parole for convicted felons. In an immediate reaction to this news, the president of the Socialist Party, Steve Stevaert, tabled a motion to end this regulation, contrary to his longstanding party manifesto (Hooghe and Teepe 2007, p. 969).

Parties such as the Christian Democratic Party of Belgium protested against the proliferation of VAAs, arguing in the light of the aforementioned episode that these tools would fuel further a populist approach to politics and election campaigns (Wall et al. 2009). While testing the validity of such an argument lies beyond the purposes of this chapter, it is worth pointing those instances in which political parties actually embraced a "populist" approach *vis-à-vis* VAAs. It is the case, for example, of the Dutch Christian Democratic Appeal. Observers noted that during the 2006 parliamentary election campaign the party did not answer the

StemWijzer statements on the basis of their manifesto, but rather submitted those answers that were more likely to be the most popular. Indeed, the justifications provided by the party for their positions appeared tailor-made to confront the main opponents' positions (van Praag 2007). An analysis of the Lithuanian case speaks further of the VAAs's (potential) encouragement to the adoption of ideologically unconstrained policy positions on behalf of parties (Ramonaite 2010; *contra*: Schwarz et al. 2010). Against this background, a number of developers have adopted a number of strategies to cope with the risk of false/inconsistent issue placement by parties. Most notably, the *EU Profiler* relied on a two-step interaction whereby parties were indeed asked to position themselves on the statements, but their responses were subject to corrections by the makers based on a hierarchy of available sources to derive the actual position of the party on that statement.

Second, they may not only distort their real positions, but simply lie about them in order to maximise an expected electoral advantage. However, as the self-positioning of parties in the EP 2009 elections showed, there is little evidence for this kind of behaviour, with only small discrepancies usually emerging—and for a small proportion of cases only—between parties and experts (see Trechsel and Mair 2011). Third, instead of passively waiting for a VAA questionnaire to be developed, they may proactively try to shape the latter. In Germany, this is institutionalised in the *Wahl-O-Mat*, where representatives of political parties collaboratively co-shape the questionnaire (Marschall et al. 2010). Finally, a rather radical impact on political parties could be measured, e.g. during the 2009 EP elections in Greece. Here, the interaction with the Greek country team of the *EU Profiler* led the Green Party to change its initial position on a statement in virtue of the convincing evidence brought forward by the *EU Profiler* country team (Trechsel and Mair 2011).

Impact on Users: Political Attitudes and Behavior

As made clear in the Section "Impact on Electoral Competition: Parties and Party Systems", the impressive numbers of users visiting VAAs during election campaigns have rendered political parties increasingly more careful in their relationship with the VAAs. This attention can be most easily explained by the parties' "gut feeling" that VAAs do have an effect on voters' choice in elections (Walgrave et al. 2008). Indeed, in recent years a growing number of academic studies have been devoted to this topic. Questions about VAAs' ability to affect the behavior—or attitudes and preferences—of their users have commonly been framed within issue voting theories.[2] Issue voting refers to the assumption that vote choice is determined by the individual voter's proximity/distance to the

---

[2] For a richer discussion of the relationship between VAAs and issue voting, see Garzia (2010).

position of the parties on salient issues (Downs 1957). In order to link their policy preferences to party positions, however, voters need not only to have preferences, but also a sufficient amount of information available regarding the policy stances of the parties in the electoral competition (Carmines and Huckfeldt 1996). In this respect, political information can be either generated directly by the supply side (i.e. the parties) or indirectly. VAAs fall in this second category of information-provision mechanisms. Like traditional media, they relay information about parties' positions to voters. Unlike other sources, however, they provide *tailor-made* political information (Alvarez et al. 2012). Voters do not simply go to a VAA website to inform themselves about parties' positions, but to match their personal political profile with the parties' offer (Boogers and Voerman 2003). In other words, VAAs reveal to the user the structure of the political competition *in light of her own preferences.*

The theoretical approach to the study of potential effects of VAAs on partisan preferences builds on both these strands of literature. In particular, Alvarez et al. (2012) developed the concept of "representative deficit" from the degree to which users fail to match the political supply—the lower the match between the user's issue preferences and the parties' offer, the higher the representative deficit. Their reasoning stems from the intuition that the revealed proximity between the user and the parties may, under certain conditions, lead the user to a learning process that eventually affects his partisan preferences. The representative deficit is precisely the conditioning mechanism that makes users more likely to take their revealed preferences into account. A low representative deficit is, in a way, a clear self-portrait. It shows the users that "their" party (i.e. a party that greatly overlaps with their ideological profile) does indeed exist and, in doing so, it might lead them to reshape their patterns of party preference in favor of the ideologically closest party. By the same token, a higher representative deficit—signaling the vaguer contours of the match between voters and the political offer—can be thought to lower the probability of revealed preferences to affect voters' partisan preferences.

The "representative deficit" theory does not only help explaining switching of party preferences after exposure to VAAs, but can also account for changing patterns of electoral mobilization at the individual level. The mobilizing effect of VAAs is hypothesized to operate on users in two orthogonal ways. On the one hand, a perfect match between the user and one of the parties may incite him to turn out and vote, as he sees his personal preferences quite well mirrored by the partisan offer. Quite to the contrary, a user finding himself in some corner of the political space where no party can be found may feel a sense of "political solitude", and this could exert in turn a negative effect on his willingness to take part in the election.

VAA providers have great confidence in the mobilizing capacity of these tools (Ruusuvirta et al. 2009), and many VAAs are actually developed as an attempt to mobilize voters and increase turnout (Marschall 2005). Empirical evidence provides preliminary confirmation to this expectation. Studies of the impact of *Wahl-O-Mat* usage in German federal elections consistently find one *Wahl-O-Mat* user out of ten declaring to feel more motivated to vote than before using the VAA

(Marschall 2005; Marschall et al. 2010). Further evidence in this direction comes from the Swiss case (Ladner and Pianzola 2010). An analysis of *smartvote* 2007 data found as much as 40 % of users declaring that using the VAA had a "decisive or at least slight influence on their decision to go to the polls" (Fivaz and Nadig 2010, p. 184). According to this study, the overall turnout in the 2007 federal election may have been some 5 % lower had these voters not been mobilized by *smartvote* (ibid.). Similar conclusions are reported in Ruusuvirta et al. (2009) analysis of Dutch national election study data. As a best estimate, they conclude that VAA usage increased turnout at the 2006 election by 3 % (Ruusuvirta et al. 2009, p. 18). VAAs have been found to exert an effect on individual propensity to turn out also in supranational, i.e. European elections. A study by Dinas et al. (2011) could show that even after controlling for a set of socio-demographic, attitudinal and behavioral variables, the probability to participate in European elections is about 14 % higher for VAA users as compared to non-users. In the same contribution, the authors could also empirically verify the impact of the representative deficit on mobilization.

The VAA literature also features a growing body of studies dealing with the actual effect of the tool on users' party preference and vote choice. According to the available evidence, the large majority of users would seem to remain unaffected by the VAA in terms of changing their mind regarding their preferred party. A recent cross-national analysis finds indeed that only a minority (i.e. about 8 %) of VAA users switched their top-party preference to become consistent with the top-party proposed by the application (Alvarez et al. 2012). Similar results are reported in national case studies from Belgium (Walgrave et al. 2008; Nuytemans et al. 2010), Finland (Mykkänen et al. 2007), Germany (Marschall 2005), the Netherlands (Boogers 2006; Wall et al. 2012), and Switzerland (Ladner et al. 2010). Again, the size of the representative deficit seems to play an important role in linking VAA exposure to preference change: the smaller the deficit, the higher the probability for switching allegiances (Alvarez et al. 2012).

Although conceptually and empirically distinct from choice, preferences are assumed to feed into the mechanism that enables choice. To be sure, at every given time point there can be multiple preferences, but except in open list systems, such as Switzerland, Luxembourg or Finland, there can only be one choice. For this reason, preferences can be thought to be more responsive (that is, malleable) to the external stimulus provided by the voting advice *vis-à-vis* actual vote choice. On the basis of a multi-wave (i.e. pre/post electoral) panel of Flemish voters, Walgrave et al. (2008) demonstrate that the reported intention to change vote choice in accordance with the advice provided is not always matched with actual changes in voting behavior. As they find

> only half of the people who said [*Doe de Stemtest*] made them doubt about their vote (8 %) actually changed preferences. For the other half, [*Doe de Stemtest*] inspired doubt but did not have electoral consequences. Even among the small group of people saying that [*Doe de Stemtest*] really made them change their mind (1 %), one-third did not change their mind at all and remained loyal (Walgrave et al. 2008, pp. 65–66).

As it appears then, voters do not uncritically follow the advice obtained by the VAA—regardless of how much it simplifies the political decision-making process. After all, VAAs are only *one* among many competing information sources available to voters during a campaign. Yet, such small-scale, direct forms of impact do not exclude the possibility for VAAs to exert more subtle, indirect effects on users. In the longer run, VAAs might help improving users' sense of identification with another party, thus facilitating change of party choice in the future. Similarly, VAAs can draw the user's attention to a party beyond the one(s) he considered voting for, as well as to "minor" parties receiving only limited exposure in contemporary campaign dynamics (Walgrave et al. 2009).

VAAs have been also found to exert *cognitive* effects on their users. In the light of the key role played by political issues in the VAA-logic, users have been found to give more weight to issue-related considerations in their voting calculus as compared to non-users (Walgrave et al. 2008). Significant VAA-effects have been witnessed also in the domain of information-seeking behavior. A number of post-test surveys conducted among *Wahl-O-Mat* users in Germany show that between 50 and 60 % of respondents declare to be motivated to collect further political information after having performed the VAA (Marschall 2005; Marschall et al. 2010). Similar figures are reported in the cases of Finland (Mykkänen et al. 2007) and the Netherlands (Boogers 2006).

Impact on the Discipline: Party Politics and Democratic Representation

The spread of VAAs among voters and across political systems has opened up novel possibilities for social and political science research. The data gathered from the huge number of users visiting VAA websites before election can be used in many ways. For instance, one can produce refined measurements of campaign dynamics based on daily addition of detailed preference voicing on a large-*n* scale. Research in this domain is only in its infancy (among the few exceptions, see: Hooghe and Teepe 2007; Çarkoğlu et al. 2012; Dufresne et al. 2012) but it can be expected to grow substantially in the near future. At the present stage, VAA's most relevant contribution to the discipline rests probably with the important number of parties' issue positions coded across time and space by VAA developers.

The ability to locate parties in the ideological space has always represented a central feature in the comparative study of party systems (Laver 2001). Since the pioneering work of Downs (1957) the capacity to locate parties in a common policy space has been traditionally used to understand coalition formation processes and the patterns of partisan voting in legislatures. This also facilitates cross-national comparison of party systems. Various methods have been derived by political scientists to empirically determine parties' positions on issues. Nowadays, this research domain is dominated by two sets of techniques: expert surveys

(Castles and Mair 1984; Mair 2001; Benoit and Laver 2006) and manifesto/program coding (Klingemann et al. 2006). In both cases, party positions are established by professionals outside the parties—qualified researchers in the case of expert surveys and expert coders in the case of manifesto studies. Both techniques bear advantages as well as drawbacks (for a review, see Marks 2007). The experts that are requested to position parties are asked to do so in light of their demonstrable knowledge in the field, yet they are not asked to justify their placings nor to cite evidence for those placings. Manifesto coding is apparently more transparent: the codes used are in fact attributed to publicly available party documents. Even in this case, however, it is not always straightforward (and at times not possible) to trace the coder's decision to employ a specific coding category to a concrete piece of text.

Against this background, VAAs broke new ground in party research. To the best of our knowledge, none of the available expert and manifesto codings carried out throughout the years have been checked with the parties themselves—in contrast to many VAAs. As previously mentioned, parties and candidates taking part in VAAs are either asked to authoritatively self-place themselves on the issues (e.g. *StemWijzer/smartvote* family) or to collaborate with the developers in the two-step process of party placement (e.g. *EU Profiler*). Such a multitude of party positions can fruitfully contribute to our understanding of old and new cleavage lines that structure the party space, overcoming or supporting the left–right dichotomy (Lobo et al. 2010; Gemenis 2013; Otjes et al. 2011). In this respect, the *EU Profiler* project represents literally a breakthrough in cross-national party research. With more than 270 European parties coded across as many as 30 different issues, the *EU Profiler* database allows for an empirically-driven identification of party families within the EU. Such an analysis might point to alternative ways in grouping the parties in Europe which might not necessarily correspond to the already existing party family structure. The successful experience of *EU Profiler* does also provide encouragement for further experiments in party self-coding. In several instances, the correspondence between coder placement and party self-placement was closer than between expert judgments and manifesto scores in previous comparative analyses (Trechsel and Mair 2011).[3]

Further than the placement of parties on a wide array of political issues, VAA generated data can also provide insights on the extent to which parties translate their pre-electoral positions into policy-making once in power (Skop and Michal 2010). By comparing what parties stand for and what government actually produces, we can more easily assess how representative governments are responsive to the demands and preferences of the electorate. Furthermore, in countries where candidate-based voting systems are in place (e.g. in Finland, Switzerland and

---

[3] On more than 2,300 of the issue positions coded in the *EU Profiler* (i.e., *circa* 83 % of the total) there was complete agreement between the coders and the parties themselves, while on a further 344 issues the discrepancy only stretched to one position on the scale (the difference between "completely agree" and "tend to agree," for example, rather than between "agreement" and "disagreement").

Luxembourg) VAA data can be fruitfully employed in the study of intra-party cohesion (Schwarz et al. 2010).

Finally, VAA data can be—and has been—used in analyses of elite-mass congruence (Talonen et al. 2011; Wheatley et al. 2012). Traditional analyses of the ideological positions of the general population commonly resort to traditional surveys. Note, however, that one of the major problems linked to VAA research in this field is, for obvious reasons, the highly non-representativeness of VAA usage (Vassil 2011: Nonetheless, VAAs would seem to feature a number of advantages *vis-a-vis* more traditional research tools. For one thing, VAAs are able to attract a much wider number of respondents as compared to the typical-*n* of mass election survey. Even more importantly, they allow comparisons of the issue positions of parties and voters *using the same data source*. In turn, this can help understanding the working and effectiveness of representative government by means of a straightforward measurement of the extent to which parties and voters are mutually congruent (Trechsel and Mair 2011).

Conclusions: The Future of VAAs

Over the last decade, the internet has become an ever more important platform for election campaigns in contemporary democracies, supplementing traditional media such as television, radio and newspapers, as well as playing a vital role within the realm of political communication on different levels of social stratification (Chadwick and Howard 2009). For many citizens, political online communication has turned into a major—and for some the only—source of political information, communication and participation (Zittel and Fuchs 2007; Norris 2008).

The proliferation of ICTs has borne profound effects on campaigning. Amongst them, we highlight the growing loss of control candidates and parties have over the message due to the emergence of increasingly relevant non-partisan actors in electoral politics. Internet-based technologies allow voters to satisfy certain informational needs efficiently and independently from the parties. Nowadays, it is increasingly common for voters, in Europe and elsewhere, to compare their own positions with the political offer by resorting to Voting Advice Applications. VAA usage allows voters to look into their "political mirror" and detect a summary of their preferences, carefully matched with the ideological profile of parties and/or candidates running in the election. Never before was this possible on such a large scale and in such detail. The popularity of VAAs shows the extent to which voters are asking for such indirect campaign information. As it has been observed, VAAS can be considered "the first phenomenon really to use the interactive and personalized capabilities of the internet for political purposes" (Hooghe and Teepe 2007, p. 981).

Research has generated considerable evidence that in Western democracies the emergence of the internet has resulted in a significant change within political behaviour, especially in voting behaviour (Wagner and Gainous 2009; Leighley 2010). Internet-based applications such as VAAs make no exception to this trend. The present VAA literature, as reviewed in this chapter, shows that the behaviour of users is indeed affected by their exposure to VAAs. Users are more likely to take part in elections as compared to non-users, and a growing body of evidence would seem to support the idea that VAAs bear a mobilizing potential of themselves. The "representative deficit" notion helps illustrating the mechanism under which users can be mobilized—or made to abstain—by the tool. As shown by Dinas et al. (2011), the closer the match between the user and the political offer, the higher the probability of believing in the elections and therefore participating. This, in turn, has strong underpinnings to the way representative democracy works. If taking part in elections becomes a function of the overlap between the personal issue preferences of voters and the political offer, a system in which only the well-represented participate could be envisaged. The extent to which such a trend may spread in the future remains to be seen. In this respect, however, VAAs provide social scientists with an extremely potent tool to map these developments.

In a similar vein, VAAs have been found to exert a direct effect on users' party preferences and vote choice. Previous research shows that a non-negligible proportion of VAA users is willing to 'move' their vote in accordance with the advice obtained. The robustness of these findings is however limited due to the inherent endogeneity within users' subjective evaluations of the influence exerted by VAA usage. In fact, the great majority of analyses of VAA effects rely on opt-in surveys administrated to users right after their VAA experience. Apart from being subject to a heavy self-selection bias, these kind of data can also overestimate to a substantial extent the actual effect exerted by VAA usage on the voting decision. As Walgrave et al. (2008) demonstrated, the reported intention to change vote choice in accordance with the advice provided is not always matched with actual changes in voting behaviour.

In order to better understand the actual impact of VAAs on users (and on election outcomes in turn) there is much to expect from experimental research designs. Here, we deliberately take the view offered by Angrist and Phischke (2009) and urge future research on VAAs to think in the framework of causality (*What is the causal relationship of interest?*) and in the framework of experiments (*What would the experiment capturing this causal effect look like?*). Observational studies are needed as far as no other kind of data is available, but as soon as social scientists can devise alternative data collection enterprises (as it is the case with VAAs) then randomized experiments should be the gold standard. Most recently, studies in Estonia (Vassil 2011) and Switzerland (Pianzola et al. 2012) have pioneered in the experimental design.

A better understanding of the extent to which VAAs are able to affect their users should, in our view, be placed high on the research agenda of comparative political behaviour scholars. If a substantial part of users is affected by VAAs, then it goes without saying that these applications should be taken seriously by political scientists, especially in the light of their rapid spread among European electorates. Moreover, a number of socio-political trends common to all European societies lead us to expect that VAAs might play an ever more decisive role in the future. As modern Western societies turn out to be more heterogeneous and individualized, processes of dealignment will pursue as will the decline of party identification and cleavage voting (Franklin et al. 1992; Dalton and Wattenberg 2000). Issue voting might become more relevant in the future. VAAs fit this tendency, as they offer a 'cheap' cue for the supposedly increasing number of voters who base their voting decision on a comparison between the parties' policy offers and their own policy preferences.

In political terms, VAAs bear also the potential to foster longstanding debates about transnational democracy (Lacey 2012). The rise of supranational VAAs, in particular, provides citizens with the possibility to compare their own policy views not only with national parties, but also with parties competing outside their own country. On the basis of *EU Profiler* generated data, a current research project at the EUI provides preliminary evidence that a wide majority of European voters would find a better match (i.e. a lower "representative deficit") with a political party from an European country other than their own (Bright et al. 2014). Large efforts are also being devoted in the direction of embedding VAAs within Web 2.0 structures. Thanks to these technological advances, VAAs will eventually be able to match users also among themselves (Trechsel 2012). The possibility to "connect" citizens on the basis of their political affinities opens up exciting, and yet uncharted, prospects for the future of democratic representation, and leads us to wonder whether democracy would still be so "unthinkable" without political parties.

References

Alvarez RM, Levin I, Mair P, Trechsel AH (2012) Party preferences in the digital age: the impact of voting advice applications. Paper prepared for the conference "responsive or responsible? Parties, democracy and global markets. A conference in honour of Peter Mair", Florence, 26–28 Sept 2012

Angrist J, Pischke J-S (2009) Mostly harmless econometrics: an empiricist's companion. Princeton University Press, Princeton

Benoit K, Laver M (2006) Party policy in modern democracies. Routledge, London

Boogers M (2006) Enquete bezoekers Stemwijzer, unpublished paper, Universiteit van Tilburg, Tilburg

Boogers M, Voerman G (2003) Surfing citizens and floating voters: results of an online survey of visitors to political web sites during the Dutch 2002 general elections. Inf Polit 8(1–2):17–27

Breuer F (2010) The EU Profiler: a new way for voters to meet parties and to understand European elections. In: Gagatek W (ed) The 2009 elections to the European parliament—country reports. European Union Democracy Observatory, Florence, pp 27–31

Bright J, Garzia Di, Lacey J, Alexander HT (2014). Trans-nationalising Europe's voting space. EUDO Working Paper RSCAS 2014/02.

Çarkoğlu A, Vitiello T, Moral M (2012) Voting advice applications in practice: answers to some key questions from Turkey. Paper prepared for the 26th annual conference of the Italian Society of Political Science, Rome, 13–15 Sept 2012

Carmines EG, Huckfeldt R (1996) Political behavior: an overview. In: Goodin RE, Klingemann H-D (eds) A new handbook of political science. Oxford University Press, New York, pp 223–254

Castles FG, Mair P (1984) Left–right political scales: some 'expert' judgements. Eur J Polit Res 12(1):73–88

Cedroni L, Garzia D (eds) (2010) Voting advice applications in Europe: the state of the art. Scriptaweb, Napoli

Chadwick AJ, Howard PN (eds) (2009) Routledge handbook of internet politics. Routledge, London

Dalton RJ, Wattenberg MP (eds) (2000) Parties without partisans: political change in advanced industrial democracies. Oxford University Press, Oxford

de Graaf J (2010) The irresistible rise of Stemwijzer. In: Cedroni L, Garzia D (eds) Voting advice applications in Europe. The state of the art. ScriptaWeb, Napoli, pp 35–60

Dinas E, Alexander HT, Kristjan V (2011) A look into the mirror preferences, representation and electoral participation. Paper presented at the conference Internet, Voting and Democracy, Laguna Beach, CA

Downs A (1957) An economic theory of political action in a democracy. J Polit Econ 65(2):135–150

Dufresne Y, Eady G, Hove J, Loewen P, van der Linden C (2012) Avoiding the traps in VEAs. Pre-campaign market research and micro-level weighting adjustments. Paper prepared for the 22nd world congress of political science, Madrid, 8–12 July 2012

Farrell D, Schmitt-Beck R (eds) (2008) Non-party actors in electoral politics: the role of interest groups and independent citizens in contemporary election campaigns. Nomos, Baden–Baden

Fivaz J, Nadig G (2010) Impact of voting advice applications (VAAs) on voter turnout and their potential use for civic education. Policy Internet 2:7

Franklin MN, Mackie TT, Valen H (eds) (1992) Electoral change: responses to evolving social and attitudinal structures in Western societies. Cambridge University Press, Cambridge

Garzia D (2010) 'The effects of VAAs on users' voting behaviour: an overview. In: Cedroni L, Garzia D (eds) Voting advice applications in Europe. The state of the art. ScriptaWeb, Napoli, pp 13–33

Garzia D, Marschall S (2012) Voting advice applications under review: the state of research. Int J Electron Gov (article in press)

Gemenis K (2013) Estimating parties' policy positions through voting advice applications: Some methodological considerations. Acta Politica 48:268–295

Hooghe M, Teepe W (2007) Party profiles on the web: an analysis of the log files of non-partisan interactive political internet sites in the 2003 and 2004 election campaigns in Belgium. New Media Soc 9(6):965–985

Klingemann H-D, Volkens A, Budge I, Bara J, McDonald MD (2006) Mapping policy preferences II: parties, electorates and governments in Eastern Europe and the OECD 1990–2003. Oxford University Press, Oxford

Lacey J (2012) Must Europe be Swiss? On the idea of a voting space and the possibility of a multilingual demos. Br J Polit Sci 44:61–82

Ladner A, Pianzola J (2010) Do voting advice applications have an effect on electoral participation and voter turnout? Evicence from the 2007 Swiss Federal Elections. In: Tambouris E, Macintosh A, Glassey O (eds) Electronic participation. Proceedings of Second IFIP WG 8.5 international conference, ePart 2010, Lausanne, Switzerland, Aug 29–Sept 2, 2010. Springer, Berlin, pp 211–224

Ladner A, Felder G, Fivaz J (2010) More than toys? A first assessment of voting advice applications in Switzerland. In: Cedroni L, Garzia D (eds) Voting advice applications in Europe. The state of the art. ScriptaWeb, Napoli, pp 91–123

Laver M (ed) (2001) Estimating the policy position of political actors. Routledge, London

Leighley JE (ed) (2010) The oxford handbook of American elections and political behavior. Oxford University Press, Oxford

Lobo MC, Vink M, Lisi M (2010) Mapping the political landscape: a vote advice application in Portugal. In: Cedroni L, Garzia D (eds) Voting advice applications in Europe. The state of the art. ScriptaWeb, Napoli, pp 143–185

Mair P (2001) Searching for the position of political actors: a review of approaches and a critical evaluation of expert surveys. In: Laver M (ed) Estimating the policy position of political actors. Routledge, London, pp 10–30

Marks G (ed) (2007) Special symposium: comparing measures of party positioning: expert, manifesto, and survey data. Elect Stud 26(1):1–141

Marschall S (2005) Idee und Wirkung des Wahl-O-Mat. Aus Politik und Zeitgeschichte 55(51–52):41–46

Marschall S, Schmidt CK (2010). The impact of voting indicators: the case of the German Wahl-O-Mat. In: Cedroni L, Garzia D (eds) Voting advice applications in Europe. The state of the art. ScriptaWeb, Napoli, pp 65–104

Mykkänen J, Moring T, Pehkonen J (2007) Tutkimus vaalikoneiden käytöstä ja suhtautumisesta vaalikoneisiin: vaalikoneet koetaan hyödyllisiksi. Helsingin Sanomain säätiö, Helsinki

Norris P (2008) Getting the message out: a two-step model of the role of the internet in campaign communication flows during the 2005 British general election. J Inf Technol Polit 4:3–13

Nuytemans M, Walgrave S, Deschouwer K (2010) Do the vote test: the Belgian voting aid application. In: Cedroni L, Garzia D (eds) Voting advice applications in Europe. The state of the art. ScriptaWeb, Napoli, pp 125–156

Otjes S, Louwerse T (2011) Spatial models in voting advice applications. Paper presented at the 10th Politicologenetmaal, Amsterdam, 9–10 June 2011

Pianzola J, Trechsel AH, Vassil K, Schwerdt CK, Alvarez MR, (2012) The effect of voting advice applications (VAAs) on political preferences. Evidence from a randomized field experiment. Paper prepared for the 2012 APSA Conference, New Orleans

Ramonaite A (2010) Voting advice applications in Lithuania: promoting programmatic competition or breeding populism? Policy Internet 2(1):117–147

Ruusuvirta O (2010). Much ado about nothing? Online voting advice applications in Finland. In: Cedroni L, Garzia D (eds) Voting advice applications in Europe. The state of the art. ScriptaWeb, Napoli, pp 47–77

Ruusuvirta O, Rosema M (2009) Do online vote selectors influence electoral participation and the direction of vote? Paper presented at the European consortium for political research (ECPR) general conference, Potsdam, 10–12 Sept 2009

Schwarz D, Schädel L, Ladner A (2010) Pre-election positions and voting behaviour in parliament: consistency among Swiss MPs. Swiss Polit Sci Rev 16(3):533–564

Skop M (2010) Are the voting advice applications (VAAs) telling the truth? Measuring VAAs quality: case study from the Czech Republic. In: Cedroni L, Garzia D (eds) Voting advice applications in Europe. The state of the art. ScriptaWeb, Napoli, pp 199–230

Stiff J, Mongeau P (2003) Persuasive communication. The Guilford Press, New York

Talonen J, Sulkava M (2011) Analyzing parliamentary elections based on voting advice application data. In: Gama J, Bradly E, Hollmén J (eds) Advances in intelligent data analysis. 10th international symposium, IDA 2011, Porto, Portugal, Oct 2011. Springer, Heidelberg, pp 340–351

Trechsel AH (2012) Conceptualising a voter-to-voter preferences matching tool for the 2014 european parliamentary elections. Mimeo, European University Institute

Trechsel AH, Mair P (2011) When parties (also) position themselves: an introduction to the EU profiler. J Inf Technol Polit 8(1):1–20

van Praag P (2007) De stemwijzer: hulpmiddel voor de kiezers of instrument van manipulatie?. Lezing Amsterdamse Academische Club, Amsterdam

Vassil K (2011) Voting smarter? The impact of voting advice applications on political behavior, unpublished doctoral dissertation

Wagner KM, Gainous J (2009) Electronic grassroots: does online campaigning work? J Legis Stud 15(4):502–520

Walgrave S, Nuytemans M, Pepermans K (2009) Voting aid applications and the effect of statement selection. West Eur Polit 32(6):1161–1180

Walgrave S, van Aelst P, Nuytemans M (2008) Do the vote test: the electoral effects of a popular vote advice application at the 2004 Belgian elections. Acta Polit 43(1):50–70

Wall M, Krouwel A, Vitiello T (2012) Do voters follow the recommendations of voter advice application websites? A study of the effects of Kieskompas.nl on its users vote choices in the 2010 Dutch legislative elections. Party Polit

Wall M, Sudulich ML, Costello R, Leon E (2009) Picking your party online: an investigation of Ireland's first online voting advice application. Inf Polit 14(3):203–218

Wheatley J, Carman C, Mendez F, Mitchell J (2012) The dimensionality of the Scottish political space: results from an experiment on the 2011 Holyrood elections, Party Polit

Zittel T, Fuchs D (eds) (2007) Participatory democracy and political participation: can participatory engineering bring citizens back in?. Routledge, New York

Digital Media and the 2010 National Elections in Brazil

Jason Gilmore and Philip N. Howard

Abstract Over the past decade, digital and mobile media have significantly changed the system of political communication in Brazil. An increasing number of Brazilian candidates have begun to use websites and social networking applications as an integral part of their overall campaign efforts. To explore how these "new" media tools are used at all levels of campaigns for national office, we built an original dataset of media used by political campaigns in the 2010 elections in Brazil. We investigate factors such as a candidate's use of Web and social networking sites in conjunction with other traditional influences such as incumbency and party affiliation in order to get a robust understanding of the different roles that digital media tools are beginning to play in Brazilian elections. In this chapter, we ask two questions. First, does digital media provide some competitive advantage to minor party candidates facing off against major party candidates with higher profile and more resources? Second, do challenger candidates get any electoral advantage against incumbents for using the Internet, social media, or mobile media strategies in their campaigning?

Introduction

Systems of political communication around the world have significantly evolved over the last decade. The introduction of digital media has given political parties worldwide new tools for logistics and new ways of reaching potential supporters. There is a large body of research on the impact of digital media on campaigns and elections in advanced democracies (Chadwick 2006; Chadwick and Howard 2009; Davis 1999; Foot and Schneider, 2006; Howard 2006; Howard 2011), but there

J. Gilmore · P. N. Howard (✉)
Department of Communication, University of Washington, Seattle, WA, USA
e-mail: pnhoward@uw.edu

B. Grofman et al. (eds.), *The Internet and Democracy in Global Perspective*,
Studies in Public Choice 31, DOI: 10.1007/978-3-319-04352-4_4,
© Springer International Publishing Switzerland 2014

have also been important changes to the practices of political campaigning in emerging democracies. Through this study of digital media by political candidates in Brazil's 2010 elections, we analyze some of the latest trends in order to advance our understanding of how electoral competition has evolved in a developing Latin American democracy with the advent of these new media technologies.

Political life in Brazil has evolved significantly since its period of authoritarianism. Mische (2007) eloquently states that the particular challenge for Brazil has not simply been to allow electoral competition, but to develop a culture of partisanship and party affiliation. Developing democratically, in Brazil's case, has meant elaborating new projects, repertoires, and institutional forms for political action. Without political parties, citizens would lack the intermediary organizations that buffer relations between the individual and the state. Without some form of partisanship, the competing political forces might polarize to the extent that fragile democratic transitions do not deepen (Mische 2007). Since the privatization of much of the telecommunications industry in 1998, an important part of this new culture of political communication has increasingly involved digital media (Bagchi et al. 2003).

Digital Media and the Political Culture of Modern Brazil

Brazil is sometimes thought of as an emerging democracy, but the elections of 2010 demonstrate that democratic institutions are deeply entrenched in that country. This is the sixth round of national elections since the military dictatorship gave way to electoral democracy in 1985. The logistical challenges of administering the vote in a large country of over one hundred million voters are immense, and the electoral laws create interesting opportunities for challenger candidates to win seats—especially in the lower house. Political culture, in an important way, is highly developed precisely because candidates for office compete rigorously for votes. Campaign dynamics certainly vary by the level of office, but on the whole Brazil is a healthy, functioning electoral democracy. In part, this is because television became one of the ways in which political candidates competed for public support beginning with Frenando Collor de Mello's election in 1989. Television is still the primary media by which citizens have contact with major political figures (Boas 2005). Nonetheless, digital media and social networking applications have become a crucial means by which Brazilians encounter and interact with local, subnational, and national political candidates.

Brazil is particularly interesting for the study of the role of these new media technologies in emerging democracies because it is home to one of the world's most diverse, vibrant, and active online communities. In recent years, digital media have played an ever more important role in Brazil's unique system of political communication (Gilmore 2012). Brazil's population is exceptionally mobile, and the roll out of hard line telephone connections exceptionally slow. This has meant that while Internet access is an increasingly important part of the media diet for the middle and upper class, mobile telephones have become ubiquitous across the social spectrum. With more than 72 million Internet users, a number that grew by almost 10 million users over the last 2 years (Internet World Stats 2010), Brazil houses the fourth largest population of online users and there are no signs of stagnation in its pervasive growth. Additionally, Brazilians are frequently among the top ten national user groups of social media sites such as Twitter and YouTube, representing 4 and 3.5 % of international users, respectively.[1] More specifically, Brazilian participation in the social networking site Orkut (52 % of international users) is unmatched in the world and Facebook (1.3 % of international users) has recently begun to take hold despite Orkut's corner on the Brazilian social networking market. With this growing evidence about how "wired" the Brazilian electorate is becoming, it is increasingly necessary to bridge the gap in research on how this digital activity translates into the political realm.

The 2010 Campaigns in Brazil

On October 3, 2010 Brazil held elections for President, Senate, Governor, and the lower house of Congress, known as the Chamber of Deputies. Certainly, a large portion of campaign expenditures for higher levels of office when to purchasing television ads, but the Internet was not simply a logical tool for coordinating campaign volunteers. It was used for raising funds for campaign coffers, distributing original political content not found in other media, and data mining. Presidential campaigns are among the most high profile and well resourced. They tend to have aggressive Internet, social networking, and mobile campaign strategies, and often imitate each other's campaign innovations. More information for the study of electoral politics is the character of campaign at the level of Governor, Senate, and Federal Deputy races. It is at these levels that multiple candidates vie for public attention, do innovative things with digital media, and may get some measurable advantage from investments in campaign technology. The use of digital media in political campaigns in Brazil has yet to reach the levels of most developed countries, yet with the Brazilian population's fascination with these "new" technologies politicians are beginning to scamper to meet the public's demand. In the array of national electoral races, candidates use digital media tools in varying degrees of sophistication. This is more relevant, however, of the campaigns for presidency, governorships, and for the Senate than for the lower house of Congress or for state and local elections.

In the campaigns for the presidency, digital media is ubiquitously used and wielded with high levels of sophistication as the candidates are able to afford not only Web developer teams who put together highly interactive websites and the like, but they also tap into teams of content producers who work around the clock to keep their respective candidates' online presence "fresh" for the voting public. On one hand, they hire teams of video producers around the country who crafted a wide range of distinct campaign videos on a daily basis for posting on the candidates' Web, YouTube, Facebook, and Orkut sites. On the other hand, they have teams whose sole purpose is to manage each candidate's social media sites and who work tirelessly to fill candidate pages with constant updates, blogposts, and tweets around the clock. These new media teams are highly educated and try to outdo each other in a number of creative ways throughout the campaign season. For instance, Worker's Party candidate Dilma Rousseff's new media team went as far as to set up a Facebook-style social media site called Dilmaweb where ideally campaign team members would network with a wide array of political allies including other Workers' Party candidates, community organizers, bloggers, voters, as well as voters themselves in order to better coordinate their on-the-ground campaigns. In contrast, the digital media team for Green Party candidate, Marina Silva, created and highly promoted their interactive community organizing application called "Case de Marina" on the candidate's website where supporters and organizers could register their own address as one of Marina's "casas" (houses) and then locate other similar residences in their vicinity in order to facilitate neighborhood networking and organizing.

At the level of races for governor and senate, the pervasive use of digital media for campaigns was similar to their presidential hopefuls, with 97 % of all viable candidates having at least a basic form of online campaign presence, but the online campaigns themselves were nowhere near as sophisticated. In contrast to the diverse and interactive websites of the presidential candidates, websites for governor and senate candidates tended to be more informative than interactive. In some cases, candidates even preferred to use free blog sites such as Wordpress to house their official campaign websites and in one case, a sure-of-himself incumbent senator decided against building an official candidate website, and relied solely on social media for his online campaign presence. The use of social media sites was also pervasive in these races, but opening an Orkut or Facebook account or page is a different matter than actively and strategically using it for campaign purposes. Overall, 97 % of all senator and governor candidates had some form of social media or microblogging presence on the Web, however, in the case of Facebook (54 % of users), for example, only about 20 % of candidates updated their page on a daily basis and only about 30 % posted anything more than simple text-only messages. In the case of Twitter, which was used by more than 90 % of all governor and senate candidates, daily use was better than with Facebook, but still only 60 % of candidates "tweeted" on a semi-regular basis.

In the case of the lower house of the Brazilian congress, the story was quite different, principally because of the system by which candidates are elected. Specifically, the races for all 513 seats in the Brazilian Chamber of Deputies are tied to one of the 26 states or the Federal District and not to small districts within states where only a choice few candidates would compete for single seats. In other words, each state has a long, unstructured list of candidates from all participating parties who compete among themselves for the entire allotted amount of seat available in the lower house. According to Samuels (2001b), this makes for candidate centric campaigns where competition is fierce and everyone is seeking innovative ways to set themselves apart from the pack of candidates.

In the 2010 elections, one example of this type of candidate differentiation stood above the rest. In the state of São Paulo where there was already an over-populated pack of 1,169 candidates competing for 70 seats, a famous children's entertainer decided to run in his clown-type costume and under his stage name of Tiririca as a way of both mocking the electoral system and setting himself apart from his competitors. Tiririca quickly became well known for strange campaign tactics including a series of campaign ads featuring the candidate in clown cos-tume acting silly manner. All of these ads quickly went viral on YouTube and coupled with Tiririca's dynamic online campaign, including an interactive website and a popular Twitter feed, he was not only able to set himself apart from his competitors, but also on election day he was the top vote getter both nationally and more importantly in his home state of São Paulo. Tiririca, however, was but one of many candidates who employed strange or unorthodox campaign strategies. Another widely known campaign gimmick featured Rosemar Luiz da Rosa Lopes from the state of São Paulo who changed his candidate name to Rosemar Barack Obama and used the slogan "Sim você pode" (Yes you can) in all of his campaign propaganda to try and draw on the American president's international popularity for his own political gains. Alternatively, the YouTube videos of two women from the states of Rio de Janeiro and São Paulo went viral for very different reasons. The candidate videos featuring Mulher Melão (Melon Woman) and Mulher Pera (Pear Woman), named these ways for either their physical resemblance to the fruit or the fruit's resemblance to a specific body part they possessed, were widely reposted and tagged because of the way they used their sex appeal to attempt to win votes. For the most part, however, campaign antics such as these—with the obvious exception of Tiririca—were not what carried the day at the polls on October 3, 2010. According to Ames, Baker and Rennó (2008), Brazilian voters have historically tended to vote on the issues and therefore seek out candidates that best represent their own interests. It was those who were able to effectively communicate their campaign positions to voters—albeit in a memorable way—who had the best chance in setting themselves apart in the minds of the voting public. Another advantageous way to do this was through the use of savvy digital media campaigns.

According to Gilmore (2012), candidates for the lower house who chose to use digital media tools for their campaigns provided voters—who were frequently overwhelmed with an unwieldy pack of candidates to chose from—with avenues by which to find out more information about a given candidate and their political positions. Digital media tools were further advantageous to candidates due to their low usage among candidates at this level. Unlike at the level of senator or governors where 97 % of all candidates used digital media for their campaigns, only 40 % of candidates nationwide for the lower house had any form of online campaign presence. Candidate websites, by and large, had simple structures and tended to have only a few pages of information on the candidate. Only a choice few has url addresses could be quickly associated with candidate's name or party, whereas the majority included the name of the free blog site where they constructed the site. Social media sites were even less commonly used, with only 31 % of candidates, and there was no real consistency in how they were used. Orkut was the most commonly used site, yet only 13 % of candidates had a strong presence on this particular social media site. Candidates' second choice was Facebook, yet only 10 % of candidates even had a presence on the social media site and of that 10 %, less than 20 % regularly updated their pages. The exception for the lower house races was Twitter, which was used by almost 30 % of candidates. In fact, Twitter was used in a very distinct manner than the other social media tools online, specifically because it provided candidates with a sort of hypodermic needle connection with voters through its easy connection on voters' mobile devices. Twitter allowed candidates the ability to feed voters with bite-sized bits of information into voter mobile devices that they could then take into the voting booths with them. This was specifically useful because of the fact that voters had to remember the candidate's four-digit candidate or "urn" numbers in order to vote for them (Gilmore 2012). Because of this function, the bulk majority of candidate tweets in the last days building up to the elections contained only the candidate's name and their "urn" number, which could then be used as a sort of mobile and digital crib sheet that would remind voters of how to vote for a specific candidate.

Data and Methods

All analysis for the current study is drawn from an original dataset created during a month-long field visit to Brazil which tracks the political use of digital media tools for the top 69 viable gubernatorial candidates, the top 84 viable senatorial candidates and from a randomly sampled set of 1,000 candidates for the lower house of the Brazilian Congress in the 2010 national election held on October 3, 2010. In the case of gubernatorial and senatorial campaigns, only candidates who were seen as viable contenders for their respective seats were selected. Viability was determined by identifying all candidates who were performing well in the polls leading up to the races. Candidates in the case of the lower house of Congress were proportionately selected from all 26 Brazilian states as well as the Federal District, which is treated as a state during national congressional races. This portion of the dataset, therefore, represents roughly 20 % of the 5,283 viable candidates nationwide competing for the 513 total open seats in the lower house of the Brazilian Congress. Such a large sample was chosen because it allowed for each state, regardless of size, to have a sufficiently large representation of candidates in the final dataset. Candidates were then selected in a three-part process. First, we determined the percentage of congressional seats allotted to each individual state. That percentage was then used to determine the amount of candidates that would be sampled from each state's pool of candidates. For example, the states of Goiás and Minas Gerais are allotted 3 and 10 % of the total seats in the lower house of Congress, respectively; therefore 30 candidates were selected from Goiás and 100 for Minas Gerais. Finally, we randomly sampled these sets of candidates from the official, and publicly available, list of viable candidates for each state from the Brazilian Superior Electoral Court website, Brazil's official electoral commission.

Demographic and campaign information about each individual candidate including age, gender, party, and coalition affiliation, and campaign spending, was also collected from the Brazilian Superior Electoral Court website. The study population was comprised with a significantly larger male (83 %) population than female. Age of the candidates was recorded in years and ranged from 21 to 87 (*Mdn* = 48, SD = 11.08). Because candidates hailed from 1 of 28 distinct political parties, "party affiliation" as a variable was recoded into three categories: small (30 %); medium-sized (45 %); and large (25 %) parties. In addition, a candidate's coalition affiliation was coded into one of four categories: unaffiliated (26 %); in a coalition with other small or medium parties (27 %); in a coalition with the two minor of the four large parties (10 %); and in a coalition with one of the two top parties (37 %).

All data linked to an individual candidate's campaign Web presence were collected during the final 2 weeks of campaigning before the national election on October 3, 2010. All searches for candidate Web pages were conducted on Brazil's top search engine (http://google.com.br) and consisted of two steps. First, the candidates' full names were entered into the search engine along with the state they were running in. Second, if there were no results for candidate websites, a second search was conducted where the candidates' urn (candidate) names and electoral numbers were entered into the search engine. These methods were chosen in order to emulate the experience an everyday Brazilian might have in searching for any given political candidate online. In each search, the first four pages of results were examined in-depth in order to identify whether or not the candidate had a campaign website. Furthermore, because many candidates used free blog sites such as Wordpress or Blogger for their main campaign Web presence, blogs in these cases were also coded as websites. These sites also helped in identifying if candidates used any social media sites as well for campaign purposes because in many cases links to these sites were clearly apparent on the candidates' home pages. In cases where there were no links to social media sites or when candidates were found to not have a campaign website, separate searches were conducted for each candidate on the following social media sites: Twitter, Facebook, Orkut, and YouTube. The final outcome variable measured whether or not the each candidate won their respective election. Data for this variable was collected from the final election tallies from the Brazilian Superior Electoral Court website.

Digital Media and Electoral Advantage

Studies of electoral advantage and political communication in other countries recommend two reasonable questions for understanding contemporary political culture in Brazail. In some countries, it has been suggested that digital media provides minor parties with some electoral advantage against major parties. Candidates from minor parties may have smaller campaign budgets, and being unable to pay for ads in television and radio broadcast, may find the Internet an effective way to marshall unexpected resources. Sometimes, minor parties may do surprisingly well given their relative lack of resources. Similarly, candidates who have never held office may have a better chance of beating an incumbent, if they can effectively use social media to activate their social networks on election day.

Such electoral advantages may be particularly valuable in countries dominated by a single, large, entrenched political party. Although Brazil is not a one-party government, there are a set of complex coalitional relations between parties that make for a complex political landscape. In 2010, there were three influential candidates for President, 69 viable candidates for Governor, 84 candidates for Senate, and 6,015 candidates for Lower House. In the context of Brazil, there are four "Major Parties" which are the largest and most influential political parties. They include the PSDB, DEM, PMDB, and former President Ignacio Lula da Silva's Workers Party, the PT. Furthermore, all other parties, including those who hold a minor share of political seats in the Brazilian Congress as well as those that are new or up-coming, can be best defined as being "Minor Parties" in comparison to the largest four. To search for contrasts between the varied ways, a campaign may choose to use digital media in their strategy, we make three distinctions. Internet campaign strategies include a candidate's use of an official website. Because candidates across the races used self-produced websites and free blog sites similarly, we made no distinction between blog sites and official websites unless there was a marked differentiation in their use. Social media campaign strategies included a candidate's use of any of three distinct social media sites including Facebook, YouTube, and the widely popular Orkut. Finally, Mobile Media campaign strategies included a candidate's use of the microblogging site Twitter, which was the most frequently used nonofficial website for campaign purposes.

Does Digital Media Provide Minor Parties with Some Electoral Advantage?

To explore these questions, we first contrasted the winning and losing candidates, at several levels of competition, by party size and digital communication strategy (See Table 1). This table reveals that for Major Party candidates, the vast majority of those who won their race, across all levels of office, were likely to have integrated digital media into their overall campaign strategies. The contrast between winners and losers was particularly stark for winning candidates for Governor, who used social and mobile media much more than their opponents, winning candidates for Senator who used social media much more than their opponents, and winning candidates for the Federal House of Deputies who used Internet, social, and mobile media much more than their opponents.

Table 1 Winning and losing candidates in Brazil 2010, by race, party size, and campaign strategy

	Major party (winners/losers)	Minor party (winners/losers)	All parties (winners/losers)
Governor			
Internet	95/91	100/95	96/93
Social media	90/71	100/90	93/81
Mobile media	100/86	100/95	100/91
Senator			
Internet	94/89	95/82	94/87
Social media	82/63	85/64	80/63
Mobile media	85/84	91/91	87/87
Federal deputy			
Internet	88/38	80/28	84/30
Social media	45/17	43/9	44/11
Mobile media	82/33	67/21	75/24
All			
Internet	91/47	86/31	89/35
Social media	64/26	57/13	61/16
Mobile media	86/42	76/24	82/29

Source Author's calculations based on data from the Brazil 2010 election

Furthermore, all of the winning governors who had the backing of minor parties had successful Internet, social, and mobile media strategies. Senators from minor parties who won office had better organized social media campaigns than losers. For federal deputies, the contrast between winners and losers is most stark: winning minor party candidates invested in Internet, social, and mobile media campaigns significantly more than their opponents. Altogether, election winners seemed to have invested more in Internet, social, and mobile media strategies than their opponents. But in particular, sophisticated use of social media like Facebook and Orkut was an important part of the success of Senate campaigns, and mobile media strategy made a dramatic difference for anyone running for Federal Deputy.

As we can see in Table 1, use of digital media in the governor and senate races, the use of digital media was all but ubiquitous. In the case of the lower house of Congress, however, the disparities are quite apparent. In the case of Major party candidates, 88 % of winning candidates had at least some form of digital media campaign presence, usually also paired with a mobile media strategy. Losing candidates, by contrast, had generally weak digital media strategies. Although a digital media strategy might seem to be a cost-effective way for minor party candidates who cannot afford major television ads to reach their supporters, minor party candidates were slightly less invested in digital media strategies. Overall, the most important components of digital media strategy were having a dedicated

Table 2 Challengers and incumbents in Brazil 2010, by race, party size, and campaign strategy

	Incumbents (winners/losers)	Challengers (winners/losers)
Governor		
Internet	92/100	100/92
Social media	100/80	87/81
Mobile media	100/100	100/89
Senator		
Internet	94/71	95/91
Social media	91/57	89/65
Mobile media	75/86	92/87
Federal deputy		
Internet	80/67	89/29
Social media	43/37	45/11
Mobile media	67/54	84/23
All		
Internet	84/72	93/33
Social media	58/47	63/15
Mobile media	73/67	89/27

Source Author's calculations based on data from the Brazil 2010 election

URL and activating support networks with mobile phones. Social media was important for many of the winning campaigns, but not as ubiquitous as the other two kinds of digital campaign tools.

Does Digital Media Provide Newcomers with Some Electoral Advantage?

We then contrasted impact of digital media use in campaigns between challenger and incumbent candidates across three levels of elected office (See Table 2). In total, 1,153 candidate campaigns were studied. Of these, 118 were incumbents seeking reelection. Being an incumbent often means having the advantage of patronage networks and an experienced campaign team.

Table 2 shows that in almost every instance, the incumbents who lost their office invested less in Internet, social, and mobile campaign strategy than other incumbents who won. The most notable exception concerns the use of mobile media by incumbents for Senate, for whom such investments may not have contributed much to victory. For challenger candidates—often people new to electoral politics—using digital media was particularly important. Indeed, winning challenger candidates across in every level of government, and especially at the level of lower House of Deputies, tended to have more aggressive digital media campaigns than losing candidates. Overall, the evidence here suggests that digital media tools offered both incumbent and challenger candidates with a clear competitive advantage.

Conclusion

In this study, we have argued that the Brazilian political campaign sphere is a recently ripe atmosphere in which to study the use of new media technologies for campaign purposes. According to Gilmore (2012), this is specifically true because Brazilian politicians are still discovering the potential that "new" technologies have in political campaigns. The present research, however, points to but a new facet of an old art form. In Brazil specifically, political campaigns are multifaceted endeavors, which are affected by a number of influences. For instance, Samuels (2001a) argues that incumbents hold a unique advantage in Brazilian elections. This is true at all levels of elections, but specifically at the level of the lower house of Congress because they are rarely challenged head on by a newcomer candidate. Challenger candidates then, tend to establish new niches where there is either no presiding incumbent or they seek ways to trim off voters from a number of established niches. Scholars (Benoit and Marsh 2010; Samuels 2001c, 2002) have noted, however, that new candidates face an uphill battle in generating enough votes and have traditionally had to rely heavily on generating campaign funding in order to forge new niches and gain enough name recognition in the already saturated electorate market. Digital media then, as we have illustrated, is a new tool that can help bridge this gap in part and can provide challenger candidates an inexpensive, if not free, option that can help them establish new constituencies.

Alternatively, we have illustrated how digital media can have an impact in leveling the playing field for smaller political parties. Affiliation with certain political parties has traditionally lent considerable legitimacy to a given candidate's campaign. Specifically, candidates from larger parties have tended to reap increased legitimacy in the minds of the voting public (Ames et al. 2008). For instance, in the 2010 elections, 55 % of candidates elected to office in the race for the lower house of Congress came from one of the four largest parties (PT, PSDB, DEM, PMDB) while 45 % came from the other 22 political parties. With 28 distinct parties nationwide to choose from in most every state race, certain parties tend to enjoy higher voter recognition, and therefore legitimization, than others. In an attempt to address this imbalance, however, many parties join political coalitions as a way of increasing their legitimacy to the voting public (Ames 2001). In the late 1990s and early 2000s specifically, coalitions were seen a legitimate way for smaller party candidates to borrow legitimacy from the larger, more established, political parties and were argued to be an influence on election outcomes (Ames 2001). Over the past decade, however, coalitions have become more the rule than the exception and therefore may not be leveling the playing field quite as much as they once did, leaving smaller party candidates to find new and innovative ways establish their individual legitimacy in the eyes of the Brazilian voting public. And while digital media campaigns by no means replace the immediate legitimacy that an association with powerful parties may have, they do provide candidates with new ways of engaging with voters directly and without having to rely on the massive party machinery to forge their own constituency.

Finally, the findings in this study point to the difference in how distinct types of digital sites can have on a candidate's performance on election day. The findings in this study then suggest that certain Internet sites can be better suited for political campaign purposes than others and that this most likely varies depending upon the political and electoral systems, as well as culture. Specifically, we illustrate how having a mobile media campaign on a site such as Twitter is a more strategically beneficial tactic then using more traditional social media sites such as Facebook and Orkut. These findings suggesting that perhaps tools that are more pervasive, or to a certain extent *in*vasive, in the lives of the voting public, are specifically well suited for populations where mobile phone use is as extensive as in the case of Brazil. Additionally, these findings also suggest that different cultures may consume their politics through distinct types of media and that no site alone is best suited for campaign purposes across the globe. Overall, however, the evidence presented here supports the argument that social networking sites such as Twitter and Facebook are fostering new styles of conversation between candidates and voters and that these new connections can play a central role in shoring up voter support.

End Notes

All information about international website usage accessed from Alexa at http://www.alexa.com.

Acknowledgments The authors would like to thank Bernard Grofman and Alexander Treschel for the invitation to participate in the Conference on Internet, Voting, and Democracy hosted by the Center for the Study of Democracy at the University of California at Irvine in May of 2011.

References

Ames B (2001) The deadlock of democracy in Brazil. University of Michigan Press, Ann Arbor

Ames B, Barker A, Rennó LR (2008) Quality of elections in Brazil: policy, performance, pageantry, or pork? In: Kingstone PR, Power TJ (eds) Democratic Brazil revisited. University of Pittsburgh Press, Pittsburgh

Bagchi K, Solis A, Gemoets L (2003) An empirical study of telecommunication product adoption in Latin America and the Caribbean. Elect J Inf Syst Dev Countries 15(3):1–17

Benoit K, Marsh M (2010) Incumbent and challenger campaign spending effects in proportional electoral systems the Irish elections of 2002. Polit Res Q 63:1

Boas TC (2005) Television and neopopulism in Latin America: Media effects in Brazil and Peru. Lat Am Res Rev 40(2):27–49

Chadwick Andrew (2006) Internet politics: states, citizens, and new communication technologies. Oxford University Press, New York

Chadwick AJ, Howard PN (eds) (2009) Routledge handbook of internet politics. Routledge, London

Davis R (1999) The web of politics: the internet's impact on the American political system. Oxford University Press, New York

Foot KA, Schneider SM (2006) Web campaigning. MIT Press, Cambridge

Gilmore J (2012) Ditching the pack: digital media in the 2010 Brazilian congressional campaigns. New Media and Society 14(4):617–633

Howard PN (2006) New media campaigns and the managed citizen. Cambridge University Press, New York and Cambridge

Howard PN (2011) The digital origins of dictatorship and democracy: information technology and political Islam. Oxford University Press, New York

Internet World Stats (n.d.) Brazil: internet stats and telecom market report, http://www.internetworldstats.com/sa/br.htm. Accessed Dec 2010

Mische A (2007) Partisan publics: Communication and contention across Brazilian youth activist networks. Princeton University Press, Princeton

Samuels D (2001a) When does every penny count? Intra-party competition and campaign finance In Brazil. Party Polit 7(1):89–102

Samuels D (2001b) Incumbents and challengers on a level playing field: assessing the impact of campaign finance in Brazil. J Polit 63(2):569–584

Samuels D (2001c) Money, elections, and democracy in Brazil. Lat Am Polit Soc 43(2):27–48

Samuels DJ (2002) Pork barreling is not credit claiming or advertising: campaign finance and the sources of the personal vote in Brazil. J Polit 64(3):845–863

Campaigns and Social Media Communications: A Look at Digital Campaigning in the 2010 U.K. General Election

Michael J. Jensen and Nick Anstead

Abstract Social media are said to have the potential to transform relationships between political parties, candidates, and citizens. This chapter is a study of social media use at different levels in the 2010 United Kingdom general election to see to what extent that potential is realized. The research compares the use of Twitter by the national level of the campaign, composed of the three major parties, and their leaders, as well as the campaigns of the three major parties across the nine electoral districts in England's second city, Birmingham. It examines the candidates and parties' that various informational and engagement strategies at the national and Birmingham levels of the campaign with respect to their campaign functions. The analysis is carried out using natural language processing to computerize the content analysis. The findings reveal that social media are used at both levels, primarily for the undirectional transfer of information rather than for engagement. However, at the Birmingham level of the campaign there appears to be significantly greater emphasis on the creation of personal connections between candidates and the public than at the national level of the campaign. This suggests that lower profile candidates use social media in a compensatory manner, offsetting their limited media coverage which voters typically rely on in getting to know the candidates.

In recent years, United Kingdom-based electoral campaigns have simultaneously become increasingly centralized and functionally differentiated their communications while also promoting greater campaign engagement with electorates. There are many examples of this seeming contradiction. Campaigns have placed far greater emphasis on coordinating their communications in terms of media management (Strömbäck 2007), what might be termed a command and control structure of political communication (Anstead and Straw 2009). At the same time,

M. J. Jensen (✉)
ANZSOG Institute for Governance, University of Canberra, Canberra, ACT, Australia
e-mail: Michael.Jensen@canberra.edu.au

N. Anstead
London School of Economics and Political Science, London, UK

B. Grofman et al. (eds.), *The Internet and Democracy in Global Perspective*,
Studies in Public Choice 31, DOI: 10.1007/978-3-319-04352-4_5,
© Springer International Publishing Switzerland 2014

the 1990s saw the rise of "talk show democracy" in British and American electoral politics as increasingly political candidates made appearances with high profile popular media figures, directly engaging live studio audiences or callers (Blumler and Gurevitch 2001), while, more recently, Twitter and Facebook have become standard communication tools (Gainous and Wagner 2011; Gulati and Williams 2011). As such, campaigns appear to be moving in opposite directions, emphasizing greater control over their messaging while also placing their candidates in unscripted environments, directly engaging with voters. The questions this chapter poses are, to what extent and on what terms are supporters invited to engage with campaigns on social media, and are there differences between the national level and constituency levels of the campaign?

Political campaigns in the UK have struggled to identify useful ways in which to integrate social media communications into their operations. In the UK, neither the then prime minister, Gordon Brown, nor Conservative leader David Cameron opened personal Twitter accounts during the campaign, the latter infamously critical of Twitter as a medium that does not permit reflective communication.[1] There is limited evidence of the integration of social media platforms into the overall operations of a political campaign and at the constituency level. Apart from the Liberal Democrats, few resources were devoted to developing a social media strategy (Gibson 2010). There is a sense that social media communications matter; however, platforms such as Twitter pose significant communication management issues as relatively large numbers of Twitter users, representing an unknown quantity to campaigns, can emerge quickly and have a decisive impact on the flow of communications (Chadwick 2011). In the UK context, Twitter has become particularly important with the rise the practice of watching live political television while tweeting. This has resulted in the emergence of a relatively small but vocal "viewertariat" that has become established within British politics (Anstead and O'Loughlin 2011).

Some evidence, however, has shown that the sophistication of a campaign's social media strategy can produce significant electoral benefits. The first decade of empirical research on campaign engagement tended to validate the normalization thesis, auguring limited potential for Web-based communications to expand the reach and effectiveness of online campaigning due to selective exposure and the attitudinal antecedents of political Web use (Bimber and Davis 2003; Hoff 2010; Margolis and Resnick 2000; Sunstein 2001; Ward and Gibson 2009). However, more recent work has identified links between a campaign's online presence and electoral outcomes particularly for smaller, less bureaucratized parties, and those with little or no parliamentary representation (Cardenal 2011; Karpf 2012; Sudulich and Wall 2010). These effects appear particularly robust for social media campaign communications (Gibson and McAllister 2011).

---

[1] "Sweary David Cameron illustrates dangers of informal interview." *The Guardian* July 29, 2009. Although it should be noted that Cameron did eventually open a Twitter account in October 2012.

This research suggests that some political campaigns may be beginning to break Michels's (1966) dictum regarding the oligarchical imperative of party organization—and that in the context of a political campaign, there may be organizational benefits from online spaces of horizontal information flows. Campaigns may take advantage of the technological capacities of these media to directly communicate with supporters, solicit feedback, and create spaces where supporters may make consequential decisions for the manner in which the campaign is carried out. On the other hand, and despite the technological attributes of social media platforms, they are used to perform the traditional informational functions of campaigns by cognitively mapping the election contest, characterizing policies, and personalities. We can relate the latter set of functions with respect to the effects of campaign communications in terms of moving votes, while the former is oriented to the productive potential within communications.

To date, there is little information regarding the communicative operations occurring inside the "black box" of campaign effects. Although digital communication tools have the potential to technologically, symmetrically, and reciprocally structure interactions, they do not determine the structure of political relationships that emerge recursively through ongoing communications. The range of communication cannot be properly conceptualized if we limit ourselves to a vocabulary of media operations (Burke 1966, pp. 410–417). Even if the technologies used by campaigns enable horizontal modes of engagement, campaigns may still rhetorically invoke a hierarchical mode of political organization in social media communications. Hence, it does not follow that the use of horizontal modes of campaign communication gives rise to horizontal political relationships between campaigns and their supporters. If campaign social media communications are implicated in electoral outcomes, it is by virtue of the messages communicated via these channels rather than the technological structure.

This chapter, therefore, is a study of the content of social media communication in the context of the 2010 British general election. It examines the rhetorical positioning of electorates and the terms of campaign engagement communicated through candidate and party Facebook and Twitter communications. As the evidence of social media campaign effects is primarily concentrated in the results of less bureaucratized parties, we compare social media communications at the national level and smaller campaign organizations at the local or district level. The British general election is institutionalized through a geographic structure organized around 650 territorially defined constituencies with individual results aggregated into a national electoral outcome. Though the national party plays a greater role in U.K. district-level campaigns than in the U.S., local campaigns have distinct identities. Additionally, there are often great stratifications in resource parties devote to individual races, necessitating varying levels of local field operations. Given the variation in competitiveness across constituencies, the unique sets of issues in play, and local histories as well as the independent campaign activities of each of the candidates, there is potentially a high degree of differentiation in the communicative strategies for engagement in operation at the national level and across the individual district races.

In this chapter, we study the Twitter communications from the 2010 UK general election with respect to the structure of the campaign communications sent via social media platforms. In addition, we compare the national level social media communications with the constituencies in Birmingham, England as a case study, to identify differences between national and regional campaign dynamics. This research connects the rhetorical form of campaign communications with structural relationship that campaigns forge with supporters. We find there are variations in the organizational networks between political authorities and electorates at the national and local levels of electoral campaigns. Most notably, while a predominantly command and control structure of the campaign operates at the national level, communications at the local level are more horizontal and personal in nature.

The Structure of Communication Technologies and Campaign Communications

The study of communications in political campaigning has primarily focused on the instrumental functions involved in moving voters to cast their ballots in the desired way. Gronbeck (1978) categorizes these functions as behavioral activation, cognitive mapping, and adjustments aligning issues with candidates' personas and polities, and the assignation of legitimacy. However, he notes, campaigns also enact a series of "consummatory functions" that stand apart from the direct process of electing a candidate including the bonds they create with supporters and the spaces they create for supporters to shape the campaign. The growth of social media use creates new opportunities for campaigns to pursue both instrumental and consumptatory communications. Social media channels are unique, compared to broadcast campaign tools in that they both enable direct connections with members of a political system and they are interactive. Digital interactive spaces enable a wider range of participatory styles and modes of engagement than are otherwise available to campaigns (Bimber et al. 2012). These technological affordances have led to an emerging tension within organizations such as political parties that seek to both productively harness the creative energies of campaign supporters and at the same time "tame the liberating potential of networks of mass self-communication" (Castells 2009, p. 414). In this chapter, we identify two categories of communications: those that attempt to "tame" or control the flow of political communications by ordering issues and thematics in a favorable manner and those that enact horizontal relationships with supporters through informal communications or the creation of spaces where supporters can participate in the campaign on their own terms.

Instrumental campaign communications are monologic: they are crafted to activate, convert, and reinforce voters by connecting their concerns with a motive to vote for a candidate. Hence they are understood as a *vertically structured* relationship as they are understood in terms of the effects of these communications on voters. Gronbeck categorizes these functions as behavioral activation, cognitive adjustments, and the assignation of legitimacy. Behavioral activation includes efforts to mobilize one's supporters, convert others, and reinforce your supporters' views lest they become converted (Berelson et al. 1986; Lazarsfeld et al. 1948). Such appeals include communications that keep the campaign on the minds of voters by pointing to ongoing campaign events and other activities or claims about the importance of the election. Cognitive adjustments refer to the persuasive activities that create frames aligning voters with candidate and party positions. The flow of these communications has been linked to stabilizing voter identification and the likelihood one will vote in the desired way (Campbell et al. 1980; Converse 1962; Zaller 1989, 1996). In this way, campaigns manage and simplify the complexity of communications about the election by informing voters how to interpret the varied claims in circulation. Bestowing legitimacy entails to the ability to present a candidate as a viable and believable figure. Metacampaiging, that is, communications about the state of the campaign (e.g., who is ahead, who won a debate or a stage in a nominating process, or garnered coveted endorsements); statements from surrogates; and the ability to claim credit for previous policies are all linked to the assignation of legitimacy for a candidate.

These categories of campaign functions are principally concerned with the effects of campaign communication and the consequences for voter activation and vote reinforcement.

Social media communications are distinct from the broadcast media model that has informed traditional typologies of campaign communications based on the types of interactions they afford. Communications can also create *horizontally structured relationships* between political authorities and supporters. Communications can be structured horizontally in two ways. The first arrangement we term *political entrepreneurialism*. That is, campaigns can call for persons to take actions on behalf of the campaign while leaving supporters to define the premises of that engagement (Bimber et al. 2012). To the extent supporters are able to determine the manner in which they campaign on behalf of a cause or candidate, there is a greater degree of entrepreneurialism as individuals move from the position of consumers of campaign messages to producers of campaign communications and activity. Although campaigns have long sought to involve supporters in their field activities, campaigns have always attempted to constrain volunteers to scripts and set procedures (Nielsen 2012). For this reason, social media are unique as they provide a technological platform from which campaigns and supporters are positioned symmetrically with relatively equal capacities as receivers and senders of messages. Although it is possible to enact such relationships through other media, social media channels afford these operations within the same space in which persons are called to take up a role. Consequently, social media enables "communicative autonomy" from which individuals can operate and influence the news information cycle (Castells 2009, p. 414). This can pose a threat to a campaign's control on the channels of communication with supporters, but campaigns can also leverage this capacity by inviting supporters to voice their particular reasons for supporting the party or harnessing their supporters' collective intelligence and authenticity as persons who are not formally part of the campaign organization (Shirky 2010).

In the 2008 US election, for example, Barack Obama's online strategy was targeted not at individuals who might be potential voters for the candidate, but at those who could become active contributors of money, time, and efforts. The institutional openness that allowed even the formation of critical groups on mybarackobama.com permitted the emergence of amateur activists whose engagement was coordinated rather than commanded. The success of the Obama campaign attracted considerable attention from campaigners around the world looking for ways to likewise coordinate and integrate the decentralized activities of individuals in hopes of expanding the base of supporters beyond the ranks of traditional partisans (Anstead and Chadwick 2009; Humphrys 2011; Libert and Faulk 2009). In particular, the 2010 UK general election saw considerable growth in the use of interactive Web 2.0 environments by the major parties (Lilleker and Jackson 2010). An example of political entrepreneurialism from the 2010 UK general election would be the "#changewesee" Twitter campaign by Labour which invited individuals to tell their own stories about the positive impact of Labour policies which were then aggregated and redistributed.

A second way in which campaigns communicatively enact horizontal relationships is through *phatic* communications. Phatic communication designates communication motivated by "the use of speech for the establishing of a social bond between speaker and the spoken-to" (Burke 1969, pp. 269–270). Like calls for entrepreneurial interactions, these communications are distinguished from instrumental campaign communications by the secondary or even incidental nature of informational content. Political campaigns have long sought to improve candidate likeability such that voters can identify with the candidate as someone like them. Beyond the limited reach of retail politics, candidates have taken to informal and unscripted television appearances as a way to appear authentic and relatable (Baum 2005; Benoit 2007; Blumler and Gurevitch 2001; Blumler and Kavanagh 1999). The informality of social media affords the ability to regularly engage in such communications without the constraints of a mediating host. Examples of phatic statements during the 2010 UK election include Nick Clegg's tweet, "Just having a first look at the studio for this evening's debate. Nervous and excited? Absolutely" (April 15, 2010). Rhetorically, this statement is crafted to provide a convincing image of the candidate that citizens can relate to: a mixture of excitement and nerves before an important event. Such communications are technologically facilitated by the use of mobile applications to post on Twitter or Facebook in the moment and lend credibility to the impression that these statements are authentic representations of the candidate rather than crafted and politically calculated. In this case, however, the metadata supplied by Twitter perhaps belies the authenticity of Clegg's message as it was sent from a Web browser rather than a mobile application making it highly unlikely he was in the middle of visiting the studio at that point in time as he claimed to be. Nevertheless, the actual conditions of communication and its empirical consequences (in terms of conveying the impression of authenticity) are only incidental to whether or not it is phatic.

Personalized mobilization frames and social solidarity have become increasingly salient aspects of political mobilization. Personalized political frames refract political personalities and issues through individualized meanings and social attachments (Bennett and Segerberg 2011). In the American political system, phatic communications have reemerged as a significant form of political campaign communications. Gronbeck and Wiese (2005) note that going back to the 2004 election, digital social networks helped foster and maintain social identification between candidates and their supporters. More generally, the disembedded nature of interaction via social media place greater emphasis on phatic communications to establish rapport between persons (Miller 2008). In the context of a political campaign, these communications can humanize candidates as they may convey behind the scenes information, sentiment, and personal dimensions to the life of a politician. Hence, they engage the public by enacting a personal sphere of communication (Goodnight 1999). Broadcast media impose their own genres of campaign reporting which tend to be more formal, particularly within the British media system which places a greater emphasis on its informational role rather than the personal aspects of politicians (Blumler and Gurevitch 1995). Hence, there are reasons for campaigns to use phatic communication that stem both from within the structure of social media communication which make it more appropriate and from the overall organization of broadcast media channels which make such communication less appropriate. Hence, social media channels are more conducive to call for political entrepreneurialism and engage in phatic communications. As social media supplement the channels available to campaigns, it would appear reasonable that campaigns would rely on these channels in particular. Therefore, we offer our first two hypotheses concerning horizontal communications.

H₁: Entrepreneurial communications will be more common in campaign tweets than any category of vertical communications.

H₂: Phatic communications will be more common in campaign tweets than any category of vertical communications.

The value of decentralized activities may vary throughout a campaign. If the chief motives for engaging supporters on horizontal terms are to establish rapport, obtain feedback, and attract new recruits, the value for each of those functions is higher at the start of the campaign than toward the end when candidates are already presumably known and there is less time to obtain a pay-off from additional volunteers and feedback. Additionally, as the value of new information and volunteers declines, competing incentives for message control may become decisive in campaign communication strategies. These considerations suggest an additional hypothesis:

H₃: There will be a greater incidence of horizontally-structured communications towards the beginning of a campaign which will decline over time.

Finally, there are significant differences between the national and constituency-level campaign in the UK which can give rise to unequal incentives for social media use at each level. The Westminster model of government is party-centered. Historically, campaigns were fought at the local level where the vast proportion of communicative effort and resources were directed (Pinto-Duschinsky 1981). However, as a country-wide print media, national rail network, and finally electronic communications developed, campaigning became increasingly nationalized in tone, with far greater focus on parties and leaders. This shift in emphasis was so great that a slew of research published in the years around the millennium, arguing that constituency campaigns still retained some relevance to electoral outcomes, were considered to be revisionist (Denver and Hands 1997; Denver et al. 2002; Denver et al. 2004; Pattie et al. 1995). There is evidence that the constituency-level campaigns played a critical role in the 2010 election as a number of Labour candidates were able to fend off challenges from Conservatives effectively denying Conservatives an outright majority (Fisher et al. 2011).

Nevertheless, it is now widely accepted that modern British elections function on two levels: a national level campaign between leaders and party platforms, in which the ultimate goal is control of Parliament, and then local campaigns between individual candidates seeking to be representatives of the residents within a district. These campaign environments are far from wholly autonomous: local candidates run on the national party manifesto, retaining limited policy autonomy, while national parties also target resources at particular seats and high profile candidates (the most notable example of the former development was Conservative Vice Chairman Lord Ashcroft's decision to direct resources at marginal seats in the 2 years prior to 2010). Rhetorically, the duality is often reflected in the simultaneous invocation of national campaign themes within the context of the local election as candidates relate national electoral outcomes to local policy concerns. However, despite these links, the national and local levels are functionally differentiated within the context of an electoral campaign, both in content and outcome. Indeed, one of our sample constituencies provided a notable example in the 2010 election: the Labour MP for Birmingham Edgbaston, Gisela Stuart, retained her seat despite its perceived vulnerability based on previous electoral returns and polling, the overall swing of the election, resulting in Labour's second worst performance since 1918, and the seat's high ranking on the Conservative target list (and the attendant Conservative resources and energies that status brought the district).

The local and national campaigns can be differentiated in three senses. First, contingent factors of each constituency may give rise to unique sets of issues contested by the campaigns, revolving around substantive policy or candidate personality. Second, independent of national trends, localities may have an affinity for a particular individual, separated from the party, forcing challengers to adopt a posture notably different from other candidates within their own party. Third, while resources and media attention are significantly directed at the national level of campaigns, the local level is often dependent on labor intensive volunteer work to distribute fliers and knock on doors, campaign practices more prominent at the local level (Nielsen 2012).

The differentials in resources and media attention are significant for constituency-level campaigns. The national level of the campaign in England tends to be the focal point as the contest over government formation remains central and attracts a considerable amount of communication from political figures and media outlets. Furthermore, the UK has a highly nationalized media environment between newspapers, the BBC, and other networks which direct attention to the national campaign as that is relevant to all viewers and readers. Without regular news coverage, local candidates are often relatively unknown in comparison to the level of news coverage at the national level. Although the general policy positions of each candidate can be inferred from a candidate's party, candidate personalities are not. Therefore, constituency-level campaigns often have a great need to communicate the persona of a candidate so that voters may better identify with the candidate. Given the relatively limited resources, available to constituency-level candidates, they depend more on volunteers. As constituency-level campaign organizations are smaller than the national level, volunteers are nested within a more limited set of prior decisions that circumscribe their activities providing volunteers more dominion than exists at the national level. Social media can be a cost-effective manner in which candidates can communicate with supporters and receive feedback which provides greater incentives for political entrepreneurialsim at the constituency level than exists at the national level. These factors suggest our last three hypotheses.

H_4: The flow of communication at the national level will be greater than among the Birmingham constituencies.

H_5: The Birmingham campaign communications will contain more references inviting political entrepreneurialism than the national-level campaign.

H_6: The Birmingham campaign communications will emphasize phatic communications more than the national-level campaign.

Data and Methods

We selected Birmingham, England as a point of comparison between a constituency-level and the national-level campaign. Birmingham is not representative of other major cities, but it represents an important and interesting case as it was the site of a great deal of attention. In the context of the 2010 election, the nine constituencies in city offered a range of interesting political circumstances, especially pertinent in an election in which the opposition Conservative Party was seeking to (and, according to opinion polls, was likely to) take seats from the Labour government. Prior to polling day, Labour held eight of the seats, ranging from ultra-marginals to solidly safe seats. The city included seats such as Birmingham Edgbaston, number 39 on the Conservative Party's target list for the election.[2] The city's political make-up reflected the significance of other parties, with the Liberal Democrats defending their one seat of Solihull and competitive in others. As such, all three major parties recognized the city's significance and competed in it. Additionally, the Respect Party have a significant presence in local politics that they were hoping to transform into success in the Westminster elections. Thus, the city offered a good microcosm of what were likely to be the "big stories" on election night.[3]

Aside from these contingent reasons, however, Birmingham is significant for more conditional reasons as well. It is the second largest city in England, with an ethnically diverse population of over 1 million inhabitants.[4] Some districts are highly diverse, while others more homogeneous. Additionally, the city has been undergoing a significant amount of de-industrialization and is in the process of a transition to a postindustrial economy (Marsh et al. 2007, pp. 67–68). Mean annual salary across the constituencies is £19,321 Incomes in the individual constituencies range from £17,578 to £21,967. Although these figures are slightly below the UK median of £21,326, they are all within one standard deviation and include districts both above and below the UK average.[5]

For all these reasons, Birmingham figured prominently in the national campaigns, with party leaders and senior MPs making important addresses in the city, and it also hosted the final televised debate.[6] Candidates were called upon to address particular concerns raised by the loss of factory work as well as the needs posed by its highly heterogeneous population. Birmingham, therefore, is a city with both significant local campaign issues as well as national-level political attention.

The data are the set of all Twitter communications produced by official campaign accounts representing the three major parties and party leaders at the national level and those produced by the candidates in the nine Birmingham districts. These contain all of the tweets and Facebook posts produced over the course of the campaign between April 5, 2010 the day before the election was officially called and May 6, 2010 when the election was held.[7] As it was widely

[2] BBC News website. 2010. "Conservative Target Seats". Available at: http://news.bbc.co.uk/1/shared/election2010/results/targets/p_con.stm [accessed October 30, 2012].

[3] Indeed, this proved to especially true of Birmingham Edgbaston, which the Conservatives ultimately failed to take from Gisella Stuart, the incumbent Labour MP, with the result in the seat became somewhat embellmatic of the Tories overall failure to claim a majority.

[4] Office for Neighborhood Statistics. 2007. "Table View." Available at: http://neighbourhood.statistics.gov.uk/dissemination/LeadTableView.do;jsessionid=ac1f930d30d88207028aa2f942cea a38f4748c170251?a=3&b=276800&c=birmingham&d=13&e=13&g=373272&i=1001x1003x10 04&m=0&r=1&s=1282632693019&enc=1&dsFamilyId=1812&nsjs=true&nsck=true&nssvg= false&nswid=1024 [Accessed August 24, 2010].

[5] The data can be found at http://www.guardian.co.uk/news/datablog/2011/nov/24/wages-britain-ashe-mapped.

[6] "The Battle for No. 10 on Your Doorstep." Birmingham Post. April 8, 2010, p. 20.

[7] Although Parliament continued in session until April 12th, we treat April 6th as the start date as this is the day Gordon Brown formally asked to dissolve Parliament and the leaders of the major parties held rallies outlining their campaign themes.

known that Gordon Brown planned to call for elections on Tuesday April 6, 2010, the parties had already begun campaign messaging.

At the national level, the Twitter posts include communications from the Labour Party, the Liberal Democrats, and the Conservatives along with Nick Clegg, the Liberal Democrat leader.[8] At the local level, there were also four active Twitter accounts among the candidates: Gisela Stuart, the Labour candidate from Birmingham Edgebaston, Steve McCabe, the Labour candidate from Birmingham Selly Oak, Jerry Evans, the Liberal Democrat from Birmingham Hall Green, and Keely Huxtable, the Conservative candidate from Birmingham Northfield. These accounts cover the four national and four constituency-level level accounts representing all of the major parties. The Birmingham data also contains representatives of all the major parties. The resulting dataset includes 1322 Twitter posts: 1043 national-level tweets and 279 tweets from the Birmingham candidates. In addition to the message text, each post contains metadata with the date-time stamp, the source from which it was sent, and in the case of Twitter, whether the message was sent in reply to another user. Additional information on the data collection and coding are contained in the Appendix.

These posts represent the primary body of ongoing direct communications between parties, candidates, and supporters as their followers. The data collection was limited to public pages and profiles used for campaign purposes. Twitter provide a unique insight into the communication flows from parties and candidates to interested parties as they are direct communications that individuals must opt into receive by becoming a follower.[9] The possibility of these communications therefore requires a double selection: campaigns select particular messages with the aim of producing an appeal and followers/fans select the streams of appeals they wish to receive. The combination of these selections results in the communicative enactment of a relationship between campaigns and their online followers predicated on the terms defined within the flow of communications.

Each tweet was coded according the incidence of corresponding terms in the text. The coding was automated using natural language processing (NLP). The machine coding results yielded a success rate of 67.3 %. Additional details can be found in the Appendix. The terms selected were based on an initial human coding of a subsample from which key words were derived. Horizontal communications are composed of two terminological groups: terms that invoke spaces for entrepreneurial campaign engagement and terms indicative of phatic statements. Entrepreneurial terms included verbs enjoining persons to participate, the nominalizations of these terms, and adverbs describing conjoined political activity. Phatic terms relate to communications that express emotive states or other aspects of candidate personality as well as a nonpolitical narrative of campaign activity

---

[8] Neither Labour's Gordon Brown nor the Conservatives David Cameron had a personal Twitter account during the campaign.

[9] Facebook provides a similar opportunity; however, the use of Facebook by the candidates from the Birmingham constituencies was rather limited.

such as having just arrived to an event site, a candidate's subjective experience and reactions to the activity, and observations about the weather.[10] Although these data include both communication sent to a general audience as well as all public campaign replies to Twitter users, we do not uniformly count replies as evidence of horizontal communications as not all replies engage horizontally with supporters. The two modes of horizontal interactions between campaigns and supporters are operationalized as the following set of words.

- *Entrepreneurial.* Volunteer, together, support, us, recruit(s), join, and help.
- *Phatic.* Thank, arrive, visit, fun, nice, interesting, heading, me, excited, nervous, sunny, and weather.[11]

Additionally, we identify six categories of instrumental communications. These include claims about policy, provide information on campaign events or broadcasts of interviews or party election broadcasts (PEBs), engage in metacampaigning by indicating how the horse race dimension of the campaign should be understood and organized, and by invoking surrogates speaking on behalf of the campaign such as a retweet designated by the Twitter convention RT or a "follow Friday" suggestion of accounts to follow designated by "#FF." Recipients of these communications were often directed to seek out additional information via a supplied hyperlink. The common thread between these communications is that they organize the informational environment of the campaign enabling individuals to cognitively map issues, activities, and the overall state of the race.

- *Policy.* Environment, spending, tax(-es), bank(-s,-ing), crime, polic(-e, -ing) school(-s), nhs, Trident,[12] rural
- *Metacampaigning.* Endorse(-d), YouGov, Ipsos, poll(-s, -ing), win(-ning), won
- *Events.* PEB, live, now, BBC, ITV, channel, hust(-ings), and surger(-y, -ies)
- *Debates.* Leadersdebate, debate, post-debate
- *Surrogates.* RT, #FF
- *Hyperlinks.* http

---

[10] Observations about the weather can be particular important in areas like the West Midlands where the spring is normally damp and cool. In that climate, a spot of sunshine is often considered emotionally uplifting.

[11] Direct replies are not categorically included as the machine coder analyses batches of tweets rather than individual messages and as such is unable to reliably simultaneously differentiate between party officials and members of the public as well as determine the informational content of each message.

[12] Trident referred to a missile system the Liberal Democrats were proposing to cut.

Horizontal and Vertical Communications on Facebook and Twitter

The level of Twitter messaging varied considerably over the course of the election among both the accounts representing the national and Birmingham levels of the campaigns. The level of messaging started out slowly but accelerated over the course of the campaign. Between the four national-level Twitter accounts there were 3.73 times as many messages as produced by the 4 Birmingham-based accounts indicating a significantly higher level of communication intensity at the national level compared to the district level of the campaign. The overall distribution of messages, aggregated daily, from the national level and from the Birmingham districts are presented in Fig. 1a and b, respectively.

The daily level of tweeting appears relatively trendless apart from a general decline in tweeting that corresponds with Sundays. The district-level campaign proceeds more slowly given that, although many of the candidates were already known, the field was not officially set until April 20, 2010, the filing deadline to appear on the May 6, 2010 ballot. The Pearson correlation between the daily messaging production at the national and Birmingham levels of the campaign is 0.37 (p = 0.04) indicating that while there are some common structural attributes of the campaigns at each level such as the start of the campaign and the day of the election, messaging in the Birmingham campaign proceeded to a large degree at its own temporal rhythm. At the national level, there are three points of punctuated activity coinciding with the leaders' debates on April 15th, 22nd, and 29th. Although there are scant references to the debates at any other time in the national Twitter data, on these particular days, the number of references to the debates jumps to 80, 99, and 116 mentions, respectively. These dates accounted for 95 % of all messaging about the debates. Among the Birmingham Twitter accounts, the Leaders' Debates occupied considerably less attention, with 5, 1, and 3 debate mentions (47 % of all debate mentions) on the days in which they were held.

Overall, there is a greater presence of each category of vertical communications concerned with the instrumental campaign functions. Table 1 shows that apart from metacampaigning, the incidence of vertical campaign communications is more common than either references to political entrepreneurialism or phatic communications. Given the significant differences in the overall level of Twitter communications at the national and district levels of the campaign, we compare the incidence of each thematic element with respect to the share of terms it accounts for rather than absolute counts of terminological incidence. These results provide evidence of the relative emphasis of each terminological group for a unit of analysis. Instrumental communications in general composed a significant part of the tweeting at the national level. The daily averages for content are displayed in Table 2. On the whole, vertical communications at the national level is nearly twice as large as the proportion of vertical content among the constituencies. At the national level there were an average incidence of 0.007 references to political entrepreneurialism and 0.004 phatic references. Apart from metacampaigning,

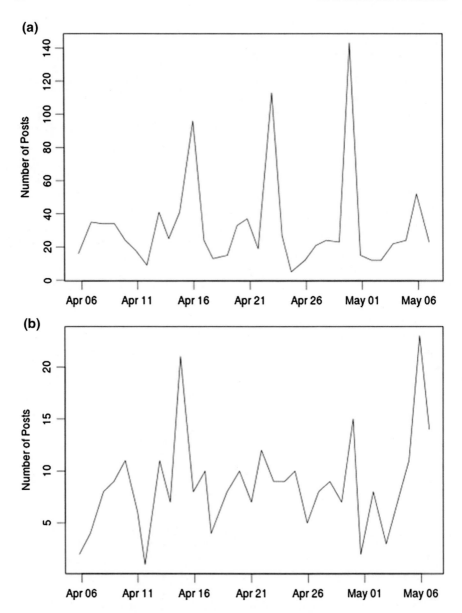

Fig. 1 **a** National Daily Twitter posts. **b** Daily Birmingham candidate Twitter posts

every category of vertical communication was more common than either entrepreneurial or phatic references. At the regional level, there were more phatic
communications than any other category apart from references to surrogates.

As a percentage of Twitter contents, there were over three times the incidence
of hyperlinks and higher levels of references to campaign events either with details

Table 1 Incidence of horizontal communications and vertical communications as a proportion of the overall communication

Entrepreneurial	Phatic	Horizontal (total)	Surrogate	Events	Metacampaign	Debate	Policy	Hyperlinks	Vertical (total)
0.007	0.004	0.011	0.012	0.009	0.001	0.011	0.008	0.023	0.064

Table 2 Average daily incidence of communication types in the national and district campaign as a proportion of the overall communication

	Entrepreneurial	Phatic	Horizontal (total)	Surrogate	Events	Metacampaign	Debate	Policy	Hyperlinks	Vertical (total)
National	0.007*	0.004***	0.011***	0.012	0.007	0.001***	0.011***	0.008	0.023***	0.062***
Birmingham	0.006	0.012	0.018	0.015	0.006	0.003	0.003	0.006	0.011	0.044

***p < 0.001

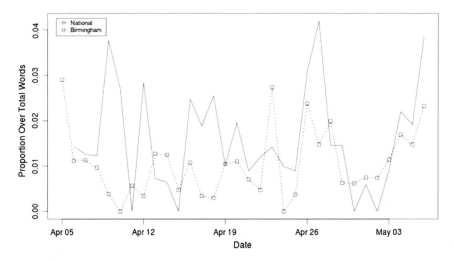

Fig. 2 Proportional incidence of horizontal communication

of where to meet a candidate or view televised appearances of party officials. Finally, surrogates were more commonly invoked at the national level than among the Birmingham sample. Policy references constituted similar proportions of the material tweeted at both the national and district levels while there was a statistically significant difference in metacampaigning at the local level as the Birmingham candidates, particularly Liberal Democrats, appealed to polling data as Nick Clegg surged in the polls or successfully competed in debates as a means indicate they have a chance of entering into government.

The level of horizontal communication is greater in the national sample than the Birmingham sample, however, most of this accounted for by differences in the quantity of entrepreneurial communications. Among the Birmingham candidates, there was a higher proportion of phatic communication than at the national level. This difference cannot be accounted for by the prevalence of parties rather than individual candidates in the national-level sample as Nick Clegg's proportion of phatic references among the body of his tweets was the same as the overall average for national-level accounts (0.004). The national-level campaigns placed greater emphasis on platforms to engage supporters in getting out their campaign message. Two examples of these efforts were evident in the tweets from the Labour party in regards to their "#changewesee" campaign inviting persons to act as surrogates tweeting about the difference Labour had made in their communities and the Conservative's initiative to crowd-source their response to Labour's manifesto. The incidence of horizontal communications at the national and constituency-levels over the course of the campaign are shown in Fig. 2.

The data represent the proportion of words (measured along the Y-axis) in each daily corpus of tweets corresponding with phatic communications or calls for entrepreneurial political participation. The national campaigns are represented in

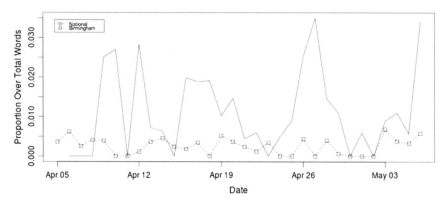

Fig. 3 Proportional incidence of Phalic communication

blue while the Birmingham campaigns are represented in red. At both levels of the campaign, there is a higher level of horizontal communications at the early stages of the campaigns, it declines until a week before the election where it rises right before the final weekend of campaigning. There is a final bump in entrepreneurial engagement on the last day candidates and parties at both levels urged supporters to talk to their friends and family and get them to vote.

Given the findings in Table 2, indicating that the two forms of horizontal communications are differentially used at national and district levels, we take a closer look at the use of these communications over time at each level. We take first the incidence of phatic communications at the national and district levels over the course of the campaign. The frequencies as a proportion of the communication content on each day are presented in Fig. 3.

At the early stages of the campaign there is a higher incidence of phatic communication at both levels, as well as toward the end of the campaign. However, the level of phatic communications are consistently higher at the district level throughout most of the campaign. Additionally, at the district level, there is an upsurge at several points throughout as candidates highlighted the social aspects of their campaign activities. Likewise, there is a higher incidence of invitations to enjoin with the campaigns as political entrepreneurs at the start of the campaign, around St. George's day, a day commemorating England's patron saint, toward the end of the last full week of the campaign and right at the end of the campaign. The results are displayed in Fig. 4.

At the national level, higher incidence of communications that encourage political entrepreneurs tend to coincide with relatively lower levels of tweet production. The incidence of the absolute incidence of these communications, however, fluctuates and the peaks and valleys of this fluctuation is evident in the data depicted in Fig. 4 (data on the absolute incidence not show). Some of the highest proportions of tweets inviting entrepreneurial interactions come toward the beginning and end of the campaign. At the district level, entrepreneurial tweets likewise appear at the beginning of the campaign but drop off considerably for

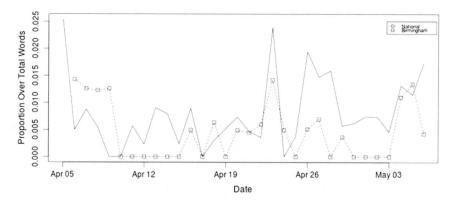

Fig. 4 Proportional incidence of enterpreneurial communication

several days until the overall campaign at the district level picks up again. At both the district and national levels of the campaigns the calls for political entrepreneurs increases toward the end of the campaign; however, in contrast to early calls which surround the recruitment of volunteers or to provide communications supportive of their party and critical of the opposition, these communications are directed at getting persons to vote.

Discussion and Conclusions

These data provide evidence that political campaigns are using social media communications for the creation of horizontal relationships with supporters. Nevertheless these relationships are highly circumscribed. Furthermore, the geographic and temporal contexts implicate the structure of campaign social media communications. Twitter communications serve multiple campaign functions that vary over the course of the campaign and these functions are different depending on whether one is concerned with the national campaign or the campaign between prospective parliamentary candidates. We will elaborate these conclusions in relation to the hypotheses posed earlier.

The first two hypotheses concerned the incidence of horizontal versus instrumental communications in Twitter messages. We find that both hypotheses are incorrect. Communications that invite political entrepreneurialism are less common than almost all of the instrumental campaign communications and likewise for phatic communications. Twitter communications contained a statistically significant higher incidence of vertical communications that aim at moving voters. As such it would appear that Twitter is not fully differentiated from the other means of communication utilized by campaigns.

The third hypothesis concerns temporal differentiations in the emphasis of social media communications. This hypothesis contends that there will be a higher incidence of horizontal communications toward the start of the campaign that will decline over time. There is little support for the hypothesis as Fig. 2 shows that at both levels of the campaign it starts with a higher proportion of horizontal communications; however, at neither the district or national levels of the campaign does this point contain the highest level of horizontal communications. Furthermore, Fig. 1a and b indicate that the volume of communications at the start of the campaign were relatively low. Hence, later on in the campaign there was both a higher emphasis and absolute incidence of horizontal communications. Given the relatively low levels of communication at the beginning of the campaign, the difference between the peaks at the start and end of the campaign may reflect more the relative inactivity overall in the Birmingham campaigns. The national-Birmingham divide persists despite the level of attention and resources that these constituencies received from the national parties. At the end of the campaign, these communications appear to have taken on a new urgency. At the national level, political entrepreneurialism climbed significantly during the last days of the campaign as campaigns focused on their get out the vote efforts. Among the Birmingham candidates, there was an increased effort at phatic communications suggesting ongoing concerns with the ability to connect with voters in their constituencies.

The final three hypotheses concern differences between social media communications at the national and district levels of the campaigns. The fourth hypothesis claimed we would encounter a higher volume of communications at the national level of the campaign than among Birmingham's candidates for Parliament. This hypothesis is borne out with finding of 3.73 times the level of communications among the four national-level Twitter accounts in comparison to the four Birmingham candidate accounts. This cannot be easily explained by differences in the tweeting practices of parties at the national level versus individual candidates at the district level. At the national level, Nick Clegg was relatively reticent, posting only 48 tweets over the course of the campaign in comparison to an average of 69.5 among the Birmingham candidates. Partly he may have benefited from the communications of the Liberal Democrat party Twitter, though this difference alone cannot account for differences in the motivations for communication.

The impact of the national-district distinction on each form of horizontal communications is the subject of our last two hypotheses. The fifth hypothesis stated that social media communications at the district level would invite political entrepreneurialism to a greater extent than at the national level. Although we suspected that the lack of campaign resources would create organizational incentives to encourage volunteers to aid the campaign on whatever terms they were willing to do so, the data presented in Table 2 contradict this hypothesis. There is no statistically significant difference in communications inviting the activities of political entrepreneurs between the national and district level. Human inspection of the tweets indicates that many messages calling for participation actually were carried out through a larger assemblage of Web-based communications and individuals to aggregate and integrate supporters' digital contributions to the campaigns. The final hypothesis stated that there would be greater levels of phatic communication among the Birmingham candidates than at the national level as these candidates were less-known quantities who did not benefit from the level of media attention given to the national campaign. The data bears out this conclusion. Furthermore, distinctions between party and candidate Twitter accounts does not explain our observation as Nick Clegg placed a similar emphasis on phatic communications as the parties. In part, the parties compensated in this regard by retweeting messages from supporters who acted as surrogates for the parties.

These findings provide support for some broader observations regarding the function and operational integration of social media communications in the context of political campaigns. In general we find that although the architecture of communication technologies are implicated in the structuring and organization of campaign communications, the structure of communications is irreducible to an accounting of the technologies. Social media communications nevertheless are involved in both information management and also the creation of a structure that can integrate decentralized activities of supporters, at least within certain parameters.

Our study of the British general election identified two informational functions of campaign social media communications. First, they were used extensively to provide a cognitive mapping of campaign themes and issues. In the hybridized setting of the Leaders' Debates. Twitter communications afforded the parties the ability to provide real time spinning of the debate, drawing attention to particular points they hoped to get across as well as providing an additional rebuttal opportunity. In the context of the 2010 UK Leaders' Debates, these communications were not trivial and generated a considerable amount of activity on online social networks (Chadwick 2011). They served a second communicative function by providing a more informal network through which the electorate could encounter the candidates. Much like the 1990s "talk show" democracy, social media provide an outlet for candidates to express their personalities and more effectively impart information about their character to the electorate. These communicative functions, both vertically structure activities like cognitive mapping and horizontal phatic communications serve strategic functions and appear highly managed by the campaigns.

Social media, however, are not solely involved in managing the campaign communication environment. There is a long history of entrepreneurial engagement with political campaigns (Nielsen 2012). Although professional staffers have organization incentives to manage the narrative and flow of communications, it has been long recognized that campaigns also depend on the efforts of supporters to persuade others and this holds true in the era of online campaigning (Berelson et al. 1986; Lazarsfeld et al. 1948; Norris and Curtice 2008). Additionally, although campaign have less control over volunteers who serve as surrogates of their messages, such surrogates can also communicate authenticity in an era of partisan media and public relations specialists. Though they are not the only means social media extend the reach of individual supporter and provide a platform through which campaigns can integrate their voices and ideas into campaign messaging and organization. Whether or not campaign uses of social media are effective in communicating authenticity and whether or not communications from supporters impact campaign priorities, strategies, and messaging are subjects for future research. In their outward effects, the campaigns waged by Labour, the Conservatives, and Liberal Democrats all demonstrated evidence that social media can and do play a role in the execution of central campaign functions—and that those functions differ across space and time.

Appendix: Data Collection

Twitter posts were collected using the twitteR module (Gentry 2012) in the R language. This captures all of the public posts from each candidate's account. Twitter posts were segmented on a daily basis and coded using natural language processing (NLP) (Bird et al. 2009). There are limitations to machine coding. The machine coding has limited ability to analyze words in relation to their contexts and to evaluate the implication of specific utterances for constituting the overall meaning of a text. We mitigate these risks as our analyses do not attempt to identify valances, selecting terms that are signified to a greater degree by the presence or absence of a term rather than the manner in which terms combine to form meanings.[13] Nevertheless, NLP significantly advances the ability to code large volumes of text that would otherwise be inaccessible if left to human coding. NLP can provide a high degree of reliability regarding the structure of a textual artifact. Furthermore, apart from its advantages in managing large volumes of data, NLP also enables the identification of patterns across large volumes of text that go beyond or are independent of the specific meanings communicated by authors (Ramsay 2005). In our case, given the highly structured nature of Twitter messages and their limited size, the occurrence of certain words can more reliably be linked to the incidence of campaign themes and communicative operations. NLP's algorithmic approach entails certain limitations: using too narrow a list of terms runs the risk of Type I, false negative errors, while using a more elaborate list of terms runs the risk of Type II, false positive errors.

Before applying NLP, all metadata was removed from the database leaving only the text of the messages. All terms were entered as lower case to match the normalization of the text. As the hypotheses under investigation relate to temporal and institutional structures or to differences between social media platforms, we take aggregates of posts rather than individual posts as our unit of analysis. After a series of tests to train the machine coder, the machine results were then verified against a second subsample of human-coded Twitter posts. A daily segment of tweets were

---

[13] Attempts to machine code semantic meanings are further problematized by the incidence of sarcasm in these data. In response to a series of reports critical of the Liberal Democrat leader, Nick Clegg, Twitter users began to sarcastically use the hashtag, "#itsnickcleggsfault" and this was later picked up by the Liberal Democrats Twitter feed as well (Chadwick 2010).

selected based on a relatively even dispersion of machine scores across each of the categories so as to not bias the testing based on a high incidence of one dimension.[14] Although these categories do not encompass the full range of communications in the samples, each tweet in the human-coded sample matched at least one of the dimensions of horizontal communications or information provision. The errors were summed with respect to the eight coding categories and calculated as a percentage of the total elements identified by human coding (Nolan 2002).

References

Anstead N, Chadwick A (2009) Parties, election campaigning, and the internet: toward a comparative perspective. In: Routledge handbook of internet politics. Routledge, London, pp 56–72

Anstead N, O'Loughlin B (2011) The emerging viewertariat and BBC Question Time television debate and real-time commenting online. Int J Press/Polit 16(4):440–462. doi:10.1177/1940161211415519

Anstead N, Straw W (2009) The change we need: what Britain can learn from Obama's victory. Fabian Society, London

Baum MA (2005) Talking the vote: Why presidential candidates hit the talk show circuit. Am J Polit Sci 49(2):213–234. doi:10.1111/j.0092-5853.2005.t01-1-00119.x

Bennett WL, Segerberg A (2011) Digital media and the personalization of collective action. Inf Commun Soc 14(6):770–799

Benoit WL (2007) Communication in political campaigns. Peter Lang, New York

Berelson B, Lazarsfeld PF, McPhee WN (1986) Voting: a study of opinion formation in a presidential campaign. University of Chicago Press, Chicago

Bimber BA, Davis R (2003) Campaigning online: the internet in US elections. Oxford University Press, New York

Bimber B, Flanagin A, Stohl C (2012) Collective action in organizations: interaction and engagement in an era of technological change. Cambridge University Press, New York

Blumler J, Gurevitch M (1995) The crisis of public communication. Taylor and Francis, New York

Blumler J, Gurevitch M (2001) Americanization reconsidered: U.K.-U.S. campaign communications across time. In: Bennett WL, Entman R (eds) Mediated politics: communication in the future of democracy. Cambridge University Press, New York, pp 380–403

Blumler JG, Kavanaugh D (1999) The third age of political communication: influences and features. Politic Commun 16(3):209–230. doi:10.1080/105846099198596

Bird S, Klein E, Loper E (2009) Natural language processing with python, 1st edn. O'Reilly Media, Sebastopol

Burke K (1966) Language as symbolic action: essays on life, literature, and method. University of California Press, Berkeley

Burke K (1969) A rhetoric of motives. University of California Press, Berkeley

Cardenal AS (2011) Why mobilize support online? The paradox of party behaviour online. Party Politics. doi:10.1177/1354068810395059

---

[14] For example, the machine coding identified references to the leaders debates with a high degree of reliability. Given the preponderance of debate-related tweets both on days when they were held, selecting a day with the debates would have biased upwards the reliability estimate. This means that the results of the test sample are likely biased downwards.

Castells M (2009) Communication power. Oxford University Press, Oxford

Chadwick A (2011) Britain's first live televised party Leaders' Debate: from the news cycle to the political information cycle. Parl Aff 64(1):24–44. doi:10.1093/pa/gsq045

Converse PE (1962) Information flow and the stability of partisan attitudes. Pub Opin Q 26(4):578–599

Denver D, Hands G (1997) Modern constituency campaigning: local campaigning in the 1992 general election. Frank Cass, London

Denver D, Hands G, Fisher J (2002) The impact of constituency campaigning in the 2001 general election. Br Elections Parties Rev 12:80–94

Denver D, Hands G, MacAllister I (2004) The electoral impact of constituency campaigning in Britain, 1992–2001. Polit Stud 52(2):289–306

Fisher J, Cutts D, Fieldhouse E (2011) The electoral effectiveness of constituency campaigning in the 2010 British general election: the 'triumph' of labour? Elect Stud 30(4):816–828

Gainous J, Wagner K (2011) Rebooting American politics: the internet revolution. Rowman & Littlefield, Lanham

Gentry J (2012) Twitter client for R. Retrieved from: http://cran.r-project.org/web/packages/twitteR/index.html

Gibson RK (2010) Open source campaigning?: UK party organisations and the use of the new media in the 2010 general election. SSRN Electron J. doi:10.2139/ssrn.1723329

Gibson RK, McAllister I (2011) Do online election campaigns win votes? The 2007 Australian "YouTube" election. Political Communication 28(2):227–244. doi:10.1080/10584609.2011.568042

Goodnight GT (1999) The personal, technical, and public spheres of argument. In: Lucaites JL, Condit M, Caudill S (eds) Contemporary Rhetorical Theory: a reader. Guiliford Press, New York, pp 251–264

Gronbeck BE (1978) The functions of presidential campaigning. Commun Monogr 45(4):268–280

Gronbeck BE, Wiese DR (2005) The repersonalization of presidential campaigning in 2004. Am Behav Sci 49(4):520–534. doi:10.1177/0002764205279754

Gulati J, Williams, CB (2011) Diffusion of innovations and online campaigns: social media adoption in the 2010 U.S. Congressional elections. SSRN eLibrary. Retrieved from http://papers.ssrn.com/sol3/papers.cfm?abstract_id=1925585

Hoff J (2010) Election campaigns on the internet. Int J E-Polit 1(1):22–40. doi:10.4018/jep.2010102202

Humphrys T (2011) How significant was the internet during the UK general election 2010? GRIN Verlag, Munich

Karpf D (2012) The Moveon effect: the unexpected transformation of American political advocacy. Oxford University Press, New York

Lazarsfeld PF, Berelson B, Gaudet H (1948) The people's choice: How the voter makes up his mind in a presidential campaign. Columbia University Press, New York

Libert B, Faulk R (2009) Barack, Inc: winning business lessons of the Obama campaign. FT Press, Upper Saddle Rive

Lilleker D, Jackson N (2010) Towards a more participatory style of election campaigning: the impact of web 2.0 on the UK 2010 general election. Policy and Internet, 2(3):69-98. doi:10.2202/1944-2866.1064

Margolis Michael, Resnick David (2000) Politics as usual? The cyberspace revolution. Sage, London

Marsh D, O'Toole T, Jones S (2007) Young people and politics in the UK: apathy or alienation?. Palgrave Macmillan, New York

Miller V (2008) New media, networking and phatic culture. Convergence: Int J Res New Media Technol 14(4):387–400. doi:10.1177/1354856508094659

Nielsen RK (2012) Ground wars: personalized communication in political campaigns. Princeton University Press, Princeton

Nolan JR (2002) Computer systems that learn: An empirical study of the effect of noise on the performance of three classification methods. Expert Systems with Applications 23(1):39–47. doi:10.1016/S0957-4174(02)00026-X

Norris P, Curtice J (2008) Getting the message out: a two-step model of the role of the internet in campaign communication flows during the 2005 British general election. J Inf Technol Polit 4(4):3–13

Pinto-Duschinsky M (1981) British political finance 1830–1980. American Enterprise Institute for Public Policy Research, Washington

Pattie CJ, Johnston RJ, Fieldhouse EA (1995) Winning the local vote: the effectiveness of constituency campaign spending in Great Britain, 1983–1992. Am Polit Sci Rev 89(4):969–983

Ramsay S (2005) In praise of pattern. Retrieved from http://digitalcommons.unl.edu/englishfacpubs/57

Shirky C (2010) Cognitive surplus: creativity and generosity in a connected age. Penguin Press, New York

Strömbäck J (2007) Political marketing and professionalized campaigning. J Polit Mark 6(2):49–67. doi:10.1300/J199v06n02_04

Sudulich ML, Wall M (2010) "Every little helps": cyber-campaigning in the 2007 Irish general election. J Inform Technol & Polit 7(4):340–355. doi:10.1080/19331680903473485

Sunstein CR (2001) Republic.com. Princeton University Press, Princeton

Ward S, Gibson R (2009) European Political Organizations and the internet mobilization, participation, and change. In: Chadwick A, Howard P (eds) Routledge handbook of internet politics. Routledge, London, pp 25–39

Zaller J (1989) Bringing converse back in: modeling information flow in political campaigns. Polit Anal 1(1):181–234

Virtual Power Plays: Social Movements, Internet Communication Technology, and Political Parties

Deana A. Rohlinger, Leslie A. Bunnage and Jesse Klein

Abstract   Drawing on interview data, participant observation, and archival research of the progressive group MoveOn.org and the conservative Tea Party Movement groups in Tallahassee, FL, this research examines how social movements use Internet Communication Technology (ICT) to affect political parties and political change in the United States. The paper consists of two analytical sections. In the first section, we examine how these groups use ICT to effectively market issues, mobilize consensus, and get citizens involved in the political process. In the second section, we outline how activist groups' use of ICT changes the relationship between social movement groups and political parties. While we do not suggest that ICT equalizes the relationship between social movements and political parties, we do show that savvy movement groups can use ICT in ways that can help activists transform a party. Additionally, we illustrate the potential for synergy between social movement and political parties in the digital age. We conclude the chapter with a discussion of how scholars might further assess the changing relationship between social movements and political parties.

> By the time Election Day arrives, millions of Americans will have contributed to a presidential candidate this year. Hundreds of political organizations—from the Sierra Club to the NRA, from MoveOn.org to the Swift Boat Veterans for Truth—will have taken an active part in the campaign, supported by Americans from every part of the political spectrum. All of this is democracy in action, and it is so commonplace that we take it for granted. Yet, this kind of mass

D. A. Rohlinger (✉) · J. Klein
Department of Sociology, Florida State University, Tallahassee, FL, USA
e-mail: deana.rohlinger@fsu.edu

L. A. Bunnage
Department of Sociology, Anthropology and Social Work, Seton Hall University, South Orange Village, NJ, USA

B. Grofman et al. (eds.), *The Internet and Democracy in Global Perspective*,
Studies in Public Choice 31, DOI: 10.1007/978-3-319-04352-4_6,
© Springer International Publishing Switzerland 2014

citizen involvement in the political process is a relatively recent phenomenon, spanning less than a half-century of our nation's history. How did it happen? And what does it suggest for this election, and for presidential elections to come? The answers can be found in the rise of what we conservatives call the "alternative" media—beginning with the conservative movement's development of political direct mail in the 1960s, followed by the growth of talk radio and cable TV news in the 1990s and, since then, by the remarkable role of the Internet in the political process. In this year's presidential election, it is the alternative media that are largely framing the issues, engaging the public, raising money, and getting out the vote. Whatever the outcome on Nov. 2, this election will be remembered as the year when these alternative media all came together to change how politics in America is practiced.

From an article published in *The Washington Post* by Richard A. Viguerie and David Franke. Published October 4, 2004

Activists, by nature, are generally optimistic. They believe that even a relatively small group of people can band together and, quite literally, change the world for the better. The relatively widespread availability of Internet Communication Technology (ICT) in the United States has fueled optimism among activists, who argue that their efforts to educate, organize, and mobilize are easier, and just as effective, in the digital age. More importantly, activists believe that they can use ICT to shape party politics and elections in the U.S. The extent to which their enthusiasm is warranted, however, is up for debate. While social scientists have investigated, and disagree over, the potential of ICT to reinvigorate political parties and engage individuals in activism beyond the armchair (Bimber 1998; Dalton and Wattenberg 2000; Rash 1997), the extent to which a social movement group's use of ICT might influence political parties remains largely unexplored.

There are a number of reasons that the relationship between social movement organizations and political parties in the digital age has not been analyzed. First, disciplinary differences cause scholars to examine how ICT affects different aspects of both the relationship between ICT and politics and the outcomes. Political scientists have done excellent work analyzing how political parties use ICT to grow support for issues and candidates and whether websites, e-mail, and the use of e-tactics can successfully alter electoral outcomes (Chadwick 2006; Dulio et al. 1999; Gainous and Wagner 2011; Gibson et al. 2003). Scholars, for instance, have found that political parties can use ICT to connect with social movement groups and amplify their campaign messages across the virtual landscape, which helps them get voters to the polls (Foot and Schneider 2002; Foot et al. 2003; Gibson and Ward 1998; Gibson and Ward 2000; Margolis et al.

1997).[1] Social movement scholars, in contrast, unpack how ICT is used to mobilize and challenge authorities and institutions (Carroll and Hackett 2006; Earl and Kimport 2008; Fisher et al. 2005). Activists, for example, can use ICT for everything from surreptitiously mobilizing workers to advocate changes in corporate policy to protesting television programs for canceling a much-loved (but unprofitable) program (Earl 2006; Raeburn 2004).[2] As a result of these different foci, very little work has been done on the interstices between the two disciplines or on how ICT affects the relationship between social movements and political parties.[3]

Second, because getting data on how activists use ICT "on the ground" in their political efforts is rife with methodological obstacles, social scientists have been slow to conduct such studies. In the best of circumstances, finding a relatively diverse pool of activists to interview about their campaigns and goals can be difficult. These challenges become more difficult still when scholars want to assess how activists in the virtual and real worlds use ICT to affect change within political institutions and party structures, particularly since some self-identified activists never get involved beyond their armchairs. Finally, it is extraordinarily difficult to assess the impacts of a social movement because they can extend beyond the policy realm. For example, social movements can affect public opinion and cultural norms (Rochon 1998; Dyke et al. 2004), induce authorities to (avoid) compliance with existing public policies (Andrews 2004; McVeigh et al. 2003), and even spillover and shape the course and content of other movements (Meyer and Whittier 1994).

---

[1] To be clear, political scientists do not agree that ICT will reinvigorate party politics or even democratize party structures. Some scholars, for instance, argue that ICT makes it easier for political parties to circulate information and engage new and existing members in decision-making processes (Bonchek 1995). Others disagree noting that in the "post-modern" era of campaigning, parties are run by consultants, who shape politicians and platforms to suit the public preference of the day but not to engage party members (Farrell and Webb 2000; Norris 2000).

[2] Here again there is not agreement regarding the ability of ICT to mobilize people to social movements. While some movement scholars argue that ICT is changing who and how citizens get involved (Earl and Kimport 2011; Rohlinger and Brown 2009), others note that ICT does little more than make communication among and coordination of activists easier (Diani 2000; Tarrow 1998).

[3] The research that does exist examines the strategic voting movement in the 2000 presidential election. In an effort to help Green Party candidate, Ralph Nader, get 5 % of the national popular vote, the benchmark for federal campaign funds, citizens decided to "swap" their votes. Nader supporters pledged their votes to Al Gore in states where the democratic candidate had a chance of beating Bush. In exchange, Gore supporters cast a vote for Nader in noncompetitive states like CA. Although the effort was unsuccessful, this e-movement serves as an important example of how activists can employ ICT to try and shape the political system Earl, Jennifer, and Alan Schussman. 2003. "The New Site of Activism: On-Line Organizations, Movement Entrepreneurs, and the Changing Locations of Social Movement Decision Making." *Research in Social Movements, Conflicts and Change* 24:155–187, Foot and Schneider (2002). "Online Action in Campaign 2000: An Exploratory Analysis of the U.S. Political Web Sphere." *Journal of Broadcasting and Electronic Media* 46:222–244, Schussman and Earl (2004). "From Barricades to Firewalls? Strategic Voting and Social Movement Leadership in the Internet Age." *Sociological Inquiry* 74:439–463.

Thus, assessing how social movement groups and activists use ICT to affect party politics is a difficult task indeed.

Drawing on interview data, participant observation and archival research of the progressive group MoveOn.org (MoveOn) and conservative Tea Party Movement (TPM) groups in Tallahassee, FL, this research takes a first step at exploring how social movements use ICT to affect political parties and political change in the United States. As we outline below, MoveOn and TPM groups are ideal for examining how ICT changes the relationship between social movements and political parties because both explicitly challenge (and seek to change) the U.S. political system and the Democratic and Republican Parties respectively. This paper is organized into two analytical sections. In Section "Social Movement Organizations and ICT" of the chapter, we examine how these groups use ICT to effectively market issues, mobilize consensus, and get citizens involved in the political process. The Section "Implications for Political Parties" of the chapter discusses how activist groups' use of ICT changes the relationship between social movement organizations and political parties. While we do not argue that ICT equalizes the relationship between social movements and political parties, we do show that savvy organizations can use ICT in ways that can ultimately help activists transform a party. Additionally, we illustrate the potential for synergy between social movements and political parties in the digital age.

MoveOn and the Tea Party Movement in Tallahassee, Florida

In order to illuminate how social movement organizations use ICT to change party structures, we analyze activist groups that share the goal of making the political system more responsive to ordinary citizens, but vary in terms of their targets, organizational form, and ideological orientation. While this research is by no means comprehensive, it arguably represents a broad range of ways that activists use ICT in their political efforts and, therefore, constitutes an important first step in analyzing the movement-party relationship. Here, we briefly introduce each of the groups included in the study and provide an overview of our data and methods.

MoveOn.org is one of the "largest and most forceful voices in digital era politics" (Fouhy 2004).[4] The organization was founded in 1998 by Wes Boyd and Joan

---

[4] MoveOn opponents agree that the group is extraordinarily effective. Republican pollster, Allan Hoffenblum, noted that in addition to organizing liberals, MoveOn is very adept at raising money, applying political pressure, and putting forward a consistent message to the public (Bernhard 2004). More colorful conservative pundits, such as Sean Hannity, argue that the organization is too successful and instead of revitalizing democracy the MoveOn "blog nuts" have taken over the Democratic Party and "control democrats with fear and intimidation" (The complete segment of "Hannity's America," which addresses the role of the Internet in progressive politics aired on April 29, 2007 and is available via You Tube at http://www.youtube.com/watch?v=ROBDpaxYxT0).

Blades, two Silicon Valley entrepreneurs, who sent an e-mail petition to about 100 friends calling on Congress to censure President Clinton for his indiscretion with Monica Lewinsky and "move on" to more pressing political issues. Their e-mail petition generated more than 400,000 replies and the couple formed MoveOn.org, a political action committee designed to affect congressional elections and, according to Boyd, bring "as much diversity to the power structure as possible. That is, ordinary citizens who can provide the countervailing influence against the notion that some kind of inside-the-beltway elite can make all our decisions" (Bernhard 2004).[5] MoveOn is specifically designed to mobilize progressives and moderate independents around a range of issues including global warming, the war in Iraq, healthcare reform, and voting rights. The organization primarily employs a top-down approach to do so. Although the day-to-day operations of MoveOn are managed entirely online, the organization is hierarchically structured with a handful of leaders and issue experts disseminating information and opportunities for involvement to its 7 million plus supporters.[6] As a result, MoveOn activities and events primarily originate at the national level and, using ICT, group leaders solicit local activists to "host" events that they manage from afar.

In contrast, the Tea Party Movement (TPM) in Tallahassee, FL is decentralized, which has resulted in the formation of several local groups. The TPM, in part, was a response to Rick Santelli's now famous rant against President Obama's mortgage rescue plan. In Tallahassee, the first TPM event took place in March 2009. Anthony, a 32-year-old conservative activist, participated in a Tea Party organized by his friend, Brendan Steinhauser (the Director of Federal and State Campaigns for FreedomWorks) outside of the White House and decided to spearhead a similar event in Florida's capital. He began by setting up a Facebook page and invited conservatives to join the group. Within a week, the page had over 500 members. The first Tea Party in Tallahassee was a success with nearly 300 in attendance and a keynote address by Dick Armey. Anthony capitalized on the "event buzz" and, using Facebook, grew the number of supporters for the movement and organized another Tea Party the following month on tax day, April 15, 2009.[7]

Although this event was also well attended and included short speeches from several state legislators, Anthony, who also works full-time, found he could not maintain the movement alone. He turned to other local conservative activists for assistance. The result was the creation of three additional local groups that support

---

[5] MoveOn also has a civic action committee, which addresses issues such as net neutrality and funding for public television and radio.

[6] According to the organizational website, MoveOn grew leaps and bounds after September 11, 2001 and the U.S. invasion of Iraq. The group reported an increase in membership from 500,000 in September 2001 to 3 million in December 2005 in the U.S. alone. In January 2013, MoveOn reported it had seven million supporters in the U.S.

[7] According to Anthony, the number of members for the Tallahassee Tea Party Facebook page has fluctuated some. At its height, there were nearly 1,500 followers. Since we have been monitoring the page, the number of members has fluctuated between 920 (in April 2010) and 830 (March 2011).

the TPM banner, but adopt different orientations to politics.[8] The first group, which we call Citizens Holding Government Accountable, is a fiscally conservative, non-partisan organization that works to "promote good conservative elected representatives to ALL levels of government." The group supports the TPM and specifically focuses on limiting government, fiscal responsibility, state's rights, and individual rights. The second organization, Christians for Responsible Government, also strongly supports the TPM platform but regards Judeo-Christian doctrine as critical to "uniting Americans" and "defending our country." The third group, Working for the American Way, integrates religious doctrine into its mission, which is to preserve "the rights and freedoms endowed by our Creator and guaranteed by our Constitution." Unlike the other groups, the primary goal of Working for the American Way is to provide a "bridge" between the TPM groups in order to increase the overall effectiveness of the movement's efforts in Florida.

In order to assess how MoveOn and the TPM groups use ICT to affect change, we employ several methods. First, we monitored organizational websites, public forums, and e-mails for all of the groups on a daily basis.[9] Second, we collected all of the media coverage on organizations. Using LexisNexis, we conducted regional and national searches as well as searches of radio, newspaper, and television transcripts for coverage including the terms "MoveOn" and "Tea Party Movement." Third, we attended dozens of meetings, rallies, and events hosted by MoveOn and local TPM groups.[10] Finally, we conducted semi-structured interviews with supporters of MoveOn and the Tallahassee TPM groups. We used a variety of methods to locate respondent including e-mail, listservs, online surveys, giving presentations at meetings, handing out flyers at events, and posting flyers in local coffee shops, on TPM Facebook sites, on campus, and in the local progressive and conservative centers. This strategy yielded a total of 19 MoveOn supporters, who were interviewed between October 2006 and April 2007 and again between December 2008 and June 2009, and 32 TPM supporters, who were interviewed between August 2010 and March 2011 and again between May 2012 and January 2013.[11]

---

[8] By local, we are referring to the immediate Tallahassee area. There are additional groups that have formed in adjacent communities. While we have monitored these groups online, seen their members at events, and conducted interviews with their members, we have not attended their meetings.

[9] The posts on public forms and Facebook were copied and pasted in a word document. This information is organized chronologically so that we can see changes over time. Since e-mails are dated and are stand alone texts, they were archived and sorted by thematic topic.

[10] We attended all MoveOn events between 2004 and 2006 and have attended all TPM group events and meetings (monthly) since April 2010. In total, we have attended 42 events, rallies, and meetings. All public meetings and events were either tape recorded or video taped so that they could be analyzed at a later date.

[11] We had some difficulty getting respondents for MoveOn because many individuals were worried about discussing the organization and their politics in the post-9/11 climate. Since the state is the largest employer in Tallahassee, FL and Jeb Bush was the governor at the time of the first interview, many individuals were concerned that their progressive politics would be "discovered" and they would lose their jobs. For a more detailed discussion see Rohlinger and Brown (2009).

Respondents were asked about their range of political experience (petitions, canvassing, protests, and so on), membership in other organizations, when and why they joined a social movement group, the kinds of activities and events (on and offline) in which they have participated, their impressions of how the group has affected their participation, and their feelings about activism and politics in the U.S. more generally. The interviews ranged in length from 25 min to 3 h. During the second interview, MoveOn and TPM supporters were asked about their current involvement in the respective organizations as well as other social movement groups and causes, reasons for their current level of involvement in various groups, their impressions of MoveOn/TPM and how it changed their participation and their feelings about activism in the U.S. more generally. We re-interviewed 13 of the 19 initial respondents from MoveOn and 24 of the 32 initial respondents from TPM groups. The follow-up interviews ranged in length from 15 to 75 min.[12] All respondents are identified with pseudonyms.

Table 1 provides an overview of the demographics of the respondents. This table only includes the demographics of those individuals whom we formally interviewed, rather than people we spoke to and informally interviewed at events and rallies. Overall, there are not remarkable differences between the supporters of MoveOn and the TPM. Supporters are diverse in terms of their age, gender, relationship, parental, and employment status but relatively homogenous in terms of their race and ethnicity. The racial and ethnic demographics are not completely representative of the Tallahassee area in which 60.42 % of the population is white, 34.24 % is African–American, 4.19 % is Latino, and 2.4 % is Asian.

Social Movement Organizations and ICT

Marketing Issues and Framing the Debate

While social movement organizations may not have direct access to policy processes, they can help shape the broader political environment in which policy debates occur through framing, or producing and mobilizing meaning on a mass scale (Benford and Snow 2000). Mass media play an important role in this regard. Social movement organizations use mass media to expand the debate around an issue, energize a movement by mobilizing a population to action, and build (and then leverage) their legitimacy in the political sphere (Gamson and Meyer 1996; Gamson and Wolfsfeld 1993; Walgrave and Manssens 2000). The opportunities for social movement organizations to promote themselves and their causes in the contemporary media environment seem endless. Social movement organizations

---

[12] Since individuals move, we were not able to locate all of the respondents 2 years after the initial interview. If an individual's contact information was no longer correct, we conducted local and national searches in an effort to locate the respondent.

Table 1 Overview of respondent demographics

	MoveOn (%)	TPM Groups (%)
Gender		
Male	47	68
Female	53	32
Age		
18–35	37	32
36–50	21	32
51 and up	42	26
Race/ethnicity		
White	89	81
Asian	11	0
Middle-Eastern	0	3
Latino	0	9
Multiracial	0	8
Relationship status		
Single	47	25
Partnered	0	6
Married	32	45
Divorced	21	19
Widowed	0	3
Employment status		
Student	21	6
Employed	74	68
Unemployed	5	6
Retired	0	22
Parental status		
No children	47	38
One child	16	22
Two or more children	37	38

Due to rounding the categories may not add up to 100 %

can target "traditional" media outlets such as print, radio, and electronic news outlets or go "virtual" and disseminate information about their causes and goals through blogs, YouTube, twitter, online radio, online news outlets, social media, or their own group websites (Atton 2007; Carroll and Hackett 2006; Gamson 1990; Rohlinger and Brown 2013; Thörn 2007). Likewise, the proliferation of venues online has dramatically changed the speed of the news cycle and the way in which information spreads across the media system (Ayres 1999; Kahn and Kellner 2004). Media venues are connected through a network of relationships (Benson and Neveu 2005; Bourdieu 1998), which allows ideas and events introduced in relatively obscure, alternative news venues online to "crossover" into mainstream venues (Bennett 2003). Savvy social movement organizations can take advantage of these linkages and move their events from sympathetic alternative news outlets to mainstream venues (Rohlinger 2007). In short, social movement organizations with a technologically and media savvy staff, can "leverage the affordances"

(Earl and Kimport 2011) of ICT and find new ways to promote their ideas across a complex, interconnected media system (Rohlinger and Brown 2013).

The changes in the media industry have altered how citizens approach politics and affect political change. Technologically savvy and politically minded individuals brought the "entrepreneurial spirit" online and into the American political system. Rather than promoting causes or platforms, these political entrepreneurs focus on selling "ideas that change the world;" a prospect that resonates with citizens across ideologies and income brackets. To be sure, the financially well-heeled (from the progressive George Soros and Steve Bing to the conservative Koch brothers) sink millions into groups like MoveOn and the TPM. However, what supporters share is the belief that political parties are dominated by "elite Washington insiders" who lack vision and are not held accountable to ordinary citizens.

For example, Andy Rappaport, a venture capitalist, felt like his donations to the Democratic Party were not being well spent. He notes:

> There is a growing realization among people who take very seriously the importance of progressive politics that the Democratic Party has kind of failed to create a vision for the country that is strongly resonant.... And our numbers—meaning Democrats as a whole—are decreasing. Our political power has been diminishing, and it's become common knowledge that the conservative movement has established a very strong, long-term foundation, whereas we've basically allowed our foundation, if not to crumble, to at least fall into a state of disrepair. So there are a lot of people thinking, What can we do about this? (Bai 2004).

The answer was to raise money (100 million) to help mobilize people to effectively advocate for progressive causes within their communities and outside of the party system. Clearly, individuals beyond the beltway and those whose income places them squarely in the middle class are willing to financially support these social movement groups. In January 2003, for instance, MoveOn asked supporters for $27,000 to fund an anti-war commercial and received $400,000 in donations (Huck 2004). Likewise, when, in 2004, MoveOn asked its supporters to hold bake sales across the U.S. and the organization raised $750,000 (Bai 2004). In short, ICT has helped alter the business model of activism. Rather than selling goals, contemporary social movement organizations market ideas to supporters and see which ones move people to action.

Some of MoveOn's and the TPM's success, then, is due to the cultural resonance of the ideas they sell. Rather than advocating a radical transformation of the political structure, the groups couch their opposition to political parties and an unresponsive government in democratic ideals and principles of the U.S. Constitution. The cultural and institutional resonance of movement ideas is important because resonant ideas appeal to broad swaths of the citizenry and are more likely to get amplified via mainstream media attention (Ferree 2003; Gitlin 1980; McAdam 1996; Snow and Benford 1988). For instance, TPM supporters blame the Republican Party for abandoning their core fiscally conservative ideals. At a Tallahassee luncheon featuring the Tea Party Patriot founders, Jenny Beth Martin (co-founder of the group) noted that she was tired of trusting the Republican Party. Instead of fiscal responsibility, she noted that Republicans:

> Abandoned the free markets, they raised taxes, they increased spending. They've done so much to infringe to influence and on our lives and take our liberty away. And, we cannot sit back and trust them to do the right thing any longer. We have to hold them accountable. We have to hold their feet to the fire.... We'll do what it takes to hold them accountable. And if they're not willing to do that, then we'll be back here in 2012 doing the same thing all over again. We'll get a new Congress who can get it right and who will keep working until they can get it right! [Audience applause].

Casting politicians and political parties as out-of-touch elites puts institutional actors on the defensive and gives social movement groups an opportunity to shape debates and set electoral agendas. To be sure, those with institutional power have a big edge in how politics are framed, particularly in mainstream media outlets (Edelman 1964; Herman and Chomsky 1988). Mainstream media, however, is drawn to conflict. Social movement organizations that can create conflict where none previously existed—and then leverage their ideas across the media industry—can benefit from the glare of the media spotlight.

Of course, social movement groups have more flexibility in terms of how they promote themselves and their issues than political parties. MoveOn, for example, is known for harnessing cultural icons to spread its political messages far and wide. MoveOn recruited movie directors (Richard Linklater, Michael Moore, and Rob Reiner), screen writers (Aaron Sorkin), actors (Scarlett Johansson and Matt Damon), and musicians (Moby, Bruce Springsteen. Pearl Jam, Dave Matthews Band, Bonnie Raitt, R.E.M., the Dixie Chicks, John Mellencamp, and a variety of punk rock bands) to promote its ideas across the media landscape before the 2004 election, generating millions in the process.[13] The Vote for Change tour, which featured many of the musicians listed above, raised several million dollars that were used to educate and mobilize progressive voters (Cornwell 2004; DeLuca 2004; Guzman 2004; Rubin and Fitzgerald 2004). Similarly, a number of conservative celebrities have embraced and promoted the ideals of the TPM including Michelle Bachman, Sarah Palin, and Glenn Beck. While the use of celebrities, political or otherwise, has its drawbacks (Meyer and Gamson 1995), using cultural elites to promote movement ideas is an effective way to leverage mass media, grow the coffers and membership of an organization, and, ultimately, affect political debates.

In sum, changes in the media industry and how movement entrepreneurs work to affect political change have happened simultaneously and as a result of the proliferation of ICT in American society. These new social movement organizations use ICT to leverage themselves across the media system and sell their ideas to the margins and the mainstream simultaneously. While this allows the activist groups to attract politically diverse supporters, MoveOn and TPM groups must find ways to mobilize consensus and action in order to engage supporters beyond their checkbooks.

---

[13] This is a partial list of the celebrities who have been involved in MoveOn.

Mobilizing Consensus

Social movement organizations also use ICT to mobilize consensus or generate support for its ideas and goals (Klandermans 1984; Klandermans 1992). This is not an easy task under the best of circumstances. Activists rarely agree on organizational priorities and conflict, left unchecked, can have disastrous results (Barasko 2004; Whittier 1995). While most federated social movement organizations adopt procedures (like voting for leadership) that allow members to participate in decision-making processes (McCarthy and Zald 1973), ICT eases the burdens of such participation and allows supporters to weigh in on organizational decisions on a more regular basis. Such participation, we find, is important because it prevents supporters from exiting the organization even when they are not completely satisfied with its course or campaigns.

MoveOn and TPM groups use ICT to engage supporters in democratic processes, which allows them to dictate the direction of the organization on a limited scale. When joining MoveOn, for example, the website asks supporters to identify those issues with which they are most interested and want to receive regular updates on.[14] Then, at least four times a year, MoveOn asks its supporters to complete a survey that is used to determine the political priorities of the organization and to participate in a virtual town hall meeting, where supporters can discuss issues and voice concerns. While local TPM groups have not used online surveys yet, ICT still plays an important role in consensus mobilization. TPM groups primarily rely on virtual democratic forums such as listservs, chat rooms, and Facebook pages to determine whether they should support a candidate and in what kind of activities the groups should sponsor (Rohlinger and Klein Forthcoming-b). For example, Anthony decided not to throw the organization's support behind Marco Rubio, who was actively seeking Tea Party support in his early bid for Florida senator, because supporters had expressed concern over Rubio's views as well as the implications of endorsing candidates during the primary on the Facebook page. Anthony described his decision not to support Rubio on the TPM Facebook site:

> I had actually put the thought [of endorsing Rubio] out there [on the Facebook page] because I thought Marco Rubio was probably the most legitimate candidate and deserved our endorsement. But even when I put the question out for the Tea Party Facebook group, "Should we endorse Marco Rubio?" I got a bunch of people saying "yeah, yeah definitely." Then, I got a lot of people saying, "I love him, but no. We should stay away from endorsing." And I had others who said, "I'm not really sure if I would endorse him." So it was kind of mixed and I thought well we're going to split this movement if we start endorsing candidates.

In short, MoveOn and TPM groups build consensus by engaging their supporters in familiar democratic processes, such as voting and debate, and giving them a voice in organizational decision-making.

---

[14] This is no longer the case. MoveOn simply asks supporters to enter their e-mail address for updates.

While these consensus-building activities may seem trivial, they enable MoveOn and the TPM groups to effectively avoid "hot button" issues, like abortion and gay rights, which have the potential to undermine the political diversity and, ultimately, the political power of the group.[15] This is an important point. Organizational supporters are cognizant of this issue avoidance, but even ardent opponents and supporters of these issues set aside their personal passion in order to maintain overall strength of the group. For example, the vast majority of respondents, and all of the local leaders, noted that it was critical for Florida TPM groups to avoid issues like gay rights and abortion. Logan, a leader of a TPM group in rural Florida, expressed personal distaste for both issues but argued that it was important for him to "set these opinions aside" so that the movement could grow its strength and influence over local and state politics. Likewise, Deborah, a 55-year-old conservative activist who has picketed as part of pro-life groups outside of abortion clinics, argued that controversial issues "could derail the central message... and take down the Tea Party Movement." She added:

> I don't know that strategically it would be the best. I think that we should concentrate more on the process... [of how] a judge becomes a judge. I think that instead of having an activist judge, you should have a judge that would adhere to the Constitution. I think that's more... it's not more important, I just think that hopefully, that would be the emphasis [of the TPM].

MoveOn supporters similarly understood the group's avoidance of controversial issues. However, respondents also noted that the organization's position could change and, more importantly, that this change would occur if it was demanded by MoveOn supporters. Marcia, a 60-year-old geologist whom we first interviewed in 2005, described the misalignment between her and MoveOn's political agenda:

> I wish the environment was at the top [of their list] but they went around all the MoveOn people and had them submit this poll about what their priorities are, and the environment wasn't really all that high...I've written to them about particular issues I've got and they do respond, so that's good. I think probably right now, the big issue is Iraq, and that's what they're focused on more than anything.

Marcia was still involved in the organization in 2008, when we interviewed her the second time, even though the environment remained low on MoveOn's list of political priorities. Her involvement was even more surprising after she expressed distaste over MoveOn's attack on General Petraeus and disappointment over the group's decision to support Barrack Obama, rather than her preference Hillary Clinton, for the Democratic presidential nomination. When asked about her continued involvement in the organization, Marcia cited the democratic process through which the decision was derived, voting, made the decision "fair" and, therefore,

---

[15] Interestingly, the success of the TPM has forced MoveOn to take up controversial issues like abortion. By changing the composition of Congress, the TPM ushered in an era of social conservative policy as well, which has included additional restrictions on abortion access through the defunding of Planned Parenthood. MoveOn attacked the proposed legislation and vigorously defended a woman's right to an abortion.

"okay." Marcia explained, "They [the MoveOn membership] took a vote, I voted. Most of the group voted. [And the group voted] to support Obama in the primaries. So I was okay with that." In a similar exchange, James, a 56-year-old psychiatrist, expressed some annoyance over MoveOn's avoidance of the abortion issue and healthcare reform as it relates to psychiatric problems. When asked why he stayed involved with the group, he cited the potential to change the agenda through their votes, e-mails, and town hall meetings. James joked, "I'm trying to persuade the MoveOn group on healthcare reform and they are trying to persuade me on other issues. So, I guess they're working on me and I'm working on them."

ICT makes it easier for social movement organizations to involve supporters in decision-making processes regarding group priorities. This is important because it allows movement groups to represent and mobilize around multiple issues and policy domains while avoiding those that are likely to fracture organizational support. Additionally, giving supporters a regular voice in the organization keeps people involved even when they are not particularly happy with the campaigns or actions of the group. Thus, rather than "exit" the group (Hirschmann 1970), supporters set aside their personal passions and support the group as a vehicle of political change.

Mobilizing Support

Some scholars are very skeptical about the ability of activist organizations to use ICT for action mobilization, or to involve supporters in group activities and events (Diani 2000; Tarrow 1998). The typical criticism of ICT-based activism is that it is "easy" and, therefore, less meaningful than protesting, for instance, which requires people to leave the safety of their living rooms. To be sure, some kinds of activism, such as challenging armed state officials, are high risk. However, what activists themselves consider high risk varies according to their personal circumstances and the political environment. Some individuals, for instance, consider online activism risky because their activities can be monitored by the government officials they work for and politically oppose. Yet, they engage online despite perceived risks (Rohlinger and Brown 2009).

Additionally, ICT helps individuals overcome barriers to activism by reducing the information and participation costs for those juggling work and family demands.[16] Signing petitions, donating money, writing letters to politicians, and calling legislators may all be relatively easy to do, but require time; a resource that is not distributed equally across the population. By offering supporters a range of activities on- and off-line in which they can engage, social movement organizations allow supporters to get involved beyond their checkbooks. For example,

---

[16] For a discussion on how "biographical availability" affects activism and political participation more generally see (Klatch 1999; McAdam 1988; Verba et al. 1995).

Janet, a 49-year-old business owner and mother of four, noted that the TPM's use of ICT made it easy for her to stay involved, "I've never physically met with any of the Tea Party Members but I can still be a part of the movement.... I can stay informed and connected... [and] I know where to contribute my money." Samantha, a 34-year-old market researcher, agreed adding that MoveOn's use of ICT made it easy for her stay involved after the birth of her daughter.

> If people just knew something they would do something...if you make it easy for them, and if you give them an action, they'll do it. And I think MoveOn has been a really good vehicle for me to do that because post child, once you have jobs...sometimes it's hard...to figure out what to do. And I...really appreciate that MoveOn takes the time... Most of what I did, pre-election, going right up to the election and post election...I probably wouldn't have done [without MoveOn]...I think it's really super that they've done things and they've used the internet positively and to let me decide that I want to still be active in politics and my community.

While Janet and Samantha had previous activist experience, the vast majority of our respondents did not. For these individuals, ICT provided a training ground for activism. A number of respondents noted that MoveOn's and the TPM's use of ICT allowed them to find their political voice and take a hand at expressing it. Deborah attributed her now regular attendance at meetings and events to the TPM community online:

> [Tea party websites, listservs and Facebook forums] provide a platform for unity and more organized communication [and action]. Being informed alone, being aware of things has increased [my] response.... If I don't know, I can't respond.... It gives me a way to fight for my country. [Respondent chokes up] To stand up for values that are really important...I was really worried....I've lost a country, because people didn't really know what was going on, and I think it's really important to educate people.

Kenneth, a 69-year-old ROTC instructor at a local high school with no experience in activism, also attributed his involvement in a local TPM group to finding his political voice online.

> I grew up in a different country than we're living in now. [I got involved because] I was really, really upset with the way we were being forced to go by people who just don't understand what makes this country great. When all this legislation started about forcing people to buy things [reference to health insurance and Obama's universal health care bill] literally I mean I could read the paper and almost get physically ill thinking about which way we were going and what's happening to this country. And, so just out of sheer frustration and anger I started dabbling in e-mails and stuff like that with people who were involved in the Tea Party.

This was no less true of MoveOn members, who attributed the group's online prodding for their attendance at seminars and house events as well as participation in rallies, lobbying, and canvassing efforts. For example, John, a 32-year-old graduate student, noted that his involvement in the "real" world increased as a result of all the information and opportunities MoveOn provided him online:

> MoveOn made me more interested in getting out there, like when John Edwards came to town. I actually made the effort to go to FAMU's campus, tracked up the hill and all around just to listen to this guy talk. It [MoveOn] made me want to go and help out on

Election Day 2004. I sat out in front of the polls and passed out little John Kerry stickers to people.... I'm pretty convinced it [MoveOn] prodded me to go and participate on election day when I could have just sat at home and not done anything. But, I wanted to see a change and [MoveOn] showed how I could do it. Honestly, I've never ever gone to volunteer for a democratic campaign in my life. [But there] I was, walking in [to headquarters] the day before the election asking, "What can I do?"

It is worth noting that the structural differences between MoveOn and TPM groups affect the ease with which individuals can learn new political skills. Event organizers, for example, receive a great deal of assistance from MoveOn, which makes it easy for novice activists to organize and host events. One respondent explained that when she planned a house event, there were "reminder e-mails," clearly indicating all of the tasks that needed to be completed. As she describes it, "it's like having your own personal assistant. It makes it very easy." Likewise, Amanda, a 52-year-old social worker, noted that when you volunteer, "it's all done for you pretty much...the paperwork, the reports, the printouts, flyers... They e-mail it to you and you print it out on your own printer and you're set to go..." She adds that the process is made simple and clear, which is important because "they make it easy for the people who don't know what they're doing and have never done this before." MoveOn also asks its more active members to take on leadership roles in their communities. Amanda described how MoveOn encouraged her to be a precinct captain.

I said "no" when they asked me [to be precinct captain]. I mean, I had absolutely no idea what I was doing. I had never done any kind of door to door thing before. But, they kept asking. They said they needed another one, so I finally did it. So, I was going in blind, but they were helpful. I might do it again depending on what the issue was and how important I thought it was.

When asked to describe her experience as precinct captain in more detail, Amanda added:

My job was to keep all the paperwork- all the reports. When you went out knocking on people's doors, you'd ask them questions and then report what their response was such as "Yes. I'm going to vote." If they told you how they were going to vote, you could document that. We were supposed to ask them that [how they were going to vote]. We weren't there to tell them how to vote.... It was interesting [the experience]. I didn't know what the response was going to be [like]. It was just so new. It was foreign to me and so it was a little scary. But, actually it [the experience] was mostly positive.

The fact that social movement organizations use ICT to mobilize support by making activism "easy" is not negative. Easy participation, in fact, may help organizations maintain themselves over time because it makes activism available to people who are otherwise obligated, provides a training ground for neophyte activists, and engages some segment of it supporters beyond the armchair. Moreover, social movement organizations that can effectively use ICT may fare better than traditional movement groups that primarily rely on a paper constituency alone because individuals can choose when and how to get involved in the group. Richard, a 53-year-old government contract analyst, summarized it best.

He explained, "Not everybody is going to go March in Washington... [MoveOn] tells people it's okay to participate at whatever level you're comfortable with."

Implications for Political Parties

The ability of activist groups to effectively leverage ICT and mobilize money and people around an array of policy issues has implications for the relationship between social movements and political parties. Typically, political parties are regarded as the arbiters of power in the political system (Schumpeter 1976). While the Republican and Democratic Parties compete for a majority at the federal and state level and woo social movement organizations in their efforts to do so, activists rarely have any real influence in party decision-making. This is particularly true in the U.S., where there are thousands of activist organizations and only two parties with which to bargain (Schattschneider 1960). Thus, while social movement organizations may shape political parties on the margin, they are far more likely to receive recognition or symbolic benefits or to have their ideas co-opted by political elites altogether than to affect policy change (Amenta et al. 1992; Gamson 1990; Piven and Cloward 1977). ICT, however, changes this strategic relationship and, specifically, makes the playing field a bit more level (albeit not entirely). Here, we outline three possible relational dynamics between social movements and political parties—competition, appropriation, and synergy—and discuss the role of ICT in each. These relational dynamics are not mutually exclusive, nor are they completely new in all cases.[17] The point here is that savvy social movement groups can use ICT to directly challenge (or change) political parties.

Competition

Although social movement organizations are not generally regarded as serious competitors by political parties, activist groups can compete with parties for members and support in the digital age. They can effectively represent issues from multiple policy domains while maintaining broad support, mobilize millions, and get supporters involved beyond the checkbook; something that political parties have struggled with for the past several decades (Dalton and Wattenberg 2000). For the reasons outlined above, political parties are most likely to feel the competitive pinch in their pocketbook as small and big donors alike turn to activist groups that they believe can quickly and effectively launch a challenge against a policy or politician.

---

[17] Of course, not all social movement organizations using ICT necessarily be in the position to engage a political party. As Earl and Kimport (2011) aptly note, like access to ICT, technological and political skill are not equally distributed across society. As a result, some movements will be better positioned than others to challenge and work with political parties on a more equal footing.

However, social movement organizations can do more than take money away from traditional party structures. They also can force parties to take up issues and offer alternative candidates. By effectively selling their ideas to a substantial segment of the voting public, activist groups can induce candidates and parties to adopt some of their frames in their efforts to win elections. While this is not new, the relative ease with which movement organizations can force candidates to take their ideas seriously is. Democratic presidential candidate, John Kerry, for instance, quickly adopted a strong anti-war stance after MoveOn and its 2.5 million supporters made it clear that ending the war in Iraq was a priority. Similarly, the Republican Party issued a "Contract with America" in September 2010 that integrated TPM ideals into sample legislation, including a "Fiscal Responsibility Act," which would require the federal government to have a balanced budget and limit taxation, and a "Citizen Legislature Act," which would impose term limits on politicians.[18]

Additionally, social movement groups can use ICT to effectively vet and support candidates, who more closely represent their values and are not approved by the party establishment. Again, while the emergence of alternative candidates is not a new phenomenon, the relative ease with which these alternative candidates can access financial resources from supporters, launch effective campaigns, and win elections is new. This was indeed the case in Florida where TP backed candidates swept the 2010 national elections (Marcio Rubio was elected to the Senate and Steve Southerland, Allen West, and Sandra Adams were elected to the House). Likewise, the TPM groups achieved astounding success at the local level.[19] In Leon County, Florida, which is predominantly Democratic, Nick Maddox, a business man and former Florida State University football player,

---

[18] The Contract with America is available at www.house.gov/house/Contract/CONTRACT.html. It is worth noting that TPM supporters are very suspicious of these appeals. Almost all of our respondents viewed Republicans as pandering for votes. For example, Joseph, a 61-year-old unemployed electronics technician, noted, "The fact that the Republican Party has tried to more or less commandeer the [TPM] platform tells me that really what they're doing is damage control…. It's basically just the same old tactics they've used all along. They know that they can't ignore their really conservative, constitutional base, but they're trying to water it [the ideas] down as much as possible. And the evidence of that is the fact that some of the new candidates who just went to Washington, they're already being thwarted and stymied and manipulated and you know just rendered impotent [by the Republican establishment]."

[19] Not all of the TPM candidates won. For example, TPM groups cultivated and promoted Steve Stewart, a business man and father of six, for Tallahassee Mayor. TPM groups and a local conservative radio host helped Stewart sell his message to the broader public, which won over many. His opponent, incumbent John Marks, however, challenged Stewart primarily using race-based arguments (Marks is African-American and Stewart is White). Marks noted that Stewart lived on the north side of town (which is sometimes referred to as FFW—Fancy, Fancy Whiteyville) and accused Stewart of "being out of touch" with the average Tallahassee citizen. Stewart tried to counter these attacks by winning an endorsement by a prominent African–American politician in town (County Commissioner Bill Proctor) and speaking before an audience on the south side of town, which is predominantly African–American, to no avail. Stewart lost the election. Despite this loss, Stewart has remained active in local politics and recently revealed an "ethical violation" made by Marks. Currently, Stewart successfully pushed for a formal investigation of the Mayor.

ousted Cliff Thaell, a liberal Democrat who served on the County Commission for 16 years. Maddox, who was discussed and promoted at TPM group meetings and events, parroted the political solutions favored by the TPM. For instance, Maddox argued that the financial success of the county would result through an investment in the private sector, "We have to work to make sure that we can help our private sector, our local small businesses. I think economic development incentives would be a good way to help those small businesses take in more employees and help our unemployment rate decrease." Of course, Florida was not the only state in which TPM groups sponsored alternative Republican candidates for various offices and won. In fact, 32 % of all TP candidates who ran for a federal office won in 2010.[20]

Appropriation

Generally speaking, social movement organizations have fewer resources available to them than institutional actors. While social movement organizations can use ICT to level the playing field a bit in terms of the financial and human resources mobilized, political parties—not activist groups—have representatives at the policy table. This fact is not lost on groups like MoveOn and the TPM, which seek to appropriate party structures as a means to achieve their goals. Supporters of MoveOn and TPM groups believe that attempts to establish a third party will fail and, instead, seek to wrest control of the existing parties from political insiders. This goal is very prominent in the Florida TPM groups, where supporters generally view career politicians unfavorably and regard a goal of the TPM as appropriating the Republican Party for their own purposes. Logan, a 68-year-old retired sales-man, noted that it was time to "take over" the Republican Party. He argued that the only way to keep the party structure honest was to make sure that politicians did not get "too comfortable" in office. Logan quipped, "Politicians are like milk. They should come with an expiration date." Diane, a 56-year-old sales repre-sentative agreed, adding that the ultimate goal of the movement is "...to replace many of the long term candidates in Washington, D.C. with more conservatives." A local leader, however, summarized it best in a post on the group's website:

> All third party attempts fail, be it Whig or Tea Party. We can look at numerous examples in history where a third party has skewed the vote and allowed someone to win who shouldn't have. Real grassroots political change happens when people join one of the major parties and influence it en mass. Why re-invent the wheel when there is a vehicle just waiting to be used?

---

[20] While some see this rate as low and, consequently, write off the TPM, we argue that these numbers reflect the variability of the movement's strength. In Florida, for example, the movement is fairly large and well organized in spite of its decentralization. This undoubtedly contributed to some of the electoral successes.

One way for a social movement organization to appropriate a political party for its own purposes is to challenge and, then, change its leadership. This is something that both MoveOn and TPM groups have done with some success. MoveOn, for instance, mobilized its supporters after the loss of the presidential election to let the Democratic Party know that the group had no intention of going quietly into the night. MoveOn leaders argued that although Kerry did not win the election, the organization was very successful at engaging progressives in the political process. More importantly, MoveOn noted that political organizing needed to move beyond pleas for campaign cash and "the boom-bust cycle of campaigns—where you build up all this grass-roots energy and then it dissipates" (Faler 2004). One way to do this, the group argued, was for the Democrats to get new leadership. Eli Pariser, the executive director of MoveOn at the time, noted that "There's a vacuum at the heart of the [Democratic] party and it's time to fill it with new energy, with people who have passion and who don't come from inside the Beltway" (Balz 2004b). MoveOn leaders specifically argued that burgeoning grassroots organizations like itself gave more than $300 million to the Kerry campaign and the Democratic National Committee, proving that the party did not need corporate cash—but needed its increasingly disaffected base—to compete with Republicans (Balz 2004b). Pariser and another MoveOn leader, Justin Ruben, publicly attacked the current DNC chairman, Terry Mc Auliffe, for his:

> Watered down, play-it-safe politics that kept the money flowing but alienated traditional
>   Democrats as well as reform-minded independents in search of vision and integrity....
> It's absolutely time for a change at the DNC. The party run by D.C. insiders with losing
> track records, who haven't been able to put forward a compelling vision for where the
> Democratic Party needs to go, isn't gonna cut it anymore (Horrigan 2004).

Pariser added that progressives were posed to wrest control of the Democratic Party from career politicians, "Now it's our party: we bought it, we own it, and we're going to take it back" (Hananel 2004).

MoveOn's message of progressive political empowerment and structural change was championed by former Vermont governor Howard Dean, who ran unsuccessfully for the Democratic presidential nomination in 2004. Dean insisted that Democrats take MoveOn seriously and sow the seeds of a grassroots revival. "We're going to build this message... from the ground up.... We have a better message, and our principles and moral values are closer to the American people than Republicans are, and now we've got to go out and run on that" (Balz 2004a). Dean won the chairmanship handily. While there were other dynamics at play in this election (e.g., the other serious contender, Tim Roemer, was pro-life and Dean publicly said that he would not run for president in 2008 if elected DNC chairman), MoveOn's presence mattered as well. With its growing membership and ability to mobilize people and money on a day's notice, MoveOn's dissatisfaction with the Democratic Party simply could not be ignored.

Arguably, the TPM has done a better job of changing the Republican Party because it has taken over local units of the state party as well as affected leadership decisions at the top. In states like Florida and Virginia, TPM groups successfully won chairmanships of the state Republican Party. Additionally, the Florida state leadership, who won using the smaller government mantra, made a point of meeting with organizational leaders and joining the TPM caucus. For example, Governor Rick Scott, who rode the small government mantra into office, broke tradition and unveiled his first state budget at a Tea Party luncheon in rural Eustis, Florida rather than the state capital.[21] According to reports, Scott began his invitation only speech by saying, "Today we present Florida's first job budget, it is designed to reduce state spending, to lower taxes and hold your state government accountable. This is the budget you asked for."[22] Additionally, Scott agreed to join the Tea Party Caucus and made a "surprise" appearance at a TPM rally on the opening day of the legislative session (March 8, 2011). In his short speech, Scott thanked the TPM for their support and urged activists to keep the pressure on politicians and the Republican Party.

> Showing up at things like this, you are changing the country because people are listening to what you're doing whether it's in Wisconsin or New Jersey or Ohio or Texas, you're changing the country. So thank you from the bottom of my heart because your showing up is making sure everybody in Tallahassee does what you elected them to do. Less government, right? [the crowd applauds and yells "yeah!"] Lower taxes? [the crowd applauds and yells "yeah!"] No high speed rail? [the crowd applauds and yells "yeah!"] It's your money. We're going to follow the Constitution. We're going to watch spending like a hawk, it's your money!... Let's get to work!

Florida Senate President, Mike Haridopolis, also spoke at the rally and discussed how he wanted to make Florida politicians subject to the same cuts (in benefits and salary) that were being proposed for other state workers. There have been leadership changes at the national level as well. Reince Priebus, a vocal Tea Party supporter who also had a lot of grassroots support, wrested control of the Republican National Committee chairmanship from an admittedly beleaguered, but far more moderate, Michael Steele.

Of course, it is possible that these appropriations of the party by social movement groups are temporary and, ultimately, the parties will find ways to co-opt MoveOn and the TPM, respectively. To some extent, this seems to have happened to the Florida TPM. In the follow-up interviews, half of our respondents, all of whom identified as Libertarians, noted that they no longer supported the TPM. All of these respondents argued that the TPM had embraced social issues like abortion, immigration, and gay marriage, and consequently become an "arm of the Republican Party." Adrian, for example, explained:

> As I predicted in the previous interview, there was a struggle between the Libertarians and the social conservatives. And, it was pretty evident that the Tea Party Movement was co-opted into the Republican Party and became an arm of it. This goes back to that CATO study I was telling you about. I was watching the results and I was like, "Wow! That's

---

[21] He repeated this move the following year as well, unveiling his budget to Tea Party Movement supporters in South Florida.

[22] Posted by reporter Irene Christou on the Phoenix Network. Available at http://phoenixnetwork.us/2011/02/08/.

exactly what happened!" [The study] basically said that Libertarians have no loyalties. They don't get along with others very well and when...when the social conservatives latched on to the Tea Party Movement, the Libertarians basically took their balls and they went home.... I took my ball and went home. I was not making this about social issues—we [Libertarians] had one issue and that was basically spending.

Nancy echoed this criticism:

Well, I feel like what is coming out of the Tea Party movement now isn't consistent with my personal philosophy, which is more Libertarian. I think that as mainstream politicians co-opted [the movement] it became xenophobic and just...the only thing that it really has in common I think with my political viewpoint at this point is its anti-tax stand—and even that has gone extreme and doesn't make sense.

The perceived co-optation of the TPM, however, should not be understood as a result of the Republican Party's political skill. As we outline elsewhere, the decentralized structure of the movement and changes in the political environment (such as the emergence of the Occupy Wall Street Movement) forced the TPM to constrict its ideological boundaries and align the movement with a Republican-friendly, socially conservative agenda (Rohlinger and Klein Forthcoming-a; Rohlinger and Klein Forthcoming-b). The Florida TPM, in short, was easy to co-opt.[23]

Synergy

Social movement organizations and political parties may also decide to cooperate and, at times, develop synergy. Here, we purposefully use the term synergy, rather than cooperation, in order to more fully capture how ICT may alter the relationship between social movement groups and political parties, particularly in the contemporary political and communications environment. Synergy, which generally refers to the dynamic where two or more agents work together and successfully produce a result that would be impossible for a single, separately operated agent to achieve on its own, can be critical during election cycles. Thus, unlike cooperation, synergy is not the result of explicit coordination but a product of a mutually beneficial relationship. Synergy is typically associated with corporations that through either vertical or horizontal integration derive new opportunities to promote a product and grow profits. However, this dynamic may be on the rise in the political world as well. Social movement organizations use ICT to mobilize money and with these funds launch campaigns that are designed, among other things, to affect election outcomes. These campaigns are not coordinated with political

---

[23] This conclusion is based on our analysis of the Florida TPM. We are not generalizing about the entire movement, nor are we arguing that all of our Republican-minded respondents agree with this interpretation. Respondents working with the Republican Party through TPM committees regard their dealings as mutually beneficial "partnerships."

parties because there is not always agreement on targets and strategy and because activist groups do not want to be subject to FEC campaign finance restrictions. Synergy, however, still can occur because social movement organizations will take up issues or launch campaigns that political parties will not and still influence elections.

This kind of synergy was visible between MoveOn and the Democratic Party in 2004. First, MoveOn sponsored ads that strategists for the Kerry campaign would not even consider. The Kerry campaign wanted to appeal to centrist swing voters "with a moderate message of strength and optimism while depicting Bush as an extremist renegade, out of step with the mainstream conservatism of the Republican base" (Lippert 2004). As a result, the campaign passed on attack ads and did so without even looking at them so that a 527 group would be free to run them; something that MoveOn did. Additionally, MoveOn sponsored an online advertising competition called "Bush in Thirty Seconds." The competition was open to all MoveOn supporters and the prize for the winning advertisement was a massive national audience for the contestant's work. MoveOn would pay to air the spot during the SuperBowl. The winning ad, titled "Child's Play," which showed children toiling at menial jobs to pay off the Bush deficit, became an Internet favorite when CBS refused to broadcast it during the Super Bowl (Gourevitch 2004). In short, while the use of creative advertising to affect election outcomes is not new (Jamieson 1996), the ability of social movement organizations to cheaply craft and effectively circulate ads throughout a culture is. Social movement organizations can draw on the talents of their supporters and potentially sink more money into circulating attack ads as a result. Likewise, the network of relationships that dominate the media industry insure that spots rejected by mainstream media outlets are circulated on the nightly news, spread virally via e-mail, and leveraged across the spectrum of sympathetic outlets.

Synergy, however, is not limited to advertising alone. Social movement organizations can also fill critical gaps left unfilled by political parties during election cycles. For example, during the 2004 election cycle, MoveOn used ICT to raise money and, then, launched a $5 million dollar "Leave No Voter Behind" campaign. The goal of the campaign was to turn out thousands of additional progressives from targeted neighborhoods in battleground states like Florida. MoveOn's efforts in this regard were critical in places like Tallahassee, where individuals interested in getting involved found the local Democratic Party structure in disrepair. A surprising number of respondents mentioned that they had contacted the Democratic Party in order to volunteer and, after not getting a response, got involved in MoveOn instead. MoveOn, in other words, provided a progressive grassroots structure that the Democratic Party was unable to supply. Marcia, who had contacted the Democratic Party directly and did not get a response, reflected:

> I don't think they [the Democratic Party] have their act together.... I wish MoveOn would take over for them, they're so organized. With MoveOn, we called for eastern Pennsylvania and Virginia and Ohio, Missouri, New Jersey. Every single one, it turns out, that the democrats won. So, I felt really positive about it...I have contacted ... the Democratic

Party and never gotten much of a response from them about volunteering and helping. So, to me, MoveOn has been very proactive and well organized.

Liam, a 37-year-old communications director, agreed noting that MoveOn really made it easy for people to get involved in the get out the vote efforts.

[T]here was a respectable, sizable group of people that got involved going door to door, participating in the election that would not have had that avenue to participate in. Either they're not involved in a union or they are put off by the politics of their local democratic executive committee or what have you. So MoveOn was there. Now a lot of those people that were out there on the street wouldn't have been there if it hadn't been for MoveOn.

The Democratic Party bridged this gap by the 2008 presidential election. In fact, the Obama campaign dedicated $9.1 million to Florida alone in its efforts to mobilize progressive voters (Kenski et al. 2010). Marcia, who is now highly involved in the Democratic Party, explained that the party had finally caught up:

MoveOn did what the Democratic Party was supposed to do, and now the Democratic Party seems to be kicking in, and doing more of the MoveOn type of stuff...[The Democratic Party is now] informing you about things. I'm getting e-mails about things..., do you want this or that..., just questions about things. And of course asking for money but, talking about various races and what the issues are...I just didn't get that from the Democratic Party before. So MoveOn has served a wonderful purpose.

Next Step?

ICT makes it easier for social movement organizations to frame political debates, mobilize consensus and support, and affect party politics in the United States. Savvy activist groups can leverage the affordances of ICT in ways that allow citizens to easily mobilize around multiple issues and give supporters voice on an organization's priorities and campaigns. With the influx of money by both big donors and small and a media system bursting with opportunity, contemporary social movement groups like MoveOn and TPM offer an alternative to the traditional party system—as well as a means through which to change it, albeit sometimes temporarily. In short, savvy movement groups can use ICT in ways that make them difficult to ignore.

This research, however, is a first attempt to empirically understand how ICT can be used to affect elections and political parties more generally. Scholars need to assess whether various organizational forms can affect parties and elections differently. Our analysis suggests, for instance, that an important strength of localized movement groups is that they can change politics and policy from the bottom up. This kind of change could have important implications over the long haul because localized vetting processes could cultivate new party leaders at the state and national level. We are not suggesting that change from the top-down is unimportant. Social movement organizations that can affect the field of candidates can alter how a political party views its constituents and role in the political system for the foreseeable future. The point here is that different kinds of social movement organizations have different advantages and that these advantages (and what groups do with them) may have long-term implications for the party. Likewise, social scientists will need to parse out how money affects the course of social movement organization, its goals, and its role in elections. MoveOn and TPM groups benefit at various points in time from an influx of financial and other resources, which may influence the agenda in more or less subtle ways.[24] Similarly, scholars will want to pay attention to party politics and the role of enterprising political neophytes who ride the wave of political dissent into office on the organizations that helped them get elected (although sometimes inadvertently). The role of money may indeed shape a social movement organization in the short and long term, and, perhaps, reveal its influence in these virtual power plays.

References

Amenta Edwin, Carruthers Bruce, Zylan Yvonne (1992) A Hero for the Aged? The Townsend Movement, The Political Mediation Model, and Old Age Policy, 1934–1959. Am J Sociol 98:308–339
Andrews K (2004) Freedom is a constant struggle. University of Chicago Press, Chicago
Atton C (2007) Current issues in alternative media research. Sociol Compass 1:17–27
Ayres J (1999) From the streets to the internet: the cyber-diffusion of contention. Ann Am Acad Polit Soc Sci 566:132–143
Bai M (2004) Wiring the vast left-wing conspiracy. In: The New York Times. New York
Balz D (2004a) Campaign for DNC chief begins; candidates say party must rebuild state chapters, offer resounding message. In: The Washington Post. The Washington Post, Washington
Balz D (2004b) DNC chief advises learning for GOP. In: The Washington Post. The Washington Post, Washington
Barasko M (2004) Governing NOW: grassroots activism in the national organization for women. Cornell University Press, Ithaca
Benford R, Snow David (2000) Framing processes and social movements: an overview and assessment. Annu Rev Sociol 26:611–639
Bennett WL (2003) Communicating global activism: strengths and vulnerabilities of networked politics. Inf Commun Soc 6(2):143–168
Benson R, Neveu Erik (2005) Bourdieu and the journalistic field. Polity Press, Malden
Bernhard B (2004) Tempest from a Teapot. LA Weekly
Bimber B (1998) The internet and political transformation: populism, community, and accelerated pluralism. Polity 31:391–401

---

[24] To my knowledge, the local TPM groups are not funded by national groups such as the Tea Party Patriots or FreedomWorks. However, outside groups occasionally help with mobilization efforts. For example, one of the rallies during the opening week of the legislature was sponsored by Americans for Prosperity, which brought TPM supporters from other parts of the state to the capital. In fact, according to our video documentation of the event, more than 90 % of the attendees were bused from other parts of Florida for the event (the FL representative from the group asked attendees to raise their hand if they had taken the free bus to Tallahassee).

Bonchek, Mark S (1995) Grassroots in cyberspace: Using computer networks to facilitate political participation. 53rd annual meeting of the midwest political science association, Vol 6. Chicago, IL

Bourdieu P (1998) On television. New Press, New York

Carroll WK, Hackett RA (2006) Democratic media activism through the lens of social movement theory. Media Cult Soc 28:83–104

Chadwick A (2006) Internet politics: states, citizens, and new communication technologies. Oxford University Press, New York

Cornwell R (2004) The boss offers kerry blue-collar support: backing from the entertainment has sometimes been a mixed. In: The Independent. Newspaper Publishing PLC, London

Dalton RJ, Wattenberg MP (eds) (2000) Parties without partisans: political change in advanced industrial democracies. Oxford University Press, Oxford

DeLuca D (2004) The pop vote. In: The Philadelphia inquirer. Philadelphia Papers LLC, Philadelphia

Diani M (2000) Social movement networks virtual and real. Inf Commun Soc 3:386–401

Dulio D, Goff D, Thurber J (1999) Untangled web: internet use during the 1998 election. Polit Sci Polit 32:53–59

Dyke V, Nella SS, Taylor V (2004) The targets of social movements: beyond a focus on the state. Res Soc Mov Conflict Change 25:27–51

Earl J (2006) Pursuing social change online: the use of four protest tactics on the internet. Soc Sci Comput Rev 20:1–16

Earl J, Kimport K (2008) The targets of online protest. Inf Commun Soc 11:449–472

Earl J, Kimport K (2011) Digitally enabled social change: activism in the internet age. MIT Press, New York

Edelman M (1964) The symbolic uses of politics. University of Illinois Press, Urbana

Faler B (2004) Kerry's E-Mail List Continues to Be a Valuable Resource. In: The Washington Post. The Washington Post, Washington

Farrell D, Webb P (2000) Political parties as campaign organisations. In: Dalton R, Wattenberg M (eds) Parties without Partisans, Oxford: Oxford University Press pp. 102–28

Ferree M (2003) Resonance and radicalism: feminist framing in the abortion debates of the United States and Germany. Am J Sociol 109:304–344

Fisher D, Stanley K, Berman D, Neff G (2005) How do organizations matter? mobilization and support for participants at five globalization protests. Soc Probl 52:102–121

Foot KA, Schneider SM (2002) Online action in campaign 2000: an exploratory analysis of the U.S. political web sphere. J Broadcast Electron Media 46:222–244

Foot KA, Schneider SM, Dougherty M, Xenos M, Larsen E (2003) Analyzing linking practices: candidate sites in the 2002 US electoral web sphere. J Comput Mediated Commun 6:0

Fouhy B (2004) MoveOn.org becomes anti-Bush online powerhouse. The Associated Press, Berkeley

Gainous J, Wagner K (2011) Rebooting american politics: the internet revolution. Rowman & Littlefield, New York

Gamson W (1990) The strategy of social protest. Dorsey Press, Homewood, IL

Gamson W, Meyer D (1996) Framing political opportunity. In: McAdam D, McCarthy J, Zald M (eds) Comparative perspectives on social movements: political opportunities, mobilizing structures, and cultural framings. Cambridge University Press, Cambridge, pp 275–290

Gamson W, Wolfsfeld G (1993) Movement and media as interacting systems. Ann Am Acad Polit Soc Sci 578:104–125

Gibson R, Ward S (1998) UK political parties and the internet: politics as usual in the new media? Havard Int J Press/Politics 3:14–38

Gibson R, Ward S (2000) New media, same impact? British party activity in cybersapce. In: Gibson R, Ward S (eds) Reinvigorating government? British politics and the internet. Ashgate, Aldershot, pp 106–129

Gibson R, Nixon P, Ward S (2003) Net gain?political parties and the internet:. Routledge, New York

Gitlin T (1980) The whole world is watching: mass media in the making and unmaking of the new left. University of California Press, Los Angeles

Gourevitch P (2004). Swingtime: former bush voters advertise their disaffection. In: The New Yorker. The Conde Nast Publications, Inc., New York

Guzman I (2004) Boss amps up tour to rock Anti-W Vote. In: Daily News. Daily News LP, New York

Hananel S (2004) MoveOn to democratic party: 'We Bought it, we own it'. The Associated Press, New York

Herman E, Chomsky N (1988) Manufacturing consent: the political economy of mass media. Pantheon Books, New York

Hirschman A (1970) Exit, voice, and loyalty: responses to decline in firms, organizations, and states. Harvard University Press, Cambridge

Horrigan M (2004) MoveOn.org steals DNC thunder. UPI, USA

Huck P (2004) Moving the masses.In: The Age. The Age Company Limited, Melbourne

Jamieson KH (1996) Packaging the president: a history and criticism of presidential campaign advertising. Oxford University Press, New York

Kahn R, Kellner D (2004) New media and internet activism: from the 'Battle of Seattle' to blogging. New Media Soc 6:87–95

Kenski K, Hardy B, Jamieson KH (2010) The Obama victory: how media, money, and message shaped the 2008 election. Oxford University Press, New York

Klandermans B (1984) Mobilization and participation: social-psychological expansions of resource mobilization theory. Am Sociol Rev 49:583–600

Klandermans B (1992) The social construction of protest and multiorganizational fields. In: Morris A, McClurg Mueller C (eds) Frontiers in social movement theory. New Haven, Yale University Press, pp 77–103

Klatch R (1999) A generation divided: the new left, the new right and the 1960s. University of California Press, Los Angles

Lippert B (2004) Barbara Lippert's critique: kerry is so very. In: AdWeek. VNU Business Media, Inc., New York

Margolis M, Resnick D, Chin-chang T (1997) Campaigning on the internet: parties and candidates on the world wide web in the 1996 primary season. Int J Press/Politics 2:59–78

McAdam D (1996) The framing function of movement tactics: strategic dramaturgy in the American civil rights movement. In: McAdam D, McCarthy J, Zald M (eds) Comparative perspectives of social movements: political opportunities, mobilizing structures, and cultural framings. Cambridge University Press, Cambridge, pp 338–355

McAdam D (1988) Freedom summer. Oxford University Press, New York

McCarthy J, Zald M (1973) The trend of social movements in America: professionalization and resource mobilization. General Learning Press, Morristown

McVeigh R, Welch M, Bjarnason T (2003) Hate crime reporting as a successful social movement outcome. Am Sociol Rev 68:843–867

Meyer D, Gamson J (1995) The challenges of cultural elites: celebrities and social movements. Sociol Inq 65:181–206

Meyer D, Whittier N (1994) Social movement spillover. Soc Probl 41:277–298

Norris P (2000) A virtuous circle: political communications in postindustrial societies. Cambridge University Press, New York

Piven FF, Cloward R (1977) Poor people's movements. Basic Books, New York

Raeburn N (2004) Changing corporate america from inside out. University of Minnesota Press, Minneapolis

Rash W (1997) Politics on the nets: wiring the political process. W.H. Freeman & Company, New York

Rochon T (1998) Culture moves: ideas, activism, and changing values. Princeton University Press, Princeton

Rohlinger D (2007) American media and deliberative democratic processes. Sociol Theor 25:122–148

Rohlinger D, Brown J (2009) Democracy, action and the internet after 9/11. Am Behav Sci 53:133–150

Rohlinger D, Brown J (2013) Mass media and institutional change: organizational reputation, strategy, and outcomes in the academic freedom movement. Mobil Int Q 18:1–27

Rohlinger D, Klein J (Forthcoming-a) Constricting boundaries: collective identity in the tea party movement. In: Naples N, Mendez J (eds) Border politics, globalization and social movements. New York University Press, New York

Rohlinger D, Klein J (Forthcoming-b) From fervor to fear: ICT and emotions in the tea party movement. In: Meyer D, Van Dyke N (eds) Understanding the tea party. Ashgate, New York

Rubin D, Fitzgerald T (2004) Working in concert against Bush: Springsteen, others to play in Philadelphia and Swing States. In: The Philadelphia Inquirer. Philadelphia Philadelphia Newspapers LLC

Schattschneider EE (1960) The semi-sovereign people. Holt, Rinehart, & Winston Inc, New York

Schumpeter J (1976) Capitalism, socialism, and democracy. Haper & Row, New York

Schussman A, Earl J (2004) From barricades to firewalls? strategic voting and social movement leadership in the internet age. Sociol Inquiry 74:439–463

Snow D, Benford R (1988) Ideology, frame resonance, and participant mobilization. Int Soc Mov Res 1:197–217

Tarrow S (1998) Fishnets, internets and catnets: globalization and transnational collective action. In: Hanagan M, Moch LP, Brake W (eds) Challenging authority: the historical study of contentious politics. University of Minnesota Press, Minneapolis, pp 228–244

Thörn H (2007) Social movements, the media and the emergence of a global public sphere: from anti-apartheid to global justice. Curr Sociol 55:896–918

Verba S, Scholzman KL, Brady H (1995) Voice and equality: civic volunteerism in american politics. Harvard University Press, Boston

Walgrave S, Manssens J (2000) The making of the white march: the media as a mobilizing alternative to movement organizations. Mobilization 5:217–239

Whittier N (1995) Feminist generations: the persistence of the radical women's movement. Temple University Press, Philadelphia

Revolutionary Cells: On the Role of Texts, Tweets, and Status Updates in Unarmed Revolutions

Daniel P. Ritter and Alexander H. Trechsel

Abstract The question of the role played by new ICTs in the 2011 revolutions in the Middle East and North Africa (MENA), particularly those of Tunisia and Egypt, triggered a heated debate among pundits and academic observers. On one side, myriad bloggers, tweeters, journalists and scholars declared these revolutions to be "2.0" in form, i.e., triggered by online activists and won thanks to the Internet. On the other side, critical voices surfaced, claiming that the Internet was merely a tool amongst others used by opponents of dictatorial regimes, and hence less relevant than Internet enthusiasts claim. With this paper we aim at contributing to this debate by going beyond these simplistic contrasts. While it is naïve to contend that the Internet and cell phone communications did not contribute to the positive outcome in Tunisia and Egypt, it would also be historically and theoretically uninformed to suggest that the absence of these technologies would have made the revolutions impossible. By comparing the unarmed revolutions of Tunisia and Egypt in 2011 to the nonviolent Iranian Revolution of 1977–79, we propose a theoretical framework that balances structural conditions with the strategic decisions made by revolutionary agents. We conclude that although new ICTs cannot be directly linked to revolutionary success, such technologies have significantly altered the way revolutions are fought and won.

D. P. Ritter
Stockholm University, Florence, Italy

A. H. Trechsel (✉)
European University Institute, Florence, Italy
e-mail: Alexander.Trechsel@EUI.eu

B. Grofman et al. (eds.), *The Internet and Democracy in Global Perspective*,
Studies in Public Choice 31, DOI: 10.1007/978-3-319-04352-4_7,
© Springer International Publishing Switzerland 2014

Introduction

The question of the role played by new ICTs in the 2011 revolutions in the Middle East and North Africa (MENA), particularly those of Tunisia and Egypt, triggered a heated debate among pundits and academic observers (Bennett-Jones 2011; Gladwell 2010; Gladwell and Shirky 2011; Tufekci 2011b). On one side, myriad bloggers, tweeters, journalists, and scholars declared these revolutions to be "2.0" in form, i.e., triggered by online activists and won thanks to the Internet (Shirky 2011; Tufekci 2011a, b). On the other side, critical voices surfaced, claiming that the Internet was merely a tool among others used by opponents of dictatorial regimes, and hence less relevant than Internet enthusiasts claim (Gladwell 2010). With this chapter we aim at contributing to this debate by going beyond these simplistic contrasts. While it is naïve to contend that the Internet and cell phone communications did not contribute to the positive outcome in Tunisia and Egypt, it would also be historically and theoretically uninformed to suggest that the absence of these technologies would have made the revolutions impossible.

In this chapter we examine the relationship between ICTs and unarmed revolutions. Defined as noninstitutionalized mass movements that cause regime change through the deliberate and strategic opposition use of nonviolent methods of struggle, such as strikes, demonstrations, and boycotts, unarmed revolutionaries have benefited greatly from the emergence of the Internet and other advanced technologies that facilitate mass mobilization. But is there reason to believe that there is a causal link between new ICTs and revolutionary success? As we will see, old ICTs were used in past unarmed revolutions as well, long before the ousters of Ben Ali and Mubarak. Through a comparison between the first unarmed revolution, that of Iran 1977–1979, and the two most recent examples in Tunisia and Egypt, we will analyze the role played by new ICTs in unarmed revolutions. We argue that although the use of new and old ICTs in unarmed revolutions are very similar, modern, Internet-based forms thereof have nevertheless altered the game in important ways.

It is puzzling that the traditional literature on revolutions quite entirely misses out on the central role played by information and communication *techniques*, not to say *technologies*. While much ink has been shed in attempts to analytically isolate the specific structural factors that cause revolutions (Foran 2005; Goldstone 1991; Goodwin 2001; Skocpol 1979; Soboul 1977; Tilly 1978), much less attention has been given to the role of the revolutionaries themselves (Selbin 1997, 2010). Even among those sociologists and political scientists who have focused on agency in revolutions, few contributions have been devoted to the role of information and communication technology in the process of regime change, nonviolent, or otherwise. This is mainly due to two interrelated facts: first, the study of revolutions has as noted above tilted heavily toward structural analyses that leave little room for the role of the actual revolutionaries, and even less for their communication tactics. Second, and perhaps more important to the argument made here, unarmed revolutions remain severely understudied. This matters, because the successful use of ICTs seems to be correlated with unarmed revolutions in particular, not their violent counterparts. Hence, a failure to recognize the nonviolent nature of the ICT revolutions would lead to a faulty understanding of the role of such technologies. With the revolutionary events in Tunisia and Egypt now firmly within the relevant universe of cases, it becomes difficult, if not impossible, for observers to ignore the role of information and communication in revolutionary processes.

While we may anticipate that events in the MENA region will increase scholarly interest in an understudied subject, unarmed revolutions have nonetheless already received some attention from researchers (Garton Ash 2009; Nepstad 2011; Ritter 2010; Schock 2005; Sharp 2005). In this chapter, we particularly draw on Ritter's (2010) notion that the emergence and success of unarmed revolutions depend on the internationalization of these struggles and the presence of an iron cage of liberalism (ICL) in the countries experiencing a "revolutionary situation" (Tilly 1978). The concept ICL is based on the insight that governments that have perished at the unarmed hands of unarmed revolutionaries share one central commonality: they tend to be autocratic regimes closely allied with democratic states. These relationships, which develop over the span of decades, initially provide autocratic leaders with both international legitimacy and economic gains in the form of grants, loans, and trade. Eventually, however, the relationship may become a burden if domestic opposition groups can highlight the discrepancy between the regime's insincere commitment to the liberal democratic principles of the patron state and its actual performance in these areas. Historically, nonviolent protesters have often been successful in making this discrepancy manifest to the world and have thus managed to trap numerous dictators in ICLs. The reason for this is quite simple: nonviolent protest is in itself little more than the expression of some of the most fundamental human and civil rights—the rights to freedom of expression and peaceful assembly. Any government officially committed to liberal values, regardless of the hypocrisy accompanying that commitment, will encounter great difficulties in its efforts to repress peaceful protesters and their messages. This is *especially* the case if the government in question is closely allied with one or more Western democracies that have their own liberal reputations to consider. Despite the absolute nature of his assertion, Downing (1996) is largely correct when he states that "a movement that is not reported does not take place" (Downing 1996, p. 22). In terms of the dynamics of the ICL, it is not enough that a state represses nonviolent protesters—the world must also be aware the repression takes place. And this is where ICTs enter the story. Fundamentally, information and communication technologies are employed by unarmed revolutionaries in two contexts: the domestic and the global. In the domestic arena, ICTs primarily serve the function of mobilization through information diffusion and protest coordination. ICTs facilitate mobilization on the ground by connecting like-minded citizens, offering nonofficial information to anybody interested in the events and inviting protesters to gather in public places, marches, or other forms of political activism. Beyond the domestic arena, ICTs aid the movement's cause by increasing global awareness of the revolutionary situation. This dynamic is illustrated in Fig. 1.

Fig. 1 The impact of ICTs in
unarmed revolutions

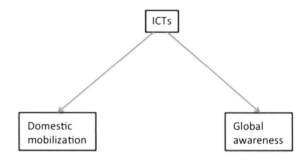

We posit that these two major effects of ICTs are central features of all unarmed revolutions. In the empirical section of this chapter, we therefore investigate to what extent both domestic mobilization and global awareness was facilitated by new ICTs specifically. The remainder of this chapter proceeds through a comparison between the world's first unarmed revolution, namely the Iranian revolution of 1977–1979 (Goodwin 2001), and the most recent ones in Tunisia and Egypt. We will show to what extent ICTs mattered in all three cases for domestic and global purposes in order to draw conclusions about the unique contributions of new ICTs. While the similarities between the cases exceed their differences, we show that digital media tied the domestic and the global arenas together in an unprecedented way. As this chapter is rather theory-building than theory-testing in form, we will not develop proper hypotheses at this point. Rather, we depart from a hunch, i.e., that new ICTs have caused the domestic and the global arenas of unarmed revolutions to become increasingly interwoven and at times even overlap one another.

From Iran to Egypt: ICTs in Unarmed Revolutions

ICTs and the Nonviolent Iranian Revolution

The Iranian Revolution is often depicted of as one of the most violent examples of regime change in the second half of the twentieth century (Arsenault 2011). But the chroniclers of the revolution overwhelmingly agree that the removal of Muhammad Reza Pahlavi—the shah of Iran—occurred without the reliance on opposition violence (Abrahamian 1982; Amjad 1989; Arjomand 1988; Bakhash 1990; Burns 1996; Cottam 1988; Daneshvar 1996; Dorman and Farhang 1987; Fischer 2003; Foran 1994; Green 1982; Hoveyda 1980; Keddie 1983; Kurzman 2004; Milani 1988; Parsa 1989; Parsons 1984; Shivers 1980; Sick 1985; Sreberny-Mohammadi and Mohammadi 1994; and Stempel 1981). Instead, Iranian protesters employed nonviolent tactics, in particular massive demonstrations and debilitating strikes, to bring the government to its knees. In the end, an alarming rate of the shah's 400,000 soldiers began to desert from the military not because they were engaged in gun battles with hostile freedom fighters, but because they day after day had to listen to their countrymen and women plead with them to join the people and stop killing their Muslim brothers (Amuzegar 1991; Arjomand 1988; Heikal 1982; Kurzman 2004). The role of communication technology in Iran's unarmed revolution has rarely received the attention it deserves, but as one of its most prominent chroniclers has declared, "national integration and improved nationwide communications were the essential preconditions of the revolution of 1979" (Arjomand 1988, p. 119).

One of the architects behind this unarmed revolutionary strategy was, perhaps surprisingly to a Western audience, Ayatollah Ruhollah Khomeini, the man who would take over after the shah and become Iran's first Supreme Leader. Khomeini realized early on that violent attacks on the state would serve little purpose. When eager Islamist guerrillas, who were engaged in a bloody and ultimately unsuccessful battle with the shah's military in the late 1960s and early 1970s, came to receive the Ayatollah's blessing for their struggle, Khomeini reprimanded the disappointed young men and informed them that "the regime would fall not when the masses took up arms but when the whole clerical stratum joined the opposition" (Abrahamian 1989, p. 150). He recognized that the shah's government with its vast military and international support would have little trouble defeating an armed uprising (Bakhash 1990; Heikal 1982; Milani 1988).

Old ICTs and Domestic Mobilization

Khomeini knew what needed to be done, but how does one go about mobilizing millions of people in a largely rural developing country, in particular when one finds oneself in exile? Well, one uses the most advanced technologies available, in this case, cassette tapes and telephone landlines. The Ayatollah's sermons and messages, recorded in exile in Iraq and later France, were smuggled into Iran. Once in Iran, Khomeini's collaborators within the religious establishment made sure the tapes were copied and distributed widely. As one commentator explains:

> tapes of Khomeini's sermons and speeches passed through the mosque network from his residence in Iraq to Qom, Iran's most holy city and the Ayatollah's home until his exile. From there, they were taken to other cities, where enterprising and friendly bazaar merchants duplicated tapes and sold them to the faithful. Beginning in 1976 the mosque network eliminated the middleman and delivered the cassettes and pamphlets which spread revolutionary doctrine directly to the sympathetic mullahs. They in turn passed it to the people in the mosques. Much of this activity went unnoticed until it was fully organized in late 1977. Strangely, there were no successful attempts on the part of the government to interfere with this network on a sustained basis. In a few sporadic cases local distributors were arrested, but this would only enrage the faithful and increase sympathy for revolutionary efforts (Stempel 1981, p. 45).

While Khomeini's messages may in some ways have been more difficult to access than the tweets and Facebook updates of 2011, Iranians found ways to spread the Ayatollah's message in creative ways by tapping into and altering existing cultural practices. For example, rather than treating their passengers to the latest developments in popular music:

> it was one symbol of the Islamic revolution in Iran that the only tapes played in long-distance trucks, in buses and taxis were the tapes of Ayatullah Khomeini. We can say that in one way the revolution was a revolution of which the technological symbol was the cassette tape (Algar 1983, p. 105).

Just like the cassette tape became the "technological symbol" of the 1977–1979 revolution, it is worth noting that 90 years earlier, during the Tobacco Rebellion of 1891, the Iranian clergy had made good use of that era's revolutionizing communication technology—the telegraph. While that struggle was far from a revolution, the clerics used technology at their disposal to mobilize the Iranian population against a proposed government concession that would give a British industrialist monopolistic rights to the entire Iranian tobacco industry (Keddie 2003, pp. 61–62).

The concrete effects of the opposition's tactic of distributing Khomeini's cassette tapes went beyond simply mobilizing the Iranian people. The cassette tapes also influenced the responses of the armed forces. Amuzegar (1991) has noted that:

> encouraged by Khomeini, through widely distributed cassettes, not to shoot at their Moslem brothers and sisters and to overthrow the illegitimate monarchy, army conscripts and junior officers began to question the righteousness of the task. And military commanders began doubting the unquestioned loyalty of draftees and enlisted men (Amuzegar 1991, p. 286).

In order to fully explicate the extent of the role played by the "Khomeini tapes," Taheri (1986) has shown that Parviz Sabeti, the then-head of the "anti-subversion unit" of the SAVAK, Iran's secret police, believed that over 100,000 tapes were distributed in Iran during 1978. "That meant," Taheri suggests, "that millions of Iranians were able to hear Khomeini's uncompromising condemnation of the Shah directly and were encouraged by his total lack of regard for conventional rules of politesse when speaking of 'the hated Shah, the Jewish agent, the American snake whose head must be smashed with a stone'" (1985, p. 213).

In an ironic twist in the fate of the man who famously referred to the United States as "the great Satan," Khomeini's enterprise benefitted tremendously from American Bell International's $10 billion project (paid for by the shah's government) to revamp Iran's telephone system in the mid-1970s (Stempel 1981, p. 72). Taking full advantage of the improved telephone network, Khomeini's messages to the Iranian masses "would be recorded in Paris and read over the telephone to a number of individuals in Tehran who would have tape recorders held against the telephone. They would then telephone other individuals in provincial cities who were waiting with their tape recorders, and in a brief time the message would be duplicated and circulated throughout the country" (Algar 1983, p. 105).

In addition to being used in the distribution of Khomeini's revolutionary messages and sermons, revolutionaries also relied on the telephone system to coordinate their demonstrations in different cities (Stempel 1981). In other words, and in a manner not very different from how protest events were coordinated more than 30 years later in Tunisia and Egypt, organizers used the most advanced technological means at their disposal to increase the effects of their efforts. For the shah's security forces, coordinated demonstrations in different parts of the country naturally became a difficult expression of dissent to contain.

Old ICTs and Global Awareness

The improved telephone system also allowed Iranians to keep the world, and especially Iranian living abroad, abreast of what was happening at home. Once again we see how the telephone system filled the role played by online communication technology in 2011. As cell phone calls, Tweets, and Facebook updates were used by Tunisians and Egyptians to inform the world of the progress of their revolutions, Iranians used their telephones in a similar manner. An indication of how accessible information about the revolution was to the rest of the world is represented by the virtual explosion of telephone calls between Iran and the U.S. in the years leading up to the shah's ouster. Zonis (1991), quoting James Bill, reports that while 53,597 calls were made from the United States to Iran in 1973, that number increased to 854,382 calls in 1977, an increase of over 1,600 %. The 1973 figures equal almost 9,000 h of conversation time, an already significant number. However, by 1977, that number was up to 134,000 h. While many of these calls undoubtedly were made to the roughly 50,000 Americans living in Iran at the time, it still seems quite likely that Iranians exploited their improved access to telecommunications to inform friends and family abroad about the political situation at home (Stempel 1981).

A final use of communication technology in the Iranian Revolution is represented by the radio. Similarly, to the use of the telephone system, the radio became a revolutionary tool as an inadvertent consequence of the shah's modernization scheme. Eager to rapidly develop his country to the level of the West, the shah welcomed new technology into Iran. While "in the 1960s, a radio was a luxury few people could afford... In the seventies, the situation drastically changed. More than 65 % of private households owned radios in 1976. In urban areas, the figure was more than 75 %" (Milani 1988, p. 121).

The revolutionaries made use of this development in several different ways. First, Khomeini benefitted from more or less unrestricted access to BBC radio journalists while in Parisian exile to communicate directly with the Iranian people, thus removing the need for cassette tapes (Foran 1993, p. 381). Second, when shah lifted some of the censorship restrictions on the media as a part of the liberalization measures, he hoped would save his throne, the opposition pounced on the opportunity to keep each other up to date with developments in different part of the country. "This additional means of communication... generated a sense of solidarity among different groups of strikers" at the height of the revolution in the fall of 1978 (Parsa 1989, p. 151). Knowledge that other strikers suffered the same difficulties contributed to the resilience of the strikers, thus allowing them to crucially put pressure on the regime and its finances.

As this section has shown, communication technology clearly contributed to the Iranian revolutionaries achieving their objectives. However, ICTs had a much greater impact on domestic mobilization than on the movement's efforts to raise global awareness. Old ICTs, such as cassette tapes and landlines, lack the immediate and wide-reaching capacities of the Internet. Consequently, old ICTs were less effective in internationalizing the revolution. In order to reach the international community, Iranian movement leaders had to rely on the Western media. In fact, it was not until Khomeini moved to Paris that the European and American news outlets seriously began to cover the revolution. In addition, and as further evidence of the slower transmission of the revolution to the world, Khomeini had to send some of his collaborators to the United States on "speaking tours." These trips were intended to reassure Americans that the Islamic Revolution was peaceful and that "nothing would prevent the continuation of mutually satisfactory relations with the United States" (Sick 1985, p. 112). While the revolution eventually succeeded, the shah held out for roughly a year and half. Meanwhile, Ben Ali lasted a little less than a month, and Mubarak for a mere 17 days. It seems plausible that the delayed internationalization of the revolution, explained in part by the lack of direct and effective communication tools capable of reaching the West, may help explain its relatively long duration. As we will see next, ICTs contributed similarly to domestic mobilization in Tunisia and Egypt, but the presence of new ICTs drastically accelerated the internationalization of the two revolutions.

ICTs and the Revolutions of Tunisia and Egypt

Similarly, to earlier unarmed revolutions, events in Tunisia and Egypt were characterized by mass mobilization and the eventual internationalization of the movement. Commentators emphasizing the positive impact of increased Internet penetration in Egypt and Tunisia point to the fact that Facebook groups were instrumental in the early stages of the revolutions. These online communities allowed movement leaders to coordinate dates and meeting points for the initial protests, thus increasing the likelihood of large turnouts (Hauslohner 2011; Miladi 2011). In the later stages of the revolutions, new ICTs allowed the activists, unlike their Iranian counterparts, to immediately and vividly transmit their struggles directly to the world.

New ICTs and Domestic Mobilization

In both Tunisia and Egypt, ICTs played an important role in the very early stages of the revolutions. In response to the self-immolation of Mohammed Bouazizi in the central town of Sidi Bouzid on December 17, Tunisian demonstrators took to the streets that same day (Rifai 2011). As the traditional Tunisian media was tightly controlled by the state, online activists took it upon themselves to disseminate news of these protests. Bouazizi's story was told on Facebook and other social networking sites, causing outraged Tunisians to participate in demonstrations in various parts of the country (Anderson 2011; Miladi 2011). In the early stages of the uprising, this form of citizen journalism set the revolution on a path of potential success. Although online activists continued to post directions for protesters to congregate at given locations at specific times throughout the month-long struggle, the revolution was decidedly decentralized (Beckett 2011). To imply that one cyber activist-leader, or a group thereof, was effectively pulling the strings of the revolution would therefore be to exaggerate the importance of online activism and organizing. Instead, once the initial protests had grabbed the hopes and imaginations of Tunisians, the street, not cyberspace, became the locus of organizing efforts. Bloggers continued to report on the progression of the protests and announced meeting points and times for planned demonstrations, but mobilization in the latter part of the revolution would likely have occurred even without the participation of online activists.

Similarly, online activists played a central role in organizing the January 25 Police Day protests that kicked off the Egyptian Revolution. While this protests had been planned far in advance, it acquired new meaning in the aftermath of Ben Ali's ouster. One activist told us that although organizers hoped that the recent events in Tunisia would inspire people to join the demonstration, they simultaneously remained realistic. Calls for public expression of dissent had often been issued in the past, but typically with disappointing result (Personal interview). However, the January 25 demonstrations turned out to be an unprecedented success that set the Egyptian revolution on its path to victory.

In the days preceding what had been labeled by the organizers as "Day of Wrath" or "Revolution Day," 85,000 people had committed to participating in the protests via the Facebook page called "We are all Khaled Saeed" (Hauslohner 2011). The Facebook page, which had about 400,000 members, was the brainchild of Wael Ghonim, the Google executive who became one of the faces of the revolution after his arrest in the early days of the upheaval. The actual number of demonstrators participating in the protests ultimately turned out to be significantly less than the 85,000 "registered" attendants, but it seems plausible that the large "virtual turnout" may have contributed to a larger physical turnout than would have been the case had a more modest number of Egyptian Facebook users announced their participation. In this sense ICTs played an important role in triggering the revolution as it helped generate an initial protest large enough to provide the movement with the necessary momentum. Still, as the revolution played out its course, online activism again became less and less important in organizational terms. As in Tunisia, the revolution took on a life of its own as new demonstrations were organized by the activists on the ground rather than those operating in the ether.

In terms of domestic participation, both Egypt and Tunisia display a similar dynamic in which the Internet with its bloggers and Facebook users played an important catalyzing role. As the events progressed, however, the streets replaced the Web as the main source of organizational activity. With only 33 and 21 % of the population having access to the Internet in Tunisia and Egypt, respectively (Kuebler 2011), we should perhaps not expect the Web to be instrumental in maintaining large demonstrations once a critical mass of activists has taken to the streets. Rather than relying on a technology that ultimately only a relatively small portion of the movement base had access to, organizing future protest events became part of the demonstrations themselves. In the late stages of the Egyptian revolution the Tahrir Square protests were more or less continuous, making organizational activities superfluous. The inhabitants of Cairo could not escape being aware of the events that were taking place, and anybody itching to partake in the revolution knew where to go in order to be a part of the historic process unfolding before their eyes.

New ICTs and Global Awareness

Once the two revolutions had been set in motion with the help of ICTs, the technological tools at the disposal of the revolutionaries were used in a decidedly different manner. Rather than mobilizing their own citizens, online activists moved to inform the international community. Through blogs, Facebook updates, cell phone communication, and, most vividly, YouTube, activists targeted friends, family, and colleagues abroad, as well as the international media. Crucially, cyber activist worked to complement the traditional media outlets in the task of informing the world of conditions on the ground.

In Tunisia, where activists faced a more concerted government effort to censor their activities, online protesters collaborated with satellite TV channels. Al-Jazeera, which was a central player in both the Tunisian and Egyptian revolution and has done its best to encourage similar protest movements elsewhere in North Africa and the Middle East, was the most important partner of the Tunisian blogosphere. As Ben Ali's government aggressively sought to limit the public impact of its online opponents, mainly by blocking sites and stealing usernames and passwords, Al-Jazeera contributed to the opposition's efforts by reproducing tweets and status updates on their TV channels (Miladi 2011; Wagner 2011). While many of the messages were directed at Tunisians, a large portion also sought to spread information about domestic events to the international audience. As Faris Bouhafa, an ordinary Tunisian broadcasting his experiences on YouTube, put it, "I was definitely afraid at first but I wanted everything we were filming to reach the outside world. When you know nobody was going to come down here and nobody could reach us, thanks God we were able to reach them" (Al-Jazeera 2011). Crucially, the impact of these activities was to make it difficult for the world, and in particular those Western governments allied with Ben Ali, to turn a blind eye to the regime's repressive response against predominantly nonviolent protesters. For example, French popular outrage resulted in severe criticism of those French politicians who had been linked to the Ben Ali government, and even forced resignations. In the past these connections had raised little concern, but now, as a consequence of the well-reported ruthless repression of protesters, French partnership with the Tunisian government was considered highly inappropriate.

In Egypt, we again see a similar dynamic, but one in which ICTs played a less important role due to the fact that Al-Jazeera even more aggressively interjected itself into the struggle to evict Hosni Mubarak from power. Whereas the Qatari news giant relied on video and text provided by activists to relay the Tunisian revolution to the rest of the region and the world, its Egyptian coverage was composed of live reports and video provided by the organization's own journalists. Texts, tweets, and status updates continued to play a role in informing the world since Al-Jazeera's journalists and those of other news outlets could not cover every corner of the Egyptian uprising. But in relative terms new ICTs may have been less impactful in Egypt than they were in Tunisia. This is not due to the fact that the Egyptian government more aggressively pursued a policy of cyber repression, it did not, but rather to the fact that traditional ICTs were better prepared and perhaps more willing to report on events in Egypt. Rather uncharacteristically for a revolution, this one turned out to be televised.

The internationalization of the Egyptian revolution generated widespread solidarity mobilization throughout the world (The Electronic Intifada 2011). In the United States, late January demonstrations took place in New York City, Washingon, DC, Boston, Chicago, San Francisco, Tampa, Seattle, Ann Arbor, Atlanta, Columbus, Cincinnati, Dayton, Portland, Houston, Blacksburg, Norfolk, Madison, Detroit, Minneapolis, Jersey City, Queens-Astoria, and Los Angeles (Giambusso 2011; NBC Washington 2011; Szaniszlo 2011; The Electronic Intifada 2011). Meanwhile, London, Dublin, and the Hague witnessed similar protests targeting the Egyptian embassies in those cities (Cocker 2011; The Electric Intifada 2011). In addition sympathetic demonstrations took place in Canada, Australia, Venezuela, and throughout the Middle East (The Electronic Intifada). Besides encouraging Egyptian demonstrators to continue their activities, these demonstrations increased the pressure on the some governments, particularly the American one, to take a harder line in its communication with Mubarak. Thus, the internationalization of the revolution helps explain Obama's transformation from cautiously supportive of his Egyptian ally to demanding of meaningful change and eventually a political transition (Ritter 2011).

Clearly, preventing protest domestically was one of the main reasons for the Egyptian regime to take the unprecedented action of disabling both the Internet and mobile phone services at country level on January 26 (The Guardian, January 26). However, activists rapidly found myriad ways to circumvent the blackout. For instance, landlines were used to phone in tweet messages thanks to Google's makeshift alliance with Twitter's "Speak to Tweet" service. The government block lasted until February 2 when suddenly digital communication was restored. The regimes' inability to block information from spreading globally over the Internet was later complemented by the regime's incapacity to prevent information from entering Egypt. On the day before Mubarak's departure, his new vice president, Omar Suleiman, compelled his compatriots via national television to stop watching foreign broadcasts: "Don't listen to satellite television stations who are trying to create unrest and division and to weaken Egypt and distort its image" (Suleiman on February 10 2011). As we will see in the final section of the chapter, this mutual permeability between information leaving and entering a revolutionary context is one of the main effects, in our view, of new ICTs in unarmed revolutions.

Conclusions: Pushing the Theory

In order to properly assess the role played by new ICTs in the unarmed revolutions of Tunisia and Egypt it is important to distinguish between the impacts they had on the *revolutionary process* as opposed to the *revolutionary outcome*. Our central conclusion is that while new ICTs have directly altered the unarmed revolutionary process, they only have an indirect effect on the outcome thereof.

New ICTs and the Revolutionary Process

On the domestic side, new ICTs affected the revolution process in two different ways. First, they allowed for an impressive *multiplication and amplification of voices* that complicated regime efforts to control expressions of dissent. As the sheer number of voices to be silenced drastically increased, the muting capacities of the state were quickly overwhelmed, thus allowing the message of the revolution to be heard, and acted upon, by large numbers of potential protesters. Second, the *tempo of the revolution* was unarguably affected by new ICTs, as they allowed for instantaneous dispersion of news. Mass participation in news production thus facilitated mobilization and made repression more difficult to accomplish. The multiple channels of immediate communication available to the revolutionaries (mobile phones, Facebook, Twitter, and the World Wide Web in general) made the revolutions' messages impossible to contain. In short, new ICTs contributed to the diffusion of information and subsequently to the rapid mobilization of new activists.

Internationally, the same technologies were used to spread the message of the revolution beyond the borders of the revolutionary contexts. New ICTs allowed for an unprecedented *immediate international diffusion* of news. If it was difficult in the past for any government to contain information about events within a polity, it has now become almost impossible. Any information can spread virally without a real possibility for it to be quarantined. What the 2011 MENA events show is that for information and communication, borders have largely become irrelevant.

As a consequence, widespread global awareness of the struggles was achieved much more rapidly in Tunisia and Egypt than it was in Iran, with new ICTs playing crucial roles. Whereas Iranian revolutionaries, both before and during the revolution, were forced to rely on external media outlets in the United States and Europe to convey their revolutionary narrative to sympathetic audiences, Tunisian and Egyptian revolutionaries accomplished the same objective more directly through the use of new ICTs. Citizen journalists broadcasted the revolution directly to the rest of the world through their mobile phones, without having to rely on intermediary media outlets, in an example of what Trechsel (2011), building on Manin (1997) refers to as "Paparazzi Democracy."

Due to the vast on- and offline coverage of the events in Tunis and Cairo, these domestic events quickly morphed into internationalized revolutions where the boundary between revolutionary and audience becomes increasingly blurred. Today, any Internet-connected person is a potential revolutionary, regardless of their physical location. Whether you are located in Italy, the United States, or Egypt no longer makes a difference: by a click of the mouse anyone can become part of an initially domestic movement to the point where the domestic and international become indistinguishable. As a side effect of this, the language of revolution becomes English, the lingua franca of the Internet. This fact is powerfully evidenced by the impressive presence of protest signs and banners in English in virtually all MENA countries now experiencing revolutionary activities.

But the crucial difference between new and old ICTs in the process of unarmed revolution is not the independent impact new ICTs have on either the domestic or international sphere. Instead, what is "revolutionary" here is the capacity of new ICTs to tie the two together. The central contribution of new ICTs is therefore their capacity to interweave the domestic and international into a feedback loop that can accelerate the revolution. Through the use of new ICTs the revolutionary efforts of both Tunisians and Egyptians were immediately and seamlessly relayed to the world. The world, in turn, responded as immediately and seamlessly and quickly became part of the revolution. This message of support and solidarity was in turn relayed back to the protesters in Tunis and, most spectacularly, Cairo's Tahrir Square. A *non-mediated, transnational loop of protest* was created, where domestic events became global news in a glimpse of a moment, and where regime-critical statements from the White House and capitals throughout the world were received by hundreds of thousands of protesters in the streets, thus causing a what Keck and Sikkink (1998) refer to as a "boomerang effect." In short, a domestic struggle had become an international affair.

Figure 2 shows how we conceive of the impact of new ICTs on unarmed revolutions. In more abstract terms, domestic mobilization and global awareness gradually converge, with one sphere strongly influencing the other. Campaigns to increase global awareness directly feeds into the domestic protest, which, in turn, increases the effects of international public opinion and pressures from foreign governments.

Fig. 2 The impact of ICTs
2.0 in unarmed revolutions

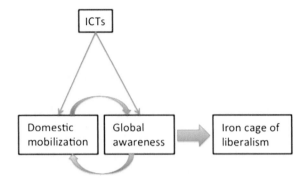

New ICTs and Revolutionary Outcomes

Can the dynamics identified in Fig. 2 also help explain revolutionary success? The answer is yes, but only indirectly and if we bring the ICL into the discussion. The processes we identified in the Iranian, Tunisian and Egyptian revolutions can be found in other contexts, too. For instance, let us briefly consider attempted unarmed revolutions of Burma in 2007 ("The Saffron Revolution" or the "Movement of the Monks") and Iran in 2009 ("The Green Revolution"). Both are excellent examples of unarmed revolutionary movements that failed despite activists' use of new ICTs. Burmese citizen journalists accepted tremendous risks in order to film the government's repression of monks and civilians. The tapes were then smuggled into neighboring Thailand, where they were uploaded to YouTube. In Iran, activists used their cell phones to document government atrocities and to make live appearances on CNN and other international media outlets. In both countries, activists were mobilized and the world informed through the opposition's use of new ICTs. Yet, both Burma and Iran represent failed unarmed revolutions, at least for the moment.

To make sense of Tunisian and Egyptian success in the face of Burmese and Iranian failure, we must go beyond the similarities (the use of new ICTs and the way they affect the interaction between global awareness and domestic mobilization) and look at the crucial structural difference between the cases. While we would suggest that new ICTs affected the *process* of all four revolutions more or less equally, we believe that the successful outcomes in Tunisia and Egypt can be explained by the presence of ICLs in Tunisia and Egypt and the lack thereof in Iran and Burma. As discussed in the introduction, ICLs only emerge in countries allied with the "democratic" nations of the West. While Tunisia and Egypt fit that profile, Burma and Iran do not find themselves in equivalent international relationships. Consequently, the governments in the latter two countries brutally repressed the opposition and the revolutions were momentarily stalled. Does this mean that new ICTs have no impact on the outcome of unarmed revolutions? Not at all, but their impact is indirect. In contexts where and an ICL is present, new ICTs can contribute tremendously to the exacerbation of the negative effects the

ICL has on an autocratic regime. To conclude, new ICTs affect the *process* of unarmed revolution, but their impact on the *outcome* is conditional on the ICL. In short, ICTs are important when they are employed under the broader context of a pre-existing ICL.

References

Abrahamian E (1982) Iran between two revolutions. Princeton University Press, Princeton

Abrahamian E (1989) Radical islam: the Iranian mojahedin. I.B. Tauris, London

Algar H (1983) Roots of the Iranian revolution. Open Press, London

Al-Jazeera (2011) The listening post. News magazine broadcast on 22 Jan 2011. http://www.youtube.com/watch?v=SfcftL-UadM. Accessed 14 April 2011

Amjad M (1989) Iran: from royal dictatorship to theocracy. Greenwood Press, New York

Amuzegar J (1991) The dynamics of the Iranian revolution: the Pahlavis' triumph and tragedy. SUNY Press, Albany

Anderson N (2011) Tweeting tyrants out of Tunisia: global internet at its best. wired.com. Published 14 Jan 2011. http://www.wired.com/threatlevel/2011/01/tunisia/all/1. Accessed 27 April 2011

Arjomand SA (1988) The turban for the crown: the islamic revolution in Iran. Oxford University Press, New York

Arsenault C (2011) Learning from past revolutions? Al-Jazeera. http://english.aljazeera.net/indepth/features/2011/02/201121616828483511.html. Published and Accessed 17 Feb 2011

Bakhash S (1990) The reign of the ayatollahs: Iran and the islamic revolution. Basic Books, New York

Beckett C (2011) After Tunisia and Egypt: towards a new typology of media and networked political change. POLIS Jounalism and Society. Published 11 Feb 2011. http://www.charliebeckett.org/?p=4033. Accessed 21 April 2011

Bennett-Jones O (2011) How cameras hidden in pens outflanked Syrian regime. BBC News. http://news.bbc.co.uk/2/hi/programmes/from_our_own_correspondent/9470481stm. Published and Accessed 30 April 2011

Burns G (1996) Ideology, culture, and ambiguity: the revolutionary process in Iran. Theor Soc 25:349–388

Cocker L (2011) Solidarity by the thousand: protesters take to the streets of London. The Morning Star. Published 30 Jan 2011. http://www.morningstaronline.co.uk/index.php/news/content/view/full/100469. Accessed 30 Mar 2011

Cottam R (1988) Iran and the United States: a cold war case study. University of Pittsburgh Press, Pittsburgh

Daneshvar P (1996) Revolution in Iran. Macmillan, New York

Dorman WA, Farhang M (1987) The U.S. press and Iran: foreign policy and the journalism of deference. University of California Press, Berkeley

Downing JDH (1996) Internationalizing media theory: transition, power, culture: reflections on media in Russia, Poland and Hungary, 1980–95. Sage, Thousand Oaks

Fischer MMJ (2003) Iran: from religious dispute to revolution. University of Wisconsin Press, Madison

Foran J (1993) Fragile resistance: social transformation in Iran from 1500 to the revolution. Westview, Boulder

Foran J (1994) A century of revolution: comparative, historical, and theoretical perspectives on social movements in Iran. In: Foran J (ed) A century of revolution: social movements in Iran. University of Minnesota Press, Minneapolis, pp 223–237

Foran J (2005) Taking power: on the origin of third world revolutions. Cambridge University Press, New York

Garton Ash T (2009) A century of civil resistance: some lessons and questions. In: Roberts A, Garton Ash T (eds) Civil resistance and power politics: the experience of non-violent action from Gandhi to the present. Oxford University Press, New York, pp 371–390

Giambusso D (2011) Thousands gather near UN in New York to support anti-government protests in Egypt. The Star-Ledger. Published 29 Jan 2011. http://www.nj.com/news/index. ssf/2011/01/thousands_gather_in_new_york_c.html. Accessed 30 Mar 2011

Gladwell M (2010) Small change: why the revolution will not be tweeted. The New Yorker (online). Published 4 Oct 2010. http://www.newyorker.com/reporting/2010/10/04/101004fa_ fact_gladwell. Accessed 15 Mar 2011

Gladwell M, Shirky C (2011) From innovation to revolution. Foreign Affairs (March/April). http://www.foreignaffairs.com/articles/67325/malcolm-gladwell-and-clay-shirky/ from-innovation-to-revolution. Accessed 14 April 2011

Goldstone JA (1991) Revolution and rebellion in the early modern world. University of California Press, Berkeley

Goodwin J (2001) No other way out: states and revolutionary movements, 1945–1991. Cambridge University Press, New York

Green JD (1982) Revolution in Iran: the politics of countermobilization. Praeger, New York

Hauslohner A (2011) Is Egypt about to have a facebook revolution? Time.com. Published 24 Jan 2011. http://www.time.com/time/world/article/0,8599,2044142,00.html. Accessed 25 April 2011

Heikal M (1982) Iran: the untold story: an insider's account of America's Iranian adventure and its consequences for the future. Pantheon Books, New York

Hoveyda F (1980) The fall of the shah. Wyndham Books, New York

Keck ME, Sikkink K (1998) Activists beyond borders: advocacy networks in social politics. Cornell University Press, Ithaca

Keddie NR (1983) Iranian revolutions in comparative perspective. Am Hist Rev 88(3):579–598

Keddie NR (2003) Modern Iran: roots and results of revolution. Yale University Press, New Haven

Kuebler J (2011) Overcoming the digital divide: the internet and political mobilization in Egypt and Tunisia. CyberOrient 5(1). http://www.cyberorient.net/article.do?articleId=6212. Accessed 24 April 2011

Kurzman C (2004) The unthinkable revolution in Iran. Harvard University Press, Cambridge

Manin B (1997) The principles of representative government. Cambridge University Press, Cambridge

Miladi N (2011) Tunisia: a media-led revolution? Aljazeera.net. Published 17 Jan 2011. http://english. aljazeera.net/indepth/opinion/2011/01/2011116142317498666.html. Accessed 25 April 2011

Milani MM (1988) The making of Iran's islamic revolution: from monarchy to islamic republic. Westview Press, Boulder

NBC Washington (2011) Egyptian-Americans take to D.C. streets. Published 31 Jan 2011. http:// www.nbcwashington.com/news/local/Egyptian-Americans-Take-to-DC-Streets-114857819. html. Accessed 30 Mar 2011

Nepstad SE (2011) Nonviolent revolutions: civil resistance in the late 20th century. Oxford University Press, New York

Parsa M (1989) Social origins of the Iranian revolution. Rutgers University Press, New Brunswick

Parsons A (1984) The pride and the fall: Iran 1974–1979. Jonathan Cape, London

Rifai R (2011) Timeline: Tunisia's uprsing. Al-Jazeera. Published 23 Jan 2011. http://english. aljazeera.net/indepth/spotlight/tunisia/2011/01/201114142223827361.html. Accessed 15 April 2011

Ritter DP (2010) Why the Iranian revolution was nonviolent: internationalized social change and the iron cage of liberalism. Dissertation, University of Texas, Austin

Ritter DP (2011) Obama, Mubarak, and the iron cage of liberalism. openDemocracy. Published 10 Feb 2011. http://www.opendemocracy.net/daniel-ritter/obama-mubarak-and-iron-cage-of-liberalism

Schock K (2005) Unarmed insurrections: people power movements in nondemocracies. University of Minnesota Press, Minneapolis

Selbin E (1997) Revolution in the real world: bringing agency back. In: Foran J (ed) Theorizing revolutions. Routledge, New York, pp 123–136

Selbin E (2010) Revolution, rebellion, resistance: the power of story. Zed Books, New York

Sharp G (2005) Waging nonviolent struggle: 20th century practice and 21st century potential. Extending Horizons, Boston

Shirky C (2011) The political power of social media: technology, the public sphere, and social change. Foreign Affairs (January/February). http://www.foreignaffairs.com/articles/67038/clay-shirky/the-political-power-of-social-media. Accessed 12 April 2011

Shivers L (1980) Inside the Iranian revolution. In: Albert DH (ed) Tell the American people: perspectives on the Iranian revolution. Movement for a New Society, Philadelphia, pp 56–78

Sick G (1985) All fall down: America's tragic encounter with Iran. Penguin Books, New York

Skocpol T (1979) States and social revolutions: a comparative analysis of France, Russia, and China. Cambridge University Press, New York

Soboul A (1977) A short history of the French revolution, 1789–1799. University of California Press, Berkeley

Sreberny-Mohammadi A, Mohammad A (1994) Small media, big revolution: communication, culture, and the Iranian revolution. University of Minnesota Press, Minneapolis

Stempel JD (1981) Inside the Iranian revolution. Indiana University Press, Bloomington

Szaniszlo M (2011) Advocates stage local rally to back protesters. The Boston Herald. Published 30 Jan 2011. http://bostonherald.com/news/regional/view/20110130advocatesstage_local rally_to_backprotesters/srvc=home&position=1. Accessed 30 Mar 2011

Taheri A (1986) The spirit of Allah: Khomeini and the islamic revolution. Adler & Adler, Bethesda

The Electronic Intifada (2011) Global mobilization in support of Egyptian uprising. Published 31 Jan 2011. http://electronicintifada.net/content/global-mobilization-support-egyptian-uprising/9206. Accessed 29 Mar 2011

Tilly C (1978) From mobilization to revolution. Addison-Wesley, Reading

Trechsel AH (2011) Paparazzi democracy. On the effects of digital media on representative government. Mimeo. European University Institute, Florence

Tufekci Z (2011a) Can 'leaderless revolutions' stay leaderless: preferential attachment, iron laws and networks. Technosociology. Published 14 Feb 2011. http://technosociology.org/?p=366. Accessed 21 Mar 2011

Tufekci Z (2011b) Why the 'how' of social organizing matters and how gladwell's latest contrarian missive falls short. Technosociology. Published 4 Feb 2011. http://techno sociology.org/?p=305. Accessed 21 Mar 2011

Wagner B (2011) Push-button-autocracy: deconstructing internet censorship and control. Paper presented at the 4th symposium for human rights in the Mediterranean

Zonis M (1991) Majestic failure: the fall of the shah. University of Chicago Press, Chicago

References

Abrahamian E (1982) Iran between two revolutions. Princeton University Press, Princeton

Abrahamian E (1989) Radical islam: the Iranian Mojahedin. I.B. Tauris, London

Algar H (1983) Roots of the Iranian revolution. Open Press, London

Al-Jazeera (2011) The listening post. News magazine broadcast on 22 Jan 2011. http://www.youtube.com/watch?v=SfcftL-UadM. Accessed 14 April 2011

Alvarez RM, Hall TE (2004) Point, click and vote: the future of internet voting. Brookings Institution Press, Washington

Alvarez RM, Hall TE, Trechsel AH (2009) Internet voting in comparative perspective: the case of Estonia. PS: Polit Sci Polit 42:497–505

Alvarez RM, Levin I, Mair P, Trechsel AH (2012) Party preferences in the digital age: the impact of voting advice applications. Paper prepared for the conference on responsive or responsible? Parties, democracy and global markets, a conference in honour of Peter Mair. Florence, 26–28 Sept 2012

Alvarez RM, Mair P, Trechsel AH (2011) The effect of voting advice applications on party preferences (Unpublished manuscript)

Amenta E, Carruthers B, Zylan Y (1992) A hero for the aged? The townsend movement, the political mediation model, and old age policy, 1934–1959. Am J Sociol 98:308–339

Ames B (2001) The deadlock of democracy in Brazil. University of Michigan Press, Ann Arbor

Ames B, Barker A, Rennó LR (2008) Quality of elections in Brazil: policy, performance, pageantry, or pork? In: Kingstone PR, Power TJ (eds) Democratic Brazil revisited. University of Pittsburgh Press, Pittsburgh

Amjad M (1989) Iran: from royal dictatorship to theocracy. Greenwood Press, New York

Amuzegar J (1991) The dynamics of the Iranian revolution: the Pahlavis triumph and tragedy. SUNY Press, Albany

Anderson N (2011) Tweeting tyrants out of Tunisia: global internet at its best. http://www.wired.com/threatlevel/2011/01/tunisia/all/1. Published on 14 Jan 2011 and Accessed on 27 April 2011

Andrejevic M (2011) The work that affective economics does. Cult Stud 25(4–5):604–620

Andrews K (2004) Freedom is a constant struggle. University of Chicago Press, Chicago

Angrist J, Pischke J-S (2009) Mostly harmless econometrics: an empiricist's companion. Princeton University Press, Princeton

Arjomand SA (1988) The turban for the crown: the islamic revolution in Iran. Oxford University Press, New York

Arsenault C (2011) Learning from past revolutions? Al-Jazeera. http://english.aljazeera.net/indepth/features/2011/02/201121616828483511.html. Published and Accessed 17 Feb 2011

Atton C (2007) Current issues in alternative media research. Sociol Compass 1:17–27

Ayres J (1999) From the streets to the internet: the cyber-diffusion of contention. Ann Am Acad Polit Soc Sci 566:132–143

Bagchi K, Solis A, Gemoets L (2003) An empirical study of telecommunication product adoption in Latin America and the Caribbean. Elect J Inf Syst Dev Countries 15(3):1–17

B. Grofman et al. (eds.), *The Internet and Democracy in Global Perspective*,
Studies in Public Choice 31, DOI: 10.1007/978-3-319-04352-4,
© Springer International Publishing Switzerland 2014

Bai M (2004) Wiring the vast left-wing conspiracy. The New York Times. New York

Bakhash S (1990) The reign of the ayatollahs: Iran and the islamic revolution. Basic Books, New York

Balz D (2004a) Campaign for DNC chief begins; candidates say party must rebuild state chapters, offer resounding message. The Washington Post, Washington

Balz D (2004b) DNC chief advises learning for GOP. The Washington Post, Washington

Barasko M (2004) Governing NOW: grassroots activism in the national organization for women. Cornell University Press, Ithaca

Beck PA et al (2004) The social calculus of voting: Interpersonal, media, and organizational influences on presidential choices. Am Polit Sci Rev 96(01):57–73

Beckett C (2011) After Tunisia and Egypt: towards a new typology of media and networked political change. POLIS J Soc http://www.charliebeckett.org/?p=4033. Published on 11 Feb 2011 and Accessed on 21 April 2011

Benford R, Snow D (2000) Framing processes and social movements: an overview and assessment. Annu Rev Sociol 26:611–639

Bennett WL (2003) Communicating global activism: strengths and vulnerabilities of networked politics. Inf Commun Soc 6(2):143–168

Bennett WL, Segerberg A (2011) Digital media and the personalization of collective action. Inf Commun Soc 14(6):770–799

Bennett-Jones O (2011) How cameras hidden in pens outflanked Syrian regime. BBC News. http://news.bbc.co.uk/2/hi/programmes/from_our_own_correspondent/9470481stm. Published and Accessed on 30 April 2011

Benoit WL (2007) Communication in political campaigns. Peter Lang, New York

Benoit K, Laver M (2006) Party policy in modern democracies. Routledge, London

Benoit K, Marsh M (2010) Incumbent and challenger campaign spending effects in proportional electoral systems the Irish elections of 2002. Polit Res Q 63:1

Benson R, Neveu E (2005) Bourdieu and the journalistic field. Polity Press, Malden

Berelson B, Lazarsfeld PF, McPhee WN (1986) Voting: a study of opinion formation in a presidential campaign. University of Chicago Press, Chicago

Bernhard B (2004) Tempest from a teapot. In: LA Weekly

Biesecker BA (2000) Addressing postmodernity: Kenneth Burke, rhetoric, and a theory of social change. University of Alabama Press, Tuscaloosa

Bimber B (1998) The internet and political transformation: populism, community, and accelerated pluralism. Polity 31:391–401

Bimber B (1999) The internet and citizen communication with government: does the medium matter? Polit Commun 16(4):409–428

Bimber BA (2003) Information and American democracy: technology in the evolution of political power. Cambridge University Press, New York

Bimber B, Davis R (2003) Campaigning online: the internet in US elections. Oxford University Press, New York

Bimber B, Flanigan AJ, Stohl C (2005) Reconceptualizing collective action in the contemporary media environment. Commun Theor 15(4):365–388

Bimber B, Stohl C, Flanagin AJ (2009) Technological change and the shifting nature of political organization. In: Chadwick A, Howard PN (eds) Handbook of internet and politics. Routledge, New York, pp 72–85

Bird S, Klein E, Loper E (2009) Natural language processing with python, 1st edn. O'Reilly Media, Sebastopol

Blumler JG, Gurevitch M (1995) The crisis of public communication. Routledge, New York

Boas TC (2005) Television and neopopulism in Latin America: media effects in Brazil and Peru. Lat Am Res Rev 40(2):27–49

Bochsler D (2010) Can internet voting increase political participation? Remote electronic voting and turnout in the Estonian 2007 parliamentary elections. Paper prepared at the conference on internet and voting. Fiesole, 3–4 June

Bonchek M (1995) Grassroots in cyberspace: using computer networks to facilitate political participation. Paper presented at the annual meeting of the midwest political science association. Chicago, Illinois. http://www.scribd.com/doc/82147418/Grass-Roots-in-Cyberspace-Bonchek -1995. Accessed on 20 Jan 2013

Boogers M (2006) Enquete bezoekers Stemwijzer (unpublished paper). Universiteit van Tilburg, Tilburg

Boogers M, Voerman G (2003) Surfing citizens and floating voters: results of an online survey of visitors to political web sites during the Dutch 2002 general elections. Inf Polit 8(1–2):17–27

Boulianne S (2009) Does internet use affect engagement? A meta-analysis of research. Polit Commun 26(2):193–211

Bourdieu P (1998) On television. New Press, New York

Breuer F (2010) The EU profiler: a new way for voters to meet parties and to understand European elections. In: Gagatek W (ed) The 2009 elections to the European parliament— country reports. European Union Democracy Observatory, Florence, pp 27–31

Breuer F, Trechsel AH (2006) Report for the council of Europe, E-voting in the 2005 local elections in Estonia. European University Institute, Florence

Burke K (1966) Language as symbolic action: essays on life, literature, and method. University of California Press, Berkeley

Burke K (1969) A rhetoric of motives. University of California Press, Berkeley

Burns G (1996) Ideology, culture, and ambiguity: the revolutionary process in Iran. Theor Soc 25:349–388

Capling A, Nossal KR (2001) Death of distance or tyranny of distance? The internet, deterritorialization, and the anti-globalization movement in Australia. Pac Rev 14(3):443–465

Çarkoğlu A, Vitiello T, Moral M (2012) Voting advice applications in practice: answers to some key questions from Turkey. Paper prepared for the 26th annual conference of the Italian society of political science. Rome, 13–15 Sept 2012

Carmines EG, Huckfeldt R (1996) Political behavior: an overview. In: Goodin RE, Klingemann H-D (eds) A new handbook of political science. Oxford University Press, New York, pp 223–254

Carroll WK, Hackett RA (2006) Democratic media activism through the lens of social movement theory. Media Cult Soc 28:83–104

Castells M (1999) Grassrooting the space of flows. Urban Geography 20(4):294–302

Castells M (2009) Communication power. Oxford University Press, Oxford

Castles FG, Mair P (1984) Left–right political scales: some 'expert' judgements. Eur J Polit Res 12(1):73–88

Cedroni L, Garzia D (eds) (2010) Voting advice applications in Europe: the state of the art. Scriptaweb, Napoli

Chadwick A (2006) Internet politics: states, citizens, and new communication technologies. Oxford University Press, New York

Chadwick A (2009) Web 2.0: new challenges for the study of E-democracy in era of informational exuberance. I/S: J Law Pol Inf Soc 5: 9–41

Chadwick A, Howard PN (eds) (2009) Routledge handbook of internet politics. Routledge, London

Cocker L (2011) Solidarity by the thousand: protesters take to the streets of London. The Morning Star. http://www.morningstaronline.co.uk/index.php/news/content/view/full/100469. Published on 30 Jan 2011 and Accessed on 30 Mar 2011

Converse PE (1962) Information flow and the stability of partisan attitudes. Pub Opin Q 26(4):578–599

Cornwell R (2004) The boss offers Kerry blue-collar support: backing from the entertainment has sometimes been a mixed. In: The independent. Newspaper Publishing PLC, London

Cottam R (1988) Iran and the United States: a cold war case study. University of Pittsburgh Press, Pittsburgh

Crozier M (2007) Recursive governance: contemporary political communication and public policy. Polit Commun 24(1):1–18

Crozier M (2010) Rethinking systems: configurations of politics and policy in contemporary governance. Adm Soc Available at: http://aas.sagepub.com/content/early/2010/07/14/0095399710377443.abstract. Accessed 18 Aug 2010

Cutts D, Webber DJ (2010) Voting patterns, party spending and relative location in England and wales. Reg Stud 44(6):735–760

Dalton RJ, Wattenberg MP (eds) (2000) Parties without partisans: political change in advanced industrial democracies. Oxford University Press, Oxford

Daneshvar P (1996) Revolution in Iran. Macmillan, New York

Davis R (1999) The web of politics: the internet's impact on the American political system. Oxford University Press, New York

de Graaf J (2010) The irresistible rise of Stemwijzer. In: Cedroni L, Garzia D (eds) Voting advice applications in Europe. The state of the art. ScriptaWeb, Napoli, pp 35–60

della Porta D, Mosca L (2005) Global-net for global movements? A network of networks for a movement of movements. J Public Policy 25(1):165–190

della Porta D, Andretta M, Mosca L, Reiter H (2006) Globalization from below: transnational activists and protest networks. University of Minnesota Press, Minneapolis

Delli Carpini MX, Williams B (2001) Let us infotain you. In: Bennett WL, Entman RM (eds) Mediated politics: communication in the future of democracy. Cambridge University Press, New York, pp 160–181

DeLuca D (2004) The pop vote. In: The Philadelphia inquirer. Philadelphia Papers LLC, Philadelphia

Delvinia (2003) Internet voting and Canadian democracy in practice: the Delvinia report on internet voting in the 2003 town of Markham municipal election

Delvinia (2007) Understanding the digital voter experience: the Delvinia report on internet voting in the 2006 town of Markham municipal election

Denver D, Hands G (1997) Modern constituency campaigning: local campaigning in the 1992 general election. Frank Cass, London

Denver D, Hands G, Fisher J (2002) The impact of constituency campaigning in the 2001 general election. Br Elect Parties Rev 12:80–94

Denver D, Hands G, MacAllister I (2004) The electoral impact of constituency campaigning in Britain, 1992–2001. Polit Stud 52(2):289–306

Diani M (2000) Social movement networks virtual and real. Inf Commun Soc 3:386–401

Dorman WA, Farhang M (1987) The US press and Iran: foreign policy and the journalism of deference. University of California Press, Berkeley

Downing JDH (1996) Internationalizing media theory: transition, power, culture: reflections on media in Russia, Poland and Hungary, 1980–95. Sage, Thousand Oaks

Downs A (1957) An economic theory of political action in a democracy. J Polit Econ 65(2):135–150

Dufresne Y, Eady G, Hove J, Loewen P, van der Linden C (2012) Avoiding the traps in VEAs. Pre-campaign market research and micro-level weighting adjustments. Paper prepared for the 22nd world congress of political science. Madrid, 8–12 July 2012

Dulio D, Goff D, Thurber J (1999) Untangled web: internet use during the 1998 election. Polit Sci Polit 32:53–59

Earl J (2006) Pursuing social change online: the use of four protest tactics on the internet. Soc Sci Comput Rev 20:1–16

Earl J, Kimport K (2008) The targets of online protest. Inf Commun Soc 11:449–472

Earl J, Kimport K (2011) Digitally enabled social change: activism in the internet age. MIT Press, New York

Earl J, Schussman A (2003) The new site of activism: on-line organizations, movement entrepreuneurs, and the changing locations of social movement decision making. Res Social Mov Conflict Change 24:155–187

Easton D (1965) A systems analysis of political life. Wiley, New York

Edelman M (1964) The symbolic uses of politics. University of Illinois Press, Urbana

Elections Canada (2011) Canada municipal jurisdiction graphs

Faler B (2004) Kerry's e-mail list continues to be a valuable resource. The Washington Post, Washington

Farrell D, Schmitt-Beck R (eds) (2008) Non-party actors in electoral politics: the role of interest groups and independent citizens in contemporary election campaigns. Nomos, Baden–Baden

Ferree M (2003) Resonance and radicalism: feminist framing in the abortion debates of the United States and Germany. Am J Sociol 109:304–344

Fischer MMJ (2003) Iran: from religious dispute to revolution. University of Wisconsin Press, Madison

Fisher D, Stanley K, Berman D, Neff G (2005) How do organizations matter? Mobilization and support for participants at five globalization protests. Soc Probl 52:102–121

Fisher J, Cutts D, Fieldhouse E (2011) The electoral effectiveness of constituency campaigning in the 2010 British general election: the 'triumph' of labour? Elect Stud 30(4):816–828

Fivaz J, Nadig G (2010) Impact of voting advice applications (VAAs) on voter turnout and their potential use for civic education. Policy Internet 2:7

Foot KA, Schneider SM (2002) Online action in campaign 2000: an exploratory analysis of the U.S. political web sphere. J Broadcast Electr Media 46:222–244

Foot KA, Schneider SM (2006) Web campaigning. MIT Press, Cambridge

Foot KA, Schneider SM, Dougherty M, Xenos M, Larsen E (2003) Analyzing linking practices: candidate sites in the 2002 US electoral web sphere. J Comput Mediated Commun 6:0

Foran J (1993) Fragile resistance: social transformation in Iran from 1500 to the revolution. Westview, Boulder

Foran J (1994) A century of revolution: comparative, historical, and theoretical perspectives on social movements in Iran. In: Foran J (ed) A century of revolution: social movements in Iran. University of Minnesota Press, Minneapolis, pp 223–237

Foran J (2005) Taking power: on the origin of third world revolutions. Cambridge University Press, New York

Fouhy B (2004) MoveOn.org becomes anti-Bush online powerhouse. The Associated Press, Berkeley

Franklin MN, Mackie TT, Valen H (eds) (1992) Electoral change: responses to evolving social and attitudinal structures in western societies. Cambridge University Press, Cambridge

Froman A, Delvinia P (2010) Personal interview, 21 Oct 2010

Gainous J, Wagner K (2011) Rebooting American politics: the internet revolution. Rowman & Littlefield, New York

Gamson W (1990) The strategy of social protest. Dorsey Press, Homewood

Gamson W, Meyer D (1996) Framing political opportunity. In: McAdam D, McCarthy J, Zald M (eds) Comparative perspectives on social movements: political opportunities, mobilizing structures, and cultural framings. Cambridge University Press, Cambridge, pp 275–290

Gamson W, Wolfsfeld G (1993) Movement and media as interacting systems. Ann Am Acad Polit Soc Sci 578:104–125

Garton AT (2009) A century of civil resistance: some lessons and questions. In: Roberts A, Garton AT (eds) Civil resistance and power politics: the experience of non-violent action from Gandhi to the present. Oxford University Press, New York, pp 371–390

Garzia D (2010) The effects of VAAs on users voting behaviour: an overview. In: Cedroni L, Garzia D (eds) Voting advice applications in Europe. The state of the art. ScriptaWeb, Napoli, pp 13–33

Garzia D, Marschall S (2012) Voting advice applications under review: the state of research. Int J Electron Gov (article in press)

Gelman A, King G (2007) Estimating incumbency advantage without bias. Am J Polit Sci 34(4):1142–1164

Giambusso D (2011) Thousands gather near UN in New York to support anti-government protests in Egypt. The Star-Ledger. http://www.nj.com/news/index.ssf/2011/01/thousands_gather_in_new_york_c.html. Published on 29 Jan 2011 and Accessed on 30 Mar 2011

Gibson R, Ward S (1998) UK political parties and the internet: politics as usual in the new media? Havard Int J Press/Polit 3:14–38

Gibson R, Ward S (2000) New media, same impact? British party activity in cybersapce. In: Gibson R, Ward S (eds) Reinvigorating government? British politics and the internet. Ashgate, Aldershot, pp 106–129

Gibson R, Rommele A (2001) Changing campaign communications: a party-centered theory of professionalized campaigning. Harvard Int J Press/Polit 6(4):31–43

Gibson R, Rommele A (2009) Measuring the professionalization of political campaigning. Party Polit 15(3):265–293

Gibson R, Rommele A (2010) Open source campaigning?: UK party organisations and the use of the new media in the 2010 general election. Paper presented to the American Political Science Association, Washington

Gibson RK, Margolis M, Resnick D, Ward SJ (2003) Election campaigning on the WWW in the US and UK: a comparative analysis. Party Polit 9(1):47–76

Gibson R, Nixon P, Ward S (2003) Net gain? Political parties and the internet. Routledge, New York

Gillan K, Pickerill J (2008) Transnational anti-war activism: solidarity, diversity and the internet in Australia, Britain and the United States after 9/11. Aust J Polit Sci 43(1):59–78

Gillan K, Pickerill J, Webster F (2008) Anti-war activism: new media and protest in the information age Basingstoke. Palgrave Macmillan, Hampshire

Gilmore J (2012) Ditching the pack: digital media in the 2010 Brazilian congressional campaigns. New Media Soc 14(4):617–633

Gitlin T (1980) The whole world is watching: mass media in the making and unmaking of the new left. University of California Press, Los Angeles

Gladwell M (2010) Small change: why the revolution will not be tweeted. The New Yorker (online) http://www.newyorker.com/reporting/2010/10/04/101004fa_fact_gladwell. Published on 4 Oct 2010 and Accessed 15 Mar 2011

Gladwell M, Shirky C (2011) From innovation to revolution. Foreign Affairs (March/April) http://www.foreignaffairs.com/articles/67325/malcolm-gladwell-and-clay-shirky/from-innovation-to-revolution. Accessed 14 April 2011

Goldstone JA (1991) Revolution and rebellion in the early modern world. University of California Press, Berkeley

Goodman N (2010) Internet voting in Canadian municipalities: what can we learn? CEU Polit Sci J 5(4):492–520

Goodman N (2011) eDemocracy and citizen engagement: the Delvinia report on internet voting in town of Markham. Paper prepared for Delvinia internet voting workshop. Ottawa, Ontario

Goodman N, Pammett JH, DeBardeleben J (2010) A comparative assessment of electronic voting. Report prepared for Elections Canada

Goodwin J (2001) No other way out: states and revolutionary movements 1945–1991. Cambridge University Press, New York

Gourevitch P (2004) Swingtime: former bush voters advertise their disaffection. In: The New Yorker. The Conde Nast Publications Inc, New York

Green JD (1982) Revolution in Iran: the politics of countermobilization. Praeger, New York

Greene A-m, Hogan John, Grieco M (2003) Commentary: e-collectivism and distributed discourse: new opportunities for trade union democracy. Ind Relat J 34(4):282–289

Gronbeck BE (1978) The functions of presidential campaigning. Commun Monogr 45(4):268–280

Gronbeck BE, Wiese DR (2005) The repersonalization of presidential campaigning in 2004. Am Behav Sci 49(4):520–534

Guzman I (2004) Boss amps up tour to rock anti-W vote. Daily News, New York

Grossman L (1996) The electronic republic: reshaping democracy in the information age. Penguin Books, London

Hananel S (2004) MoveOn to democratic party: we bought it, we own it. The Associated Press, New York

Hauslohner A (2011) Is Egypt about to have a facebook revolution? http://www.time.com/time/world/article/0,8599,2044142,00.html. Published on 24 Jan 2011 and Accessed on 25 April 2011

Heidar K (2005) Norwegian parties and the party system: steadfast and changing. West Eur Polit 28(4):807–833

Heikal M (1982) Iran: the untold story: an insider's account of America's Iranian adventure and its consequences for the future. Pantheon Books, New York

Henderson A, Bowley R (2010) Authentic dialogue? The role of friendship in a social media recruitment campaign. J Commun Manag 14(3):237–257

Herman E, Chomsky N (1988) Manufacturing consent: the political economy of mass media. Pantheon Books, New York

Hewitt L (2011) Clerks technology analyst, city of Burlington. Personal Communication, 6 May 2011

Hooghe M, Teepe W (2007) Party profiles on the web: an analysis of the log files of non-partisan interactive political internet sites in the 2003 and 2004 election campaigns in Belgium. New Media Soc 9(6):965–985

Horrigan M (2004) MoveOn.org steals DNC thunder. UPI, USA

Hortala-Vallve R, Esteve-Volart B (2011) Voter turnout and electoral competition in a multidimensional policy space. Eur J Polit Econ 27(2):376–384

Hoveyda F (1980) The fall of the shah. Wyndham Books, New York

Howard PN (2006) New media campaigns and the managed citizen. Cambridge University Press, Cambridge

Huck P (2004) Moving the masses. In: The age. The Age Company Limited, Melbourne

Internet World Stats (n.d.) Brazil: internet stats and telecom market report. http://www.internetworldstats.com/sa/br.htm. Accessed Dec 2010

Jamieson KH (1996) Packaging the president: a history and criticism of presidential campaign advertising. Oxford University Press, New York

Jarvis J (2009) What would google do? First edition first printing. Harper Business, New York

Kahn R, Kellner D (2004) New media and internet activism: from the battle of Seattle to blogging. New Media Soc 6:87–95

Kallinikos J (2006) The consequences of information: institutional implications of technological change. Edward Elgar Publishing, Cheltenham

Kallinikos J, Aaltonen A, Marton A (2010) A theory of digital objects. First Monday 15(6–7) http://firstmonday.org/htbin/cgiwrap/bin/ojs/index.php/fm/article/viewArticle/3033/2564

Keck ME, Sikkink K (1998) Activists beyond borders: advocacy networks in social politics. Cornell University Press, Ithaca

Keddie NR (1983) Iranian revolutions in comparative perspective. Am Hist Rev 88(3):579–598

Keddie NR (2003) Modern Iran: roots and results of revolution. Yale University Press, New Haven

Kenski K, Hardy B, Jamieson KH (2010) The Obama victory: how media, money, and message shaped the 2008 election. Oxford University Press, New York

Khamis S (2011) The transformative Egyptian media landscape: changes, challenges and comparative perspectives. Int J Commun 5:1159–1177

Khondker HH (2011) Role of the new media in the Arab spring. Globalization 8(5):675–679

Klandermans B (1984) Mobilization and participation: social-psychological expansions of resource mobilization theory. Am Sociol Rev 49:583–600

Klandermans B (1992) The social construction of protest and multiorganizational fields. In: Morris A, McClurg Mueller C (eds) Frontiers in social movement theory. Yale University Press, New Haven, pp 77–103

Kleinnijenhuis J, Krouwel A (2009) Dimensionality of the European issue space. Paper presented at the NCCR workshop vote advice applications. Bern, 12–13 Nov

Klingemann H-D, Volkens A, Budge I, Bara J, McDonald MD (2006) Mapping policy preferences II: parties, electorates and governments in Eastern Europe and the OECD 1990–2003. Oxford University Press, Oxford

Kohoko D (2011) Alternative voting methods. Elections Canada. Personal

Konieczny Piotr (2009) Governance, organization, and democracy on the internet: the iron law and the evolution of wikipedia. Sociol Forum 24(1):162–192

Kriesi H (2008) Political mobilisation, political participation and the power of the vote. West Eur Polit 31(1):147–168

Kuebler J (2011) Overcoming the digital divide: the internet and political mobilization in Egypt and Tunisia. CyberOrient 5(1). http://www.cyberorient.net/article.do?articleId=6212. Accessed on 24 April 2011

Kurzman C (2004) The unthinkable revolution in Iran. Harvard University Press, Cambridge

Lacey J (2012) Must Europe be Swiss? On the idea of a voting space and the possibility of a multilingual demos. Br J Polit Sci 44:61–82

Ladner A, Pianzola J (2010) Do voting advice applications have an effect on electoral participation and voter turnout? Evicence from the 2007 Swiss Federal Elections. In: Tambouris E, Macintosh A, Glassey O (eds) Electronic participation. Proceedings of Second IFIP WG 8.5 international conference, ePart 2010, Lausanne, Switzerland, Aug 29–Sept 2, 2010. Springer, Berlin, pp 211–224

Ladner A, Felder G, Fivaz J (2010) More than toys? A first assessment of voting advice applications in Switzerland. In: Cedroni L, Garzia D (eds) Voting advice applications in Europe. The state of the art. ScriptaWeb, Napoli, pp 91–123

Laver M (ed) (2001) Estimating the policy position of political actors. Routledge, London

Lawseon-Borders G, Kirk R (2005) Blogs in campaign communication. Am Behav Sci 49(4):548–559

Lazarsfeld PF, Berelson B, Gaudet H (1948) The people's choice: how the voter makes up his mind in a presidential campaign. Columbia University Press, New York

Leach DK (2005) The iron law of what again? Conceptualizing oligarchy across organizational forms. Sociol Theor 23(3):312–337

Leighley JE (ed) (2010) The oxford handbook of American elections and political behavior. Oxford University Press, Oxford

Lilleker DG (2006) Key concepts in political communication. Sage Publications, Thousand Oaks

Lilleker DG, Negrine R (2002) Professionalization: Of what? Since when? By whom? Harvard Int J Press/Polit 7(4):98–103

Lippert B (2004) Barbara Lippert's critique: Kerry is so very. In: AdWeek. VNU Business Media Inc, New York

Lobo MC, Vink M, Lisi M (2010) Mapping the political landscape: a vote advice application in Portugal. In: Cedroni L, Garzia D (eds) Voting advice applications in Europe. The state of the art. ScriptaWeb, Napoli, pp 143–185

Luhmann N (1982) The differentiation of society. Columbia University Press New York, New York

Mair P (2001) Searching for the position of political actors: a review of approaches and a critical evaluation of expert surveys. In: Laver M (ed) Estimating the policy position of political actors. Routledge, London, pp 10–30

Manin B (1997) The principles of representative government. Cambridge University Press, Cambridge

Matin-asgari A (2002) Iranian student opposition to the Shah. Mazda Publishers, Costa Mesa

Margetts H (2001) The cyber party. ECPR joint session workshops. Grenoble, France

Margolis M, Resnick D (2000) Politics as usual? The cyberspace revolution. Sage, London

Margolis M, Resnick D, Chin-chang T (1997) Campaigning on the internet: parties and candidates on the world wide web in the 1996 primary season. Int J Press/Politics 2:59–78

Marks G (ed) (2007) Special symposium: comparing measures of party positioning: expert, manifesto, and survey data. Elect Stud 26(1):1–141

Marschall S (2005) Idee und Wirkung des Wahl-O-Mat. Aus Politik und Zeitgeschichte 55(51–52):41–46

Marschall S, Schmidt CK (2010) The impact of voting indicators: the case of the German Wahl-O-Mat. In: Cedroni L, Garzia D (eds) Voting advice applications in Europe. The state of the art. ScriptaWeb, Napoli, pp 65–104

Marsh D, O'Toole T, Jones S (2007) Young people and politics in the UK: apathy or alienation?. Palgrave Macmillan, New York

McAdam D (1996) The framing function of movement tactics: strategic dramaturgy in the American civil rights movement. In: McAdam D, McCarthy J, Zald M (eds) Comparative perspectives of social movements: political opportunities, mobilizing structures, and cultural framings. Cambridge University Press, Cambridge. pp 338–355

McCarthy J, Zald M (1973) The trend of social movements in America: professionalization and resource mobilization. General Learning Press, Morristown

McVeigh R, Welch M, Bjarnason T (2003) Hate crime reporting as a successful social movement outcome. Am Sociol Rev 68:843–867

Meikle G (2002) Future active: media activism and the internet. Routledge, New York

Mercurio B (2004) Democracy in decline: can internet voting save the electoral process? John Marshall J Comput Inf Law 12(2):101–143

Meyer D, Gamson J (1995) The challenges of cultural elites: celebrities and social movements. Sociol Inq 65:181–206

Meyer D, Whittier N (1994) Social movement spillover. Soc Probl 41:277–298

Miladi N (2011) Tunisia: a media-led revolution? http://english.aljazeera.net/indepth/opinion/2011/01/2011116142317498666.html. Published on 17 Jan 2011 and Accessed on 25 April 2011

Milani MM (1988) The making of Iran's islamic revolution: from monarchy to islamic republic. Westview Press, Boulder

Milner H (2010) The internet generation: engaged citizens or political dropouts. Tufts University Press, Medford

Michels R (1999) Political parties: a sociological study of the oligarchical tendencies of modern democracy. Transaction Publishers, New Brunswick

Mische A (2007) Partisan publics: communication and contention across Brazilian youth activist networks. Princeton University Press, Princeton

Mykkänen J, Moring T, Pehkonen J (2007) Tutkimus vaalikoneiden käytöstä ja suhtautumisesta vaalikoneisiin: vaalikoneet koetaan hyödyllisiksi. Helsingin Sanomain säätiö, Helsinki

NBC Washington (2011) Egyptian-Americans take to DC streets. http://www.nbcwashington.com/news/local/Egyptian-Americans-Take-to-DC-Streets-114857819.html. Published on 31 Jan 2011 and Accessed 30 Mar 2011

Negroponte N (1996) Being digital. Hodder & Stoughton, London

Nepstad SE (forthcoming) Nonviolent revolutions: civil resistance in the late 20th century. Oxford University Press, New York

Nielsen RK (2009) The labors of internet-assisted activism: overcommunication, miscommunication, and communicative overload. J Inf Technol Polit 6(3):267–280

Nielsen RK (2011) Mundane internet tools, mobilizing practices, and the coproduction of citizenship in political campaigns. New Media Soc http://nms.sagepub.com/content/early/2011/01/26/1461444810380863.abstract. Accessed on 4 May 2011

Nielsen RK (2012) Ground wars: personalized communication in political campaigns. Princeton University Press, Princeton

Norris P (1999) On message: communicating the campaign. Sage Publications, Thousand Oaks

Norris P (2000) A virtuous circle: political communications in postindustrial societies. Cambridge University Press, New York

Norris P (2001) Digital divide: civic engagement, information poverty, and the internet. Cambridge University Press, Cambridge

Norris P (2002) Democratic phoenix: reinventing political activism. Cambridge University Press, Cambridge

Norris P (2008) Getting the message out: a two-step model of the role of the internet in campaign communication flows during the 2005 British general election. J Inf Technol Polit 4:3–13

Norris P (2012) The impact of social media on the Arab uprisings: the facebook, twitter, and youtube revolutions. Paper presented at the joint sessions of the ECPR. Antwerp, Belgium, 10–15 April

Norris P, Curtice J (2008) Getting the message out: a two-step model of the role of the internet in campaign communication flows during the 2005 British general election. J Inf Technol Polit 4(4):3–13

Nuytemans M, Walgrave S, Deschouwer K (2010) Do the vote test: the Belgian voting aid application. In: Cedroni L, Garzia D (eds) Voting advice applications in Europe. The state of the art. ScriptaWeb, Napoli, pp 125–156

Otjes S, Louwerse T (2011) Spatial models in voting advice applications. Paper presented at the 10th Politicologenetmaal, Amsterdam, 9–10 June 2011

Pammett JH, LeDuc L (2003) Explaining the turnout decline in Canadian federal elections: a new survey of non-voters. Ottawa, Elections Canada. Available at: http://www.elections.ca

Parsa M (1989) Social origins of the Iranian revolution. Rutgers University Press, New Brunswick

Parsons A (1984) The pride and the fall: Iran 1974–1979. Jonathan Cape, London

Pattie CJ, Johnston RJ, Fieldhouse EA (1995) Winning the local vote: the effectiveness of constituency campaign spending in Great Britain, 1983–1992. Am Polit Sci Rev 89(4):969–983

Pearce B (2011) Deputy Chief Election Officer, City of Vancouver. Personal Interview, 5 May 2011

Pianzola J, Trechsel AH, Vassil K, Schwerdt CK, Alvarez MR (2012) The effect of voting advice applications (VAAs) on political preferences. Evidence from a randomized field experiment. Paper prepared for the 2012 APSA conference. New Orleans

Pickerill J (2003) Cyberprotest: environmental activism on-line. Manchester University Press, Manchester

Pinto-Duschinsky M (1981) British political finance 1830–1980. American Enterprise Institute for Public Policy Research, Washington

Piven FF, Cloward R (1977) Poor people's movements. Basic Books, New York

Pollock S (2011) Program Manager, Event Readiness, Elections Ontario. Personal Interview, 10 May 2011

Raeburn N (2004) Changing corporate America from inside out. University of Minnesota Press, Minneapolis

Ramonaite A (2010) Voting advice applications in Lithuania: promoting programmatic competition or breeding populism? Policy Internet 2(1):117–147

Rash W (1997) Politics on the nets: wiring the political process. W.H. Freeman & Company, New York

Rheingold H (1993) The virtual community: homesteading on the electronic frontier. Addison Wesley, Reading. http://www.rheingold.com/vc/book/intro.html

Rheingold H (2002) Smart mob: the next social revolution. Basic Books, Cambridge

Riker WH, Ordeshook PC (1968) A theory of the calculus of voting. Am Polit Sci Rev 62(1):25–42

Rifai R (2011) Timeline: Tunisia's uprsing. Al-Jazeera http://english.aljazeera.net/indepth/spotlight/tunisia/2011/01/201114142223827361.html. Published on 23 Jan 2011 and Accessed on 15 April 2011

Ritter DP (2009) Nonviolent revolutions. In: Ness I, de Laforcade G (eds) The international encyclopedia of revolution and protest. Wiley, Oxford, pp 1205–1212

Ritter DP (2010) Why the Iranian revolution was nonviolent: internationalized social change and the iron cage of liberalism. Dissertation, University of Texas, Austin

Ritter DP (2011) Obama, Mubarak, and the iron cage of liberalism. openDemocracy. Published 10 Feb 2011. http://www.opendemocracy.net/daniel-ritter/obama-mubarak-and-iron-cage-of-liberalism

Rochon T (1998) Culture moves: ideas, activism, and changing values. Princeton University Press, Princeton

Rohlinger D (2007) American media and deliberative democratic processes. Sociol Theor 25:122–148

Rohlinger D, Brown J (2009) Democracy, action and the internet after 9/11. Am Behav Sci 53:133–150

Rohlinger D, Brown J (2013) Mass media and institutional change: organizational reputation, strategy, and outcomes in the academic freedom movement. Mobil Int Q 18:1–27

Rohlinger D, Klein J (forthcoming) Constricting boundaries: collective identity in the tea party movement. In: Naples N, Mendez J (eds) Border politics, globalization and social movements. New York University Press, New York

Rohlinger D, Klein J (forthcoming) From fervor to fear: ICT and emotions in the tea party movement. In: Meyer D, Van Dyke N (eds) Understanding the tea party. Ashgate, New York

Rubin D, Fitzgerald T (2004) Working in concert against Bush: Springsteen, others to play in Philadelphia and Swing States. In: The Philadelphia Inquirer. Philadelphia Newspapers LLC, Philadelphia

Ruusuvirta O (2010) Much ado about nothing? Online voting advice applications in Finland. In: Cedroni L, Garzia D (eds) Voting advice applications in Europe. The state of the art. ScriptaWeb, Napoli, pp 47–77

Ruusuvirta O, Rosema M (2009) Do online vote selectors influence electoral participation and the direction of vote? Paper presented at the European consortium for political research (ECPR) general conference, Potsdam, 10–12 Sept 2009

Samuels D (2001) When does every penny count? Intra-party competition and campaign finance in Brazil. Party Polit 7(1):89–102

Samuels D (2001) Incumbents and challengers on a level playing field: assessing the impact of campaign finance in Brazil. J Polit 63(2):569–584

Samuels D (2001) Money, elections, and democracy in Brazil. Lat Am Polit Soc 43(2):27–48

Samuels DJ (2002) Pork barreling is not credit claiming or advertising: campaign finance and the sources of the personal vote in Brazil. J Polit 64(3):845–863

Schattschneider EE (1960) The semi-sovereign people. Holt Rinehart & Winston Inc, New York

Schock K (2005) Unarmed insurrections: people power movements in nondemocracies. University of Minnesota Press, Minneapolis

Schumpeter J (1976) Capitalism, socialism, and democracy. Haper & Row, New York

Schussman A, Earl J (2004) From barricades to firewalls? Strategic voting and social movement leadership in the internet age. Sociol Inquiry 74:439–463

Schwarz D, Schädel L, Ladner A (2010) Pre-election positions and voting behaviour in parliament: consistency among Swiss MPs. Swiss Polit Sci Rev 16(3):533–564

Selbin E (1997) Revolution in the real world: bringing agency back. In: Foran J (ed) Theorizing revolutions. Routledge, New York, pp 123–136

Selbin E (2010) Revolution, rebellion, resistance: the power of story. Zed Books, New York

Sharp G (2005) Waging nonviolent struggle: 20th century practice and 21st century potential. Extending Horizons, Boston

Shirky C (2010) Cognitive surplus: creativity and generosity in a connected age. Penguin Press, New York

Shirky C (2011) The political power of social media: technology, the public sphere, and social change. Foreign Affairs (January/February) http://www.foreignaffairs.com/articles/67038/clay-shirky/the-political-power-of-social-media. Accessed 12 April 2011

Shivers L (1980) Inside the Iranian revolution. In: Albert DH (ed) Tell the American people: perspectives on the Iranian revolution. Movement for a New Society, Philadelphia, pp 56–78

Shulman Stuart (2009) The case against mass e-mails: perverse incentives and low quality public participation in US federal rulemaking. Policy Internet 1(1):23

Sick G (1985) All fall down: America's tragic encounter with Iran. Penguin Books, New York

Skocpol T (1979) States and social revolutions: a comparative analysis of France, Russia, and China. Cambridge University Press, New York

Skop M (2010) Are the voting advice applications (VAAs) telling the truth? Measuring VAAs quality: case study from the Czech Republic. In: Cedroni L, Garzia D (eds) Voting advice applications in Europe. The state of the art. ScriptaWeb, Napoli, pp 199–230

Smith D (2012a) President, Intelivote. Personal communication, December 5, 2012

Smith D (2012b) President, Intelivote. Personal Communication, 30 Nov 2012

Snow D, Benford R (1988) Ideology, frame resonance, and participant mobilization. Int Soc Mov Res 1:197–217

Soboul A (1977) A short history of the French revolution, 1789–1799. University of California Press, Berkeley

Sreberny-Mohammadi A, Mohammad A (1994) Small media, big revolution: communication, culture, and the Iranian revolution. University of Minnesota Press, Minneapolis

Stempel JD (1981) Inside the Iranian revolution. Indiana University Press, Bloomington

Stiff J, Mongeau P (2003) Persuasive communication. The Guilford Press, New York

Strömbäck J (2008) Four phases of mediatization: an analysis of the mediatization of politics. Int J Press/Polit 13(3):228–246

Szaniszlo M (2011) Advocates stage local rally to back protesters. The Boston Herald. http://bostonherald.com/news/regional/view/20110130advocatesstage_localrally_to_backprotesters/srvc=home&position=1. Published on 30 Jan 2011 and Accessed on 30 Mar 2011

Taheri A (1986) The spirit of Allah: Khomeini and the islamic revolution. Adler & Adler, Bethesda

Talonen J, Sulkava M (2011) Analyzing parliamentary elections based on voting advice application data. In: Gama J, Bradly E, Hollmén J (eds) Advances in intelligent data analysis. 10th international symposium, IDA 2011, Porto, Portugal, Oct 2011. Springer, Heidelberg, pp 340–351

Tarrow S (1998) Fishnets, internets and catnets: globalization and transnational collective action. In: Hanagan M, Moch LP, Brake W (eds) Challenging authority: the historical study of contentious politics. University of Minnesota Press, Minneapolis, pp 228–244

The Electronic Intifada (2011) Global mobilization in support of Egyptian uprising. http://electronicintifada.net/content/global-mobilization-support-egyptian-uprising/9206. Published on 31 Jan 2011 and Accessed on 29 Mar 2011

Thörn H (2007) Social movements, the media and the emergence of a global public sphere: from anti-apartheid to global justice. Curr Sociol 55:896–918

Tilly C (1978) From mobilization to revolution. Addison-Wesley, Reading

Trechsel AH (2007) E-voting and electoral participation. In: de Vreese C (ed) Dynamics of referendum campaigns—an international perspective. Palgrave, London, p 159–182

Trechsel AH (2011) Paparazzi democracy. On the effects of digital media on representative government. Mimeo, European University Institute, Florence

Trechsel AH (2012) Conceptualising a voter-to-voter preferences matching tool for the 2014 European parliamentary elections. Mimeo, European University Institute

Trechsel AH, Mair P (2011) When parties (also) position themselves: an introduction to the EU profiler. J Inf Technol Polit 8(1):1–20

Trechsel AH, Robert S, Kristjan V (2010) Internet voting in Estonia: a comparative analysis of four elections since 2005, report prepared for the directorate general of democracy and political affairs and the directorate of democratic institutions, Council of Europe

Tufekci Z (2011a) Can 'leaderless revolutions' stay leaderless: preferential attachment, iron laws and networks. Technosociology. http://technosociology.org/?p=366. Published on 14 Feb 2011 and Accessed on 21 Mar 2011

Tufekci Z (2011b) Why the 'how' of social organizing matters and how Gladwell's latest contrarian missive falls short. Technosociology. http://technosociology.org/?p=305. Published on 4 Feb 2011 and Accessed on 21 Mar 2011

Turpin C (2011a) Legislative Coordinator, Town of Markham. Personal Communication, 12 April 2011

Turpin C (2011b) Legislative Coordinator, Town of Markham. Personal Interview, 25 April 2011

Van D, Nella SS, Taylor V (2004) The targets of social movements: beyond a focus on the state. Res Soc Mov Conflict Change 25:27–51

van Praag P (2007) De stemwijzer: hulpmiddel voor de kiezers of instrument van manipulatie?. Lezing Amsterdamse Academische Club, Amsterdam

Vassil K (2012) Voting smarter? The impact of voting advice applications on political behavior, unpublished doctoral dissertation

Verba Sidney, Nie NH, Kim J-n (1978) Participation and political equality: a seven-nation comparison. University of Chicago Press, Chicago

Wagner B (2011) Push-button-autocracy: deconstructing internet censorship and control. Paper presented at the 4th symposium for human rights in the Mediterranean

Wagner KM, Gainous J (2009) Electronic grassroots: does online campaigning work? J Legis Stud 15(4):502–520

Walgrave S, Manssens J (2000) The making of the white march: the media as a mobilizing alternative to movement organizations. Mobilization 5:217–239

Walgrave S, van Aelst P, Nuytemans M (2008) Do the vote test: the electoral effects of a popular vote advice application at the 2004 Belgian elections. Acta Polit 43(1):50–70

Walgrave S, Nuytemans M, Pepermans K (2009) Voting aid applications and the effect of statement selection. West Eur Polit 32(6):1161–1180

Wall M, Sudulich ML, Costello R, Leon E (2009) Picking your party online: an investigation of Ireland's first online voting advice application. Inf Polit 14(3):203–218

Wall M, Krouwel A, Vitiello T (2012) Do voters follow the recommendations of voter advice application websites? A study of the effects of Kieskompas.nl on its users vote choices in the 2010 Dutch legislative elections. Party Polit

Ward S, Gibson R (2009) European political organizations and the internet mobilization, participation, and change. In: Chadwick A, Howard PN (eds) Routledge handbook of internet politics. Routledge, London, pp 25–39

Wheatley J, Carman C, Mendez F, Mitchell J (2012) The dimensionality of the Scottish political space: results from an experiment on the 2011 Holyrood elections, Party Polit

Whittier N (1995) Feminist generations: the persistence of the radical women's movement. Temple University Press, Philadelphia

Xenos MA, Foot KA (2005) Politics as usual, or politics unusual? Position taking and dialogue on campaign websites in the 2002 US elections. J Commun 55(1):169–185

Zaller J (1989) Bringing converse back in: modeling information flow in political campaigns. Polit Anal 1(1):181–234

Zittel T, Fuchs D (eds) (2007) Participatory democracy and political participation: can participatory engineering bring citizens back in?. Routledge, New York

Zonis M (1991) Majestic failure: the fall of the shah. University of Chicago Press, Chicago

Index

A
Abortion rights, 94, 95, 102
Activists, 84, 85, 86, 93, 102, 105
  online activists, 119, 120
Al-Jazeera, 120
Alternative voting method, 11, 19, 22. *See*
  Canada, Internet voting; Remote
  Internet voting
American Bell International, 116
Appropriation, 98, 100–103
  for change, 101
  to co-opt MoveOn and TPM, 102
  Florida TPM groups, 100
  Occupy Wall Street Movement, 103
  for political empowerment, 101
  Tea Party Caucus, 102
Asking Canadians Panel, 9
Assignation of legitimacy, 60, 61
Australia, 121

B
Battle in Seattle, 2
BBC, 65, 68, 117
Behavioral activation, 60, 61
Belgium, 26, 33
  Christian Democratic Party of, 30
  Flanders, 28
  multi-wave panel of Flemish voters, 33
Birmingham
  constituency-level and national-level
    campaigns, 65
  Daily Birmingham candidate Twitter posts,
    70f
  Facebook posts, 66, 67n9
  policy references, 73
  Twitter, 66, 69
Black box of campaign effects, 59
Blog sites, 90, 120

Bloggers, 49, 119
  free sites, 48, 50
  Tunisian blogosphere, 120
  Wordpress, 46
Blogposts, 46
Boycotts, 112
Brazil, 3
  2010 campaigns in, 45–47
  campaign dynamics, 44
  challengers, 52t, 53
  data and methods, 48–50
  digital media in, 43, 44–45, 47
  Dilmaweb, 46
  incumbents in, 52t, 53
  mobile population, 44
  Orkut, 45, 46, 48, 49, 50
  political culture in, 44–45
  social networking sites, 45, 48
  Tiririca's online campaign, 47
  urn numbers, 48
  winning and losing candidates in, 51t

C
Campaign communication, 58, 59, 60–65
  communication technologies in, 77
  instrumental, 75
  vertical, 69
Campaigns, 26. *See also* Horizontal
    communication; Vertical
    communication
  Brazil 2010 campaigns in, 45–47
  campaign dynamics, 34, 44
  campaign strategy, 51t, 52t
  candidates, impacts of, 20–21
  election campaigns, 29, 30
  Leave No Voter Behind, 104
  Obama's campaign, 105
  postmodern environment, 3

B. Grofman et al. (eds.), *The Internet and Democracy in Global Perspective*,
Studies in Public Choice 31, DOI: 10.1007/978-3-319-04352-4,
© Springer International Publishing Switzerland 2014

Campaigns (*cont.*)
    social media campaign effects, 59
    UK, political campaigns in, 58
Canada, Internet voting, 2, 8–9
    age and, 13, 14*f*
    Election Statute Law Amendment Act, 10
    Elections Act, 10
    and European elections, 13
    Internet ballots, party elections using, 11
    Internet ballots, use of, 15
    Internet voting, growth of, 9–11
    likelihood of voting, 19*f*
    methods of voting data, 17*f*
    middle-aged and older electors, 21–22
    public support, 11
    Town of Markham. *See* Markham;
        Markham model
    turnout of, 15–16, 16*f*
    users of, 13–15
    young voters, 19–20
Candidates, 20–21
    campaign Web, 49
    selection, 48, 49
    viability, 48
Canvassing efforts, 96
Case de Marina, 46
Child's Play (ad) , 104
Citizen engagement, 2
Citizen Legislature Act, 99
Citizens Holding Government Accountable, 88
Clinton, Hillary, 94
CNN, 124
Cognitive adjustments, 61
Communication techniques, 112
Communication technology, 60–65
Communicative autonomy, 61
Competition, 98–100
    donors and political parties, 98–99
    electoral competition, 29–31, 44
    online advertising competition, 104
Consummatory functions, 60
Consumptatory campaign communication, 58
Contract with America, 99, 99n18

D
Debates, 2, 38, 68, 69, 73, 92
    policy debates, 89
    political debates, 92, 105
Delvinia, Toronto-based company, 9
Democratic transitions, 2, 44

Demonstrations, 112, 114, 116, 119, 120
    sympathetic demonstrations, 121
Digital feedback loop, 4, 123
Digital media and electoral advantage, 49–52
    digital communication strategy, 50
    for minor parties, 50–52
    for newcomers, 52–53
    winning and losing candidates, 51*t*
Digital politics, 2
Dilmaweb, 46
Domestic mobilization, 114*f*
    and new ICTs, 114–116
    and old ICTs, 115–116
Donations, 91
Dutch Christian Democratic Appeal, 30

E
E-activism, 2
E-campaign, 3
E-democracy, 1
E-movement, 85n3
E-tactics, 84
E-voting, 10, 10n4, 13
Economic gains, 113
Egypt, 4, 111, 114, 118
    domestic mobilization, 118–119
    global awareness, 119–120
    revolutions of, 118
Elections Canada, 8, 9, 13
Electoral competition, impact of, 30–31
Electronic machines, 8
Entrepreneurial communications, 63, 73
    proportional incidence of, 73*f*
Entrepreneurial interactions, 62, 74
Entrepreneurial spirit, 91
Entrepreneurial terms, 67, 68
Estonia, 7, 18, 37
EU Profiler, 27, 29, 30, 31, 35, 38
    history and diffusion of VAAs, 28–30
    largest-scale transnational VAA, 29
EU Profiler consortium, 26, 26n1
European Union Democracy Observatory
        (EUDO) , 26n1
European University Institute (EUI) in
        Florence, 26, 26n1, 29
Events, 68, 71*t*, 72*t*, 87, 88, 89, 93, 95, 97
    domestic events, 120, 121
    in Egypt, 118, 121
    revolutionary events in, 113
    in Tunisia, 119

F
Facebook, 3, 4, 22, 62, 67n9, 93, 115, 117
   in Brazil, 43, 44, 46, 47, 48, 49, 52
   horizontal and vertical communications on.
      See Horizontal communication;
      Vertical communication
   in UK, 3, 58, 59
   TPM Facebook, 88
   We are all Khaled Saeed, 119
Finland, 26, 29, 33–35
Frequent voters, 8, 18, 22

G
Gay marriage, 102
Germany, 26, 28, 33
   Wahl-O-Mat, 26, 30, 31, 32, 34
Glasovoditel (Bulgaria), 28
Global awareness, 113*f*
   and old ICTs, 117–118
   and new ICTs, 120–121
The Green Revolution, 124

H
Heavy-VAA-user countries, 30
Helsingin Sanomat, 29
Horizontal communication, 67
   on Facebook, 69–75
   incidence of, 71*t*, 72*t*
   metacampaigning, 69
   phatic references, 69
   political entrepreneurialism, 69
   proportional incidence of, 73*f*
   on Twitter, 69–75
Horizontally structured relationships, 61, 63
Human-coded Twitter posts, 79
Hyperlinks, 68

I
ICT. *See* Internet Communication Technology
      (ICT)
Immediate international diffusion, 122
Immigration, 102
Indirect campaigning
   parties and party system, 30, 31
   party politics and demographic
      representation, 34–36
   political attributes and behavior, 31–34
Institutional power, 92
Instrumental campaign communication, 60
Intelivote, Nova Scotia-based company, 9
International legitimacy, 113

Internet ballots, 8n1. *See also* Remote Internet
      voting
Internet Communication Technology
      (ICT), 4, 84
   in action mobilization, 95–98
   activists, 85
   in consensus mobilization, 93–95
   and domestic mobilization, 115–119
   and global awareness, 117–118, 120–122
   in Iranian revolution, 114
   marketing issues, 89–92
   nonviolent revolutions, impact in, 114*f*,
      123*f*
   political scientists' view, 85n1
   proliferations of, 36
   and revolutionary outcomes, 124–125
   and revolutions of Egypt, 118–120
   and revolutions of Tunisia, 118–120
   and social issues, 102
   and social movement organizations, 89–98
Internet voting, 2, 7, 8n1. *See also* Remote
      Internet voting
   remote voting, 7
   voting turnout, 22
Internet-based forms, 112
Internet-based technologies, 36
Iran, 117
   domestic mobilization, 115–117
   global awareness, 117–118
   nonviolent revolutions of, 114
Iran's nonviolent revolution, 114
   old ICTs and domestic mobilization,
      115–117
   old ICTs and global awareness, 117–118
Issue voting, 31, 38

J
Judeo-Christian doctrine, 88

K
Kendall's tau-b, 18
Khomeini, Ayatollah Ruhollah, 115, 116
   revolutionary messages, 116
Kieskompas, Amsterdam-based company,
      26n1
Kiosks, 8

L
Leaders' Debates, 69, 77
Leave No Voter Behind" campaign, 104
Luxemburgish VAAs, 26

M
Markham, 8, 11–13
Markham model, 11–12
  Internet ballots in, 15–16
  online registrants, ballots cast, and advance
    turnout in, 12*f*
  in municipal elections of, 8
  using PIN, 12
  security measure for 2010, 12n9
  voter satisfaction, 12
  voters' age, 13, 14*f*
Mass media, 89, 90
Mass mobilization, 109, 116
Media venues, 90
Metacampaigning, 61, 68, 69, 73
Middle East, 120, 121
Middle East and North Africa (MENA) , 4,
  111, 112, 122
Movement of the Monks, 124
MoveOn.org (MoveOn), 3, 86–89, 86n4

N
National integration, 114
Natural language processing (NLP) , 67, 78
NCCR Democracy Politools network, 26n1
Netherlands, The, 13, 25, 27, 29, 30, 33, 34
Network of European Citizenship Education
  (NECE), 29
Network voting, 10, 10n6
New Democratic Party (NDP) leadership, 9
Noninstitutionalized mass movements, 112
Non-mediated, transnational loop of protest,
  123
Nonviolent protesters, 113
Nonviolent revolutions, 4, 112
Nonvoters, 18–20
  voting record, 18
  young voters, 19–20
Normalization thesis, 58

O
Obama, Barrack, 94
  mybarackobama.com, 62
  online strategy, 62
Occasional voters, 18
One stop shops, 3
Online ballots, 8n1. *See also* Remote Internet
  voting
Online communication, 4
Online news outlets, 90
Online prodding, 96
Online radio, 90

Online voting, 8n1. *See also* Remote Internet
  voting
  models, 7
Orkut, 45, 46, 48–50

P
Pahlavi, Muhammad Reza, 114
Paparazzi Democracy, 123
Party election broadcasts (PEBs), 68
Party systems
  cross-national comparison of, 34
  expert surveys, 34
  manifesto/program coding, 34
Personalized mobilization frames, 63
Phalic communication, 61
  proportional incidence of, 73*f*
Phatic terms, 67
Policy, 68
Politarena (Switzerland), 28
Political activism, 113
Political advertising, 4
Political change, 91
Political communication, 41
  command and control structure of, 57–58
Political empowerment, 101
Political entrepreneurialism, 76
Political parties, implications for, 98
  appropriation, 100–103
  competition, 96–98
  synergy, 103–105
Political skill, 103
Political solitude, 32
Polling place Internet voting, 8
Postmodern campaign environment, 3. *See
  also* Voter Advice Applications
  (VAAs)

Q
Qatari news, 121

R
Religious establishment, 115
Reminder e-mails, 97
Remote Internet voting, 8–11, 16
  electronic machines, 8
  kiosks, 8
  machines in polls, 8
  voting from remote locations, 8
Representative deficit, 32, 37, 38
Respondents
  demographics of, 89, 90*t*

political experience, 89
Revolutionary outcome, 124
  new ICTs, 124–125
Revolutionary process, 122
  new ICTs, 122–123
Revolutionary situation, 113

S
Saffron Revolution, The, 124
SAVAK, Iran's secret police, 116
Savvy social movement organizations, 90
Shah's modernization scheme, 117
Smartvote, 28, 33
Social media, 90
Social media communications, 59, 75–76, 77
Social movement organizations and ICT
  in conflict creation, 92
  conservative celebrities, 92
  marketing issues, 89–92
  mass media, 89
  mobilizing consensus, 93–95
  mobilizing support, 95–98
  political change, 92
  spending donations, 91
Social movement scholars, 85
Social solidarity, 63
StemWijzer, 26, 27, 35
  history and diffusion of VAAs, 27–29
  success of, 28
Strikes, 111
Structural change, 101
Surrogates, 68
Switzerland, 7, 25, 26
  Politarena, 28
  smartvote, 28, 35
Synergy, 103–105

T
Talk show democracy, 58, 77
Tea Party Movement (TPM), 3, 86–89
Technological symbol, 115
Telegraph, 115
Telephone voting, 10, 16
Traditional dominance, 3
Trident, 68, 68n12
Tunisia, 4, 113, 116
  domestic mobilization, 118–119
  global awareness, 119–122
  revolutions of, 118
Twitter, 2, 4, 22, 49, 90
  in Birmingham, 66, 69
  Brazilian participation, 45, 46, 48

National Daily posts, 70*f*
"Speak to Tweet" service, 121
Twitter convention RT, 68
in UK, 58
Twitter communications, 57, 58, 66, 75, 77

U
UK
  #changewesee Twitter campaign, 62
  constituency-level campaign, 65
  local level campaign, 64
  National Daily Twitter posts, 70*f*
  national level campaign, 64
  ongoing direct communications, 67
  political campaigns in, 58
  social media platforms, 59
  talk show democracy, 58
  Twitter communications, 60
  2010 general election, 2
Unemployment rate, 100
Urn numbers, 48

V
Vancouver, 10, 10n5
Venezuela, 121
Vertical communication
  on Facebook, 69–75
  incidence of, 71*t*, 72*t*
  on Twitter, 69–75
Vertically structured relationships, 60
Voting Advice Applications (VAAs) , 3, 26
  in Bulgaria (*Glasovoditel*), 28
  cognitive effects, 33
  Dutch (*Kieskompas*), 29
  EU Profiler. See EU Profiler
  future of, 36–38
  information-seeking behavior, 34
  match list, 26
  political behaviour of scholars, 37
  principle of, 26
  progressive diffusion of, 30
  snow-balling model, 29
  statement, 27*f*
  StemWijzer. SeeStemWijzer
  in Switzerland (*Politarena*), 28
Voting behavior, 13, 33

W
Wb revolution, 1
Web, 49
  Brazilian participation, 46

candidate's Web, 49
Web-based communications, 76
Westminster model of government, 64
Woman's right, to abortion, 94n15
Wordpress, 46, 49
World Wide Web, 7

Y
YouTube, 22, 49, 50, 90, 120, 124
    Brazilian participation, 45, 46, 47

Z
Zapatistas, 1

Printed by Books on Demand, Germany